# PIONEERS IN CANADA

# PIONEERS IN CANADA

SIR HARRY JOHNSTON

WITH EIGHT COLOURED ILLUSTRATIONS
E. WALL COUSINS

GYAN

*Published by*

Gyan Publishing House
5, Ansari Road
Daryaganj, New Delhi-110002
Phone: 011-47034999, 9811692060
E-mail: books@gyanbooks.com

*Distribution Network*
gyanbooks.com
India, USA, Canada, UK, Australia, France



ISBN : 978-81-212-3897-7 (PB)
First Published, London, 1912

2nd Impression 2020

*Printed at:* Gyan Press, Delhi.

# Pioneers in Canada

By SIR HARRY JOHNSTON

G.C.M.G., K.C.B.

*WITH EIGHT COLOURED ILLUSTRATIONS*
*BY E. WALL-COUSINS*

PIONEERS OF EMPIRE

BLACKIE AND SON LIMITED
LONDON GLASGOW BOMBAY
1912

c 312

TYPE OF SHIP SAILED IN BY THE ENGLISH OR FRENCH PIONEERS
IN THE SIXTEENTH CENTURY

# PREFACE

The publishers of this book asked me to write a series of works which should deal with "real adventures", in parts of the world either wild and uncontrolled by any civilized government, or at any rate regions full of dangers, of wonderful discoveries; in which the daring and heroism of white men (and sometimes of white women) stood out clearly against backgrounds of unfamilar landscapes, peopled with strange nations, savage tribes, dangerous beasts, or wonderful birds. These books would again and again illustrate the first coming of the white race into regions inhabited by people of a different type, with brown, black, or yellow skins; how the European was received, and how he treated these races of the soil which gradually came under his rule owing to his superior knowledge, weapons, wealth, or powers of persuasion. The books were to tell the plain truth, even if here and there they showed the white man to have behaved badly, or if they revealed the fact that the American Indian, the Negro, the Malay, the black Australian was sometimes cruel and treacherous.

A request thus framed was almost equivalent

to asking me to write stories of those pioneers who founded the British Empire; in any case, the first volumes of this series do relate the adventures of those who created the greater part of the British Dominions beyond the Seas, by their perilous explorations of unknown lands and waters. In many instances the travellers were all unconscious of their destinies, of the results which would arise from their actions. In some cases they would have bitterly railed at Fate had they known that the result of their splendid efforts was to be the enlargement of an empire under the British flag. Perhaps if they could know by now that we are striving under that flag to be just and generous to all types of men, and not to use our empire solely for the benefit of English-speaking men and women, the French who founded the Canadian nation, the Germans and Dutch who helped to create British Africa, Malaysia, and Australia, the Spaniards who preceded us in the West Indies, and the Portuguese in West, Central, and East Africa, in Newfoundland and Ceylon, might—if they have any consciousness or care for things in this world—be not so sorry after all that we are reaping where they sowed.

It is (as you will see) impossible to tell the tale of these early days in the British Dominions beyond the Seas, without describing here and there the adventures of men of enterprise and daring who were not of our own nationality. The majority, nevertheless, were of British stock; that is to say, they were English, Welsh, Scots, Irish, perhaps here and there a Channel Islander and a Manxman;

or Nova Scotians, Canadians, and New Englanders. The bulk of them were good fellows, a few were saints, a few were ruffians with redeeming features. Sometimes they were common men who blundered into great discoveries which will for ever preserve their names from perishing; occasionally they were men of Fate, predestined, one might say, to change the history of the world by their revelations of new peoples, new lands, new rivers, new lakes, snow mountains, and gold mines. Here and there is a martyr like Marquette, or Livingstone, or Gordon, dying for the cause of a race not his own. And others again are mere boys, whose adventures come to them because they are adventurous, and whose feats of arms, escapes, perils, and successes are quite as wonderful as those attributed to the juvenile heroes of Marryat, Stevenson, and the author of *The Swiss Family Robinson.*

I have tried, in describing these adventures, to give my readers some idea of the scenery, animals, and vegetation of the new lands through which these pioneers passed on their great and small purposes; as well as of the people, native to the soil, with whom they came in contact. And in treating of these subjects I have thought it best to give the scientific names of the plant or animal which was of importance in my story, so that any of my readers who were really interested in natural history could at once ascertain for themselves the exact type alluded to, and, if they wished, look it up in a museum, a garden, or a natural history book.

I hope this attempt to be accurate will not

frighten away young readers, who will find in between these zoological or botanical notes a variety of exciting incidents, and many a strange and fascinating glimpse of savage life; plenty of hair-breadth escapes, deeds of heroism or of bloodshed, and triumphs of courage and dogged perseverance. There will be no maudlin sentimentality about my stories; at the same time they will contain nothing that a healthy-minded boy or girl may not read unharmed. There are cannibals in *Robinson Crusoe*, and you will meet them—real ones—in these books; scalps are taken and the prisoners are tortured by Fenimore Cooper's Red Indians: well, I will show you the very originals of Fenimore's noble savages, as described by the first Europeans who met them. You shall see what the pirates of the Spanish Main and the seas of Borneo were really like; witness slave-raids in Central Africa, trials for witchcraft, deaths from thirst, and terrible episodes of almost complete starvation. Yet you shall also behold rare acts of kindness from savages towards white men and white men towards savages, attend feastings and frolics as well as deaths and scenes of torture. Your feelings shall not be unnecessarily harrowed, you will learn much of geography and natural history by the way; and, if you can have patience with the author and his desire to instruct you occasionally, you will, by reading this series of books on the great pioneers of British West Africa, Canada, Malaysia, West Indies, South Africa, and Australasia, get a clear idea of how the British Colonial Empire came to be founded.

You will find that I have often tried to tell the story in the words of the pioneers, but in these quotations I have adopted the modern spelling, not only in my transcript of the English original or translation, but also in the place and tribal names, so as not to puzzle or delay the reader. Otherwise, if you were to look out some of the geographical names of the old writers, you might not be able to recognize them on the modern atlas. The pronunciation of this modern geographical spelling is very simple and clear: the vowels are pronounced *a* = ah, *e* = eh, *i* = ee, *o* = o, *ô* = oh, *ō* = aw, *ö* = u in 'hurt', and *u* = oo, as in German, Italian, or most other European languages; and the consonants as in English.

H. H. JOHNSTON.

# CONTENTS

# LIST OF ILLUSTRATIONS

## COLOURED PLATES



## BLACK-AND-WHITE ILLUSTRATIONS

# List of the Chief Authorities

FROM WHOM THE PRINCIPAL FACTS AND INCIDENTS OF THIS BOOK HAVE BEEN DERIVED, IN ADDITION TO THE AUTHOR'S OWN RESEARCHES AND EXPERIENCES, AND INFORMATION SUPPLIED BY PROFESSOR R. RAMSAY WRIGHT, OF TORONTO UNIVERSITY

---

The Saint Lawrence Basin. By Dr. S. E. Dawson. London. 1905. Lawrence & Bullen.

Relation Originale du Voyage de Jacques Cartier au Canada en 1534; Documents inédits, &c. Publiés par H. Michelant et A. Rame. Paris. Librairie Tross. 1867.

Voyage de Jacques Cartier au Canada en 1534, &c. Par H. Michelant. Paris. 1865.

Champlain's Voyages: The Publications of the Prince Society. Boston. 1878. Three volumes.

Voyage of Verrazano, &c. By Henry C. Murphy. New York. 1875. (Also the Essay on the Journeys of Verrazano, by Alessandro Bacchiani, in the Bollettino della Società Geografica Italiana. Rome. November, 1909.)

Volume IX of the Proceedings and Transactions of the Royal Society of Canada. (For the History of Cape Breton and of the Beothiks of Newfoundland.)

The Search for the Western Sea. By Lawrence J. Burpee. London. Alston Rivers. 1908.

Travels and Explorations of the Jesuit Missionaries in New France, &c. Edited by REUBEN GOLD THWAITES. Vol. LIX. Cleveland, U.S.A. Burrows Bros. 1900.

Travels and Explorations in Canada and the Indian Territories between the years 1760 and 1776. By ALEXANDER HENRY, Esq. New York. 1809.

Voyages from Montreal on the River St. Lawrence through the Continent of North America to the Frozen and Pacific Oceans, in the years 1789 and 1793, &c. &c. By ALEXANDER MACKENZIE, Esq. London. 1801.

A Journey from Prince of Wales's Fort in Hudson's Bay to the Northern Ocean, &c. By SAMUEL HEARNE. London. 1795.

Les Bourgeois de la Compagnie du Nord-Ouest. By L. R. MASSON. Quebec. 1890. Two volumes.

New Light on the Early History of the Greater North-West: The Manuscript Journals of Alexander Henry, Jun., and of David Thompson. Edited by ELLIOTT COUES. Three Volumes. New York. Harper. 1897.

Sport and Travel in the Northland of Canada. By DAVID T. HANBURY. London. Edward Arnold. 1904.

Henry Hudson the Navigator, &c. By G. M. ASHER. London. Hakluyt Society. 1860.

The Three Voyages of Martin Frobisher. By Rear-Admiral RICHARD COLLINSON. London. Hakluyt Society. 1867.

The Voyages and Works of John Davis the Navigator. By Admiral Sir ALBERT HASTINGS MARKHAM. London. Hakluyt Society. 1880.

The Voyages of William Baffin, 1612-1622. By Sir CLEMENTS R. MARKHAM. London. 1881.

## CHAPTER I

# The White Man's Discovery of North America

So far as our knowledge goes, it is almost a matter of certainty that Man originated in the Old World—in Asia possibly. Long after this wonderful event in the Earth's history, when the human species was spread over a good deal of Asia, Europe, and Africa, migration to the American continents began in attempts to find new feeding grounds and unoccupied areas for hunting and fishing. How many thousands or hundreds of thousands of years ago it was since the first men entered America we do not yet know, any more than we can determine the route by which they travelled from Asia. Curiously enough, the oldest traces of man as yet discovered in the New World are not only in South America, but in the south-eastern parts of South America. Although the most obvious recent land connection between the Old and New Worlds is the Aleutian chain of islands connecting Kamschatka with Alaska, the ethnologist is occasionally led to think by certain evidence that there may, both earlier and later, have existed another way of reaching western America from south-eastern Asia through Pacific archipelagoes and islets now sunk below the sea. In any case it seems quite probable that men of Mongolian or Polynesian type reached America on its western coasts long before the European came from the north-east and east, and that they were helped on this long journey by touching at islands since submerged by earthquake shocks or tidal waves.

The aboriginal natives of North and South America seem to be of entirely Asiatic origin; and such resemblances as there are between the North-American Indians and the peoples of northern Europe do not arise (we believe) from any ancient colonization of America from western or northern Europe, but mainly from the fact that the North-American Indians and the Eskimo (two distinct types of people) are descended from the same human stocks as the ancient populations of the northern part of Europe and Asia.

It was—we think—from the far *north-west* of Europe that America was first visited by the true White man, though there has been an ancient immigration of imperfect "White" men (Ainu) from Kamschatka. Three or four hundred years after the birth of Christ there were great race movements in northern and central Europe, due to an increase of population and insufficiency of food. Not only did these white barbarians (though they were not as barbarous as we were led to think by Greek and Roman literature) invade southern Europe, North Africa, and Asia Minor, but from the fourth century of the Christian era onwards they began to cross over to England and Scotland. At the same time they took more complete possession of Scandinavia, driving north before their advance the more primitive peoples like the Lapps and Finns, who were allied to the stock from which arose both the Eskimo and the Amerindian.[1] All this time the Goths and Scandinavians were either learning ideas of navigation from the Romans of the Mediterranean or the Greeks of the Black Sea, or they were inventing for themselves

[1] This is a convenient name for the race formerly called "American Indian". They are not Indians (i.e. natives of India), and they are not the only Americans, since there are now about 110,000,000 white Americans of European origin and 24,000,000 negroes and negroids. The total approximate "Amerindian" or aboriginal population of the New World at the present day is 16,000,000, of whom about 111,000 live in the Canadian Dominion, and 300,000 in the United States, the remainder in Central and South America.

better ways of constructing ships; and although they propelled them mainly by oars, they used masts and sails as well.[1] Having got over the fear of the sea sufficiently to reach the coasts of England and Scotland, the Hebrides, Orkneys, and Shetlands, they became still more venturesome in their voyages from Norway, until they discovered the Faroe Archipelago (which tradition says they found inhabited by wild sheep), and then the large island of Iceland, which had, however, already been reached and settled by the northern Irish.

Iceland, though it lies so far to the north that it is partly within the Arctic Circle, is, like Norway, Scotland, and Ireland, affected by the Gulf Stream, so that considerable portions of it are quite habitable. It is not almost entirely covered with ice, as Greenland is; in fact, Iceland should be called Greenland (from the large extent of its grassy pastures), and Greenland should be called Iceland. Instead of this, however, the early Norwegian explorers called these countries by the names they still bear.

The Norse rovers from Norway and the Hebrides colonized Iceland from the year 850; and about a hundred and thirty-six years afterwards, in their venturesome journeys in search of new lands, they reached the south-east and south-west coasts of Greenland. Owing to the glacial conditions and elevated character of this vast continental island (more than 500,000 sq. miles in area)—for the whole interior of Greenland rises abruptly from the sea-coast to altitudes of from 5000 to 11,000 ft.—this discovery was of small use to the early Norwegians or their Iceland colony. After it was governed by the kingdom of Norway in the thirteenth century, the Norse colonization of south-west Greenland faded away under the attacks of the Eskimo,

[1] It is doubtful whether actual masts and sails were known in America till the coming of Europeans, though the ancient Peruvians are said to have used mat sails in their canoes. But the northern Amerindians had got as far as placing bushes or branches of fir trees upright in their canoes to catch the force of the wind.

until it ceased completely in the fifteenth century. When Denmark united herself with the kingdom of Norway in 1397, the Danish king became also the ruler of Iceland. In the eighteenth century the Norwegian and Danish settlements were re-established along the south-east and south-west coasts of Greenland, mainly on account of the value of the whale, seal, and cod fisheries in the seas around this enormous frozen island; and all Greenland is now regarded as a Danish possession.

But the adventurous Norsemen who first reached Greenland from Iceland attempted to push their investigations farther to the south-west, in the hope of discovering more habitable lands; and in this way it was supposed that their voyages extended as far as Massachusetts and Rhode Island, but in all probability they reached no farther than Newfoundland and Nova Scotia. This portion of North America they called "Vinland", more from the abundance of cranberries (*vinbær*) on the open spaces than the few vines to be found in the woods of Nova Scotia.[1]

This brings us down to the year 1008. The Icelandic Norsemen then ceased their investigations of the North-American Continent, and were too ignorant to realize the value of their discoveries. Their colonies on the coasts of Nova Scotia ("Vinland") and Newfoundland ("Estotiland") were attacked probably by Eskimos, at any rate by a short, thick-set, yellow-skinned ugly people whom the Norsemen called "Skræling",[2] who overcame the

[1] The grapes and vines so often alluded to by the early explorers of North America ripened, according to the species, between August and October. They belong to the same genus—*Vitis*—as that of the grape vines of the Old World, but they were quite distinct in species. Nowadays they are known as the Fox Grapes (*Vitis vulpina*), the Frost Grape (*V cordifolia*), the *V. æstivalis*, the *V. labruska*, &c. The fruit of the Fox Grape is dark purple, with a very dusky skin and a musky flavour. The Frost Grape has a very small berry, which is black or leaden-blue when covered with bloom. It is very acid to the taste, but from all these grapes it is easy to make a delicious, refreshing drink. Champlain, however, says that the wild grapes were often quite large in size, and his men found them delicious to eat.

[2] Perhaps from the Eastern Eskimo national name *Karalit*.

unfortunate settlers, murdered some, and carried off others into the interior.

But about this period, when Europe was going through that dismal era, the Dark Age which followed the downfall of the Roman Empire of the west, various impulses were already directing the attention of European adventurers to the Western Ocean, the Atlantic. One cause was the increased hold of Roman and Greek Christianity over the peoples of Europe. These Churches imposed fasts either for single days or for continuous periods. When people fasted it meant that they were chiefly denied any form of meat, and therefore must eat fish if they were not content with oil, bread, or vegetables. So that there was an enormous and increasing demand for fish, not only amongst those fortunate people who lived by the sea-shore, and could get it fresh whenever they liked, but among those who lived at a distance inland, and were still required to fast when the Church so directed. Of course in many parts of Europe they could get fresh-water fish from the rivers or lakes. But the supply was not equal to the demand; and fish sent up from the sea-coast soon went bad, so that the plan of salting and curing fish was adopted. The Norsemen found it a paying business to fish industriously in the seas round Iceland, Norway, Scotland, and Ireland, salt and cure the fish, and then carry it to more southern countries, where they exchanged it against wine, oil, clothing materials, and other goods. This led to the Venetians (who had absorbed so much of the carrying trade of the Mediterranean) sending their ships through the Straits of Gibraltar into the northern seas and trading with the Baltic for amber and salt fish. In the course of this trade some Venetians, such as Antonio Zeno, found their way to Norway and Iceland.[1] It is thought that by this means Venice became

[1] Antonio Zeno served as pilot to Earl Sinclair of the Faeroe Islands and of Roslyn, a Norman-Scottish nobleman who owed joint fealty to the kings of Norway and Scot-

acquainted with the records of the Icelandic voyages to North America, and that her explorers thus grew to entertain the idea of a sea journey westward, or north-westward, of Britain, bringing mariners to a New World represented by the far-eastern extension of Asia.

Christopher Columbus, the Genoese, conceived a similar idea, which also may have owed something to the tradition of the Norsemen's discovery of Vinland. But Columbus's theories were based on better evidence, such as the discovery on the coasts of the Azores archipelago, Madeira, and Portugal of strange seeds, tree trunks, objects of human workmanship, and even (it is said) the bodies of drowned savages—Amerindians—which had somehow drifted across, borne by the current of the Gulf Stream, and escaping the notice of the sharks.

Whilst Columbus was bestirring himself to find Asia across the Atlantic, a sea pilot, JOHN CABOT (Zuan Cabota)—Genoese by birth, but a naturalized subject of Venice—came to England and offered himself to King Henry VII as a discoverer of new lands across the ocean. At first he was employed at Copenhagen to settle fishery quarrels about Iceland, and probably Cabota, or Cabot, visited Iceland in King Henry's service, and there heard of the Icelandic colonies on the other side of the Atlantic, only recently abandoned.

In 1496 King Henry VII provided money to cover some of the expense of a voyage of discovery to search for the rumoured island across the ocean. The people of Bristol were ordered to assist John Cabot, and by them he was furnished with a small sailing ship, the *Matthew*, and a crew of fifteen mariners. Cabot, with his two sons, Luis and Sancio, sailed for Ireland and the unknown West in May, 1497, and, after a sea voyage quite as wonderful as that of Columbus, reached the coast of Cape Breton

land. Sinclair was so impressed with the stories of a "Newland" beyond Greenland that he sailed to find it about 1390, but only reached Greenland.

Island (or "the New Isle", as it was first named[1]) on June 24, 1497. They found "the land excellent, and the climate temperate". The sea was so full of fish along these coasts that the mariners opined (truly) that henceforth Bristol need not trouble about the Iceland trade. Here along this "new isle" were the predestined fisheries of Britain.[2]

They encountered no inhabitants, though they found numerous traces of their existence in the form of snares, notched trees, and bone netting needles. John Cabot hoisted the English flag of St. George and the Venetian standard of St. Mark; then—perhaps after coasting a little along Nova Scotia—fearful that a longer stay might cause them to run short of provisions, he turned the prow of the *Matthew* eastward, and reached Bristol once more about August 6, and London on August 10, 1497, with his report to King Henry VII, who rewarded him with a donation of £10. He was further granted a pension of £20 a year (which he only drew for two years, probably because he died after returning from a second voyage to the North-American coast), and he received a renewal of his patent of discovery in February, 1498. In this patent it is evidently inferred that King Henry VII assumed a sovereignty over these distant regions because of John Cabot's hoisting of the English flag on "the new Isle" (Cape Breton Island) in the preceding year.

[1] Cape Breton was not then, or for nearly two hundred years afterwards, known to be an island. It was thought to be part of the "island" (peninsula) of what we now call Nova Scotia, and the whole of this region which advances so prominently into the Atlantic was believed to be at first the great unknown "New Island" of Irish and English legends—legends based on the Norse discoveries of the eleventh century. Cape Breton was thus named by the Breton seaman who came thither soon after the Cabot expeditions to fish for cod. This large island is separated from Nova Scotia by the Gut of Canso, a strait no broader than a river.

[2] Dr. S. E. Dawson (*The St. Lawrence Basin*) says of this voyage: "When the forest wilderness of Cape Breton listened to the voices of Cabot's little company (of Bristol mariners) it was the first faint whisper of the mighty flood of English speech which was destined to overflow the continent to the shores of another ocean. . . ."

The new expedition of 1498 was a relatively important affair. The king assisted to finance the ventures of the Bristol captains, and five of his ships formed part of the little fleet. It is probable that John Cabot was in command, and almost certain that his young son Sebastian was a passenger, possibly an assistant pilot. The course followed lay much farther to the north, and brought the little sailing vessels amongst the icebergs, ice floes, polar bears, and stormy seas of Greenland and Labrador. Commercially the voyage was a failure, almost a disaster. The ships returned singly, and after a considerable interval of time. Nevertheless, some of the king's loans were repaid to him; and in 1501 a regular chartered company was formed (perhaps at Bristol), with three Bristolians and three Portuguese as directors. Henry VII not only gave a royal patent to this association, but lent more money to enable it to explore and colonize these new lands across the western sea.

There can be little doubt that between 1498 and 1505 these Bristol ships, directed by Italian, English, and Portuguese pilots, first revealed to the civilized world of western Europe the coasts of Newfoundland, Cape Breton Island, Nova Scotia, Massachusetts, and Delaware. They must have got as far south as the State of Delaware (according to Sebastian Cabot, their southern limit was lat. 38°), because in 1505 they were able to bring back parrots ("popyngays"), as well as hawks and lynxes ("catts of the mountaigne"), for the delectation of King Henry; and parrots even at that period could not have been obtained from farther north than the latitude of New York.[1]

But after 1505 English interest in "the Newe founde launde" and the "Newe Isle" languished; the exploration of North America was taken up and carried farther by

[1] Almost certainly this was *Conurus carolinensis*, a green and orange parrakeet still found in the south-eastern States of North America, but formerly met with as far north as New York and Boston.

Portuguese, Bretons and Normans of France, Italians, and Spaniards.[1] It revived again under Henry VIII, owing to the irresistible attraction of the Newfoundland fisheries and the knowledge that the ships from France were returning every autumn with great supplies of fish cured and salted; for an adequate supply of salt fish was becoming a matter of great importance to the markets of western Europe. In 1527 Henry VIII sent two ships under the command of John Rut to explore the North-American coast, and Captain Rut seems to have reached the Straits of Belle Isle between Newfoundland and Labrador (then blocked with ice so that he took them for a bay), and afterwards to have passed along the east coast of Newfoundland—already much frequented by the Bretons, Normans, and Portuguese—and to have stopped at the harbour of St. John's, thence sailing as far south as Massachusetts.

The Portuguese monarchy had begun to take possession of the Azores archipelago from the year 1432. These islands were probably known to the Phœnicians, and even to the Arabs of the Middle Ages; between the

[1] The name *America* probably appears for the first time in English print in the old play or masque the *Four Elements*, which was published about 1518. In a review of the geography of the Earth, as known at that period, a description is given of this vast New World across the Ocean: "But these new landys found lately, been called America, because only Americus did find them first". Americus was a Florentine bank clerk—Amerigo Vespucci—at Seville who gave up the counting-house for adventure, sailed with a Spanish captain to the West Indies and the mainland of Venezuela (off which he notes that he met an English sailing vessel, and this as early as 1499!), and then joined the first exploring voyage of the Portuguese to Brazil. He returned to Europe, and in a letter to a fellow countryman at Paris, written in the late autumn of 1502, he claimed to have discovered a New World across the Ocean. His clear statement about what was really the South American Continent aroused so much enthusiasm in civilized Europe that five years afterwards the New World was called after him by a German printer (Walzmüller) at the little Alsatian University of St. Dié. By 1518 the English writers and mariners were probably aware that the discoveries of Cabot, Columbus, and the Portuguese indicated the extension of "America" from the Arctic to the Antarctic, but not till about 1553 did the scholars and adventurers of England show themselves fully alive to the gigantic importance of this New World. Between 1530 and 1553 their attention was distracted from geography and over-sea adventure by the religious troubles of the Reformation.

fourteenth and fifteenth centuries they had been rediscovered by Catalans, Genoese, Flemings, and Portuguese; and after 1444 the Azores began to prove very useful to the sea adventurers of this wonderful fifteenth century, as they became a shelter and a place of call for fresh water and provisions almost in the middle of the Atlantic, 800 to 1000 miles due west of Portugal. Portuguese vessels sailed northwards from the Azores in search of fishing grounds, and thus reached Iceland, which they called Terra do Bacalhao.[1] They may even before Cabot have visited in an unrecorded fashion the wonderful banks of Newfoundland—an immense area of shallow sea swarming with codfish.

As soon as the news of the Cabot voyages reached the King of Portugal he arranged to send an expedition of discovery to the far north-west, perhaps to find a northern sea route to Eastern Asia. He gave the command to Gaspar Corte-Real, a Portuguese noble connected through family property with the Azores. Starting from the Azores in the summer of 1500, Corte-Real discovered Newfoundland, and called it "Terra Verde" from its dense woods of fir trees, which are now being churned into wood pulp to make paper for British books and newspapers. He then sailed along the coast of Labrador,[2] and thence crossed over to Greenland, the southern half of which he mapped with fair accuracy. His records of this voyage take particular note of the great icebergs off the coast of Greenland. His men were surprised to find that sea water frozen becomes perfectly fresh—all the salt is left out in the process. So that his two ships could

[1] *Bacalhao* in Portuguese (and a similar word in Spanish, old French, and Italian) means dried, salted fish. It comes from a Latin word meaning "a small stick", because the fish were split open and held up flat to dry by means of a cross or framework of small sticks, the Norse name "stokfiske" meant the same: stockfish or stickfish.

[2] *Labrador* (*Lavrador* in Portuguese) means a labourer, a serf. The Portuguese are supposed to have brought some Red Indians from this coast to be sold as slaves.

supply themselves with fresh water of the purest, by hacking ice from the masses floating in these Greenland summer seas. The next year he started again, but on a more westerly course. His two ships reached the coasts of New Jersey and Massachusetts, and sailed north once more to Labrador. They captured a number of Amerindian aborigines, but only one of the two ships (with seven of these savages on board) reached Portugal; Gaspar Corte-Real was never heard of again. His brother Miguel went out in search of him, but he likewise disappeared without a trace.

Nevertheless these Portuguese expeditions to North America have left ineffaceable traces in the geography of the Newfoundland coast, of which (under the name of Terra Nova[1]) the governorship was made hereditary in the Corte-Real family. Cape Race for example—the most prominent point of the island—is really the Portuguese *Cabo Raso*—the bare or "shaved" cape—and this was by the Spaniards regarded as the westernmost limit of Portuguese sovereignty in that direction. For the Spaniards were by no means pleased at the intrusion of other nations into a New World which they desired to monopolize entirely for the Spanish Crown. They did not so much mind sharing it, along the line agreed upon in the Treaty of Tordesillas, with the Portuguese, but the ingress of the English and French infuriated them. The Basque people of the north-east corner of Spain were a hardy seafaring folk, especially bold in the pursuit of whales in the Bay of Biscay, and eager to take a share in the salt-fish trade. This desire took them in the fourteenth and fifteenth centuries to Ireland and Iceland. They began to fish off the Newfoundland coasts perhaps as early as 1525. About this time also the Emperor

[1] Corte-Real's name of Terra Verde ("Greenland") was soon dropped in favour of the older English name "New Land" (Newfoundland, Terra Nova). This was at once adopted by the French seamen as "Terre Neuve".

Charles V, King of Spain, having through one great Portuguese sea captain—Magalhães (Magellan)—discovered the passage from Atlantic to Pacific across the extremity of South America, thought by employing another Portuguese—Estevão Gomez—to find a similar sea route through North America, which would prove a short cut from Europe to China. This was the famous "North-west Passage" the search for which drew so many great and brave adventurers into the Arctic sea of America between 1500 and 1853, to be revealed at last by our fellow countrymen, but to prove useless to navigation on account of the enormous accumulation of ice.

Gomez left Corunna in the winter of 1524-5, and reached the North-American coast somewhere about Florida. He probably only began to investigate closely after he passed into the broad gulf of Maine, between Cape Cod and Nova Scotia. Here he sighted from the sea the lofty mountains of New Hampshire, and steered for the mouth of the Penobscot River (which he named the River of Deer), a title which sticks to the locality—in Deer Island—at the present day). But this being no opening of a broad strait, he passed on into the Bay of Fundy (from Portuguese word, *Fundo*, the bottom of a sack or passage), explored its two terminal gulfs, then returned along the coast of Nova Scotia,[1] past Cape Sable, and so to the "gut" or Canal of Canso. Gomez realized that Cape Breton was an island (we now know that it is two islands separated by a narrow watercourse), but thought that Cabot Strait was a great bay, and guessed nothing of the Gulf of St. Lawrence, and the chance of securing for Spain the possession of this mighty waterway into the heart of North America.

From Cape North he crossed over to the south coast

[1] The name Nova Scotia was not applied to this peninsula until 1621, by the British Government. It was at first included with New Brunswick under the Spanish name of Norumbega, and after 1603 was called by the French "Acadie".

of Newfoundland, and followed this more or less till he came to Cape Race. Newfoundland was a "very cold and savage land", and Gomez decided it was no use prosecuting any farther his enquiry as to a water passage across North America, because, if it existed, it must lie in latitudes of frozen sea and be unnavigable.

At different places along the east coast of North America he kidnapped natives, and eventually returned to Spain (via Florida and Cuba) with a cargo of Amerindian slaves.

He had been preceded, by seven or eight months, in his explorations along the same coast by GIOVANNI DA VERRAZANO, a native of Florence, who as a navigator and explorer had visited the East, and had associated himself a good deal with the shipowners of Dieppe. Ever since the issue of Cabot's voyages was known—at any rate from 1504—ships from Brittany and Normandy had made their way to Cape Breton Island and Newfoundland for the cod fisheries. In 1508 a Norman named Aubert was sent out by Jean Ango—a great merchant of Dieppe of that day—to found a colony in Newfoundland. Aubert failed to do this, but he captured and brought away at least seven of the natives, no doubt of the Beothik tribe, from Newfoundland to Rouen, with their canoe, clothing, and weapons. A good many ships also went out from La Rochelle on the west coast of France, and took part in the fishing off the coast of Newfoundland: together with the ships of Brittany and Dieppe there may have been a French fishing fleet of seventy to eighty ships plying every summer season between France, Newfoundland, and Cape Breton. So that when "John from Verrazano" offered his services to Francis I to make discoveries across the ocean, which should become possessions of the French Crown, he was quickly provided with the requisite funds and ships.

Verrazano started on the 17th of January, 1524, for

the coast of North America, but I shall say little about his expedition here, because it resulted chiefly in the discovery and mapping of what is now the east coast of the United States. He reached as far as the south coast of Newfoundland, it is true; he also gave the names of Nova Gallia and Francesca to the coast regions of eastern North America, and distinctly intended to take possession of these on behalf of the French Crown. But his work in this direction did not lead directly to the creation of the French colony of Canada, because, when he returned from America, Francis I was at war with Spain, and could pay no attention to Verrazano's projects. His voyage is worth recording in the present volume only for these two reasons: he certainly put it into the minds of French people that they might found an empire in North America; and he inspired geographers for another hundred years with the false idea that the great North American Continent had a very narrow waist, like the Isthmus of Panama, and that the Pacific Ocean covered the greater part of what is now called the United States. This mistake arose from his looking across the narrow belts or peninsulas of sand in North Carolina and Virginia, and seeing vast stretches of open water to the west. These were found, a hundred years afterwards, to be merely large shallow lagoons of sea water, but Verrazano thought they were an extension of the Pacific Ocean.

Nevertheless, Verrazano's voyage developed into the French colonization of Canada, just as Cabot drew the British to Newfoundland, Columbus the Spaniards to Central and South America, and Amerigo Vespucci showed the Portuguese the way to Brazil. The modern nations of western Europe owe the inception of their great colonies in America to four Italians.

## CHAPTER II

# Jacques Cartier

Verrazano and Gomez, and probably the English captain, John Rut, had all sought for the opening of a strait of salt water—like Magellan's Straits in the far south—which should lead them through the great North-American continent to the regions of China and Japan. Yet in some incomprehensible way they overlooked the two broad passages to the north and south of Newfoundland—the Straits of Belle Isle and of Cabot—which would at any rate lead them into the vast Gulf of St. Lawrence, and thence to the St. Lawrence River and the Great Lakes; a natural system of waterways connected each with the other and all with the Mississippi and Missouri, the Arctic Ocean, and Hudson's Bay; nay, more, with the North Pacific also; so that with a few "portages", or carryings of canoes from one watershed to another, a traveller of any enterprise, accompanied by a sturdy crew, can cross the broad continent of North America at its broadest from sea to sea without much walking.

Estevão Gomez noticed Cabot Straits between Cape Breton and Newfoundland, but thought them only a very deep bay. John Rut and others discerned the Straits of Belle Isle as a wide recess in the coast rather than the mouth of a channel leading far inland. And yet, after thirty years of Breton, English, and Portuguese fishing operations in these waters, there must have been glimmerings of the existence of the great Gulf of St. Lawrence behind Newfoundland; and JACQUES CARTIER (or Quartier), who had probably made already one voyage to Newfoundland (besides a visit to Brazil), suspected that between Newfoundland and Labrador there lay the opening of the great sea passage "leading to China". He proposed himself to Philippe de Chabot, the Admiral of France, as the leader of a new French adventure to find the North-west Passage, was accepted by King Francis, and at the age of forty-three years set out, with two ships, from St. Malo in Brittany, on April 20, 1534, ten years after Verrazano's voyage, and reached the coast of Newfoundland after a voyage of only twenty days. As he sailed northwards, past the deeply indented fiords and bays of eastern Newfoundland (the shores of which were still hugged by the winter ice), he and his men were much impressed with the incredible numbers of the sea fowl settled for nesting purposes on the rocky islands, especially on Funk Island.[1] These birds were guillemots, puffins, great auks,[2] gannets (called by Cartier *margaulx*), and probably gulls and eider duck. To his sailors—always hungry and partly fed on salted provisions, as seamen were down to a few years ago—this inexhaustible supply of fresh food was a source of great enjoyment. They were indifferent, no doubt, to the fishy flavour of the auks and the guillemots, and only noticed that they were splendidly fat. Moreover, the birds attracted Polar bears "as large as cows and as white as swans". The bears would swim off from the shore to the islands (unless they could reach them by crossing the ice),

[1] Funk Island—called by Cartier "the Island of Birds"—is only about 3 miles round, and 46 feet above the sea level. It is 3 miles distant from the coast.

[2] The Great Auk (*Alca impennis*), extinct since about 1844 in Europe and 1870 in Labrador, once had in ancient times a geographical range from Massachusetts and Newfoundland to Iceland, Ireland, Scotland, N.E. England, and Denmark. Perhaps nowhere was it found so abundantly as on the coasts of Eastern Newfoundland and on Funk Island hard by. The Great Auk was in such numbers on the north-east coast of Newfoundland that the Amerindians of that country and of southern Labrador used it as fuel in the winter time, its body being very full of oil and burning with a splendid flame. The French seamen called it *pingouin* ("penguin") from its fatness, and this name was much later transferred to the real penguins of the southern seas which are quite unrelated to the auks.

and the sailors occasionally killed the bears and ate their flesh, which they compared in excellence and taste to veal.

Passing through the Straits of Belle Isle, Cartier's ships entered the Gulf of St. Lawrence. They had previously visited the adjoining coast of Labrador, and there had encountered their first "natives", members of some Algonkin tribe from Canada, who had come north for seal fishing (Cartier is clever enough to notice and describe their birch-bark canoes). After examining the west coast of Newfoundland, Cartier's ships sailed on past the Magdalen Islands (stopping every now and then off some islet to collect supplies of sea birds, for the rocky ground was covered with them as thickly as a meadow with grass).[1] He reached the north coast of Prince Edward Island, and this lovely country received from him an enthusiastic description. The pine trees, the junipers, yews, elms, poplars, ash, and willows, the beeches and the maples, made the forest not only full of delicious and stimulating odours, but lovely in its varied tints of green. In the natural meadows and forest clearings there were red and white currants, gooseberries, strawberries, raspberries, a vetch which produced edible peas, and a grass with a grain like rye. The forest abounded in pigeons, and the climate was pleasant and warm.

Later on he coasted New Brunswick, and paused for a time over Chaleur Bay, hoping it might be the opening to the strait across the continent of which he was in search; but finding it was not, he continued northwards till he had almost rounded the Gaspé Peninsula, a course which would have led him straight away into the wonderful discovery of the St. Lawrence River, but that, being forced by bad weather into Gaspé Bay, and perhaps hindered by fog, instead of entering the St. Lawrence he sailed right across to Anticosti Island. After

[1] On the shores of these islands they noticed "several great beasts like oxen, which have two tusks in the mouth similar to those of the elephant". These were walruses.

that, being baffled by bad weather and doubtful as to his resources lasting out, he decided to return to France through the Strait of Belle Isle.

So far he had failed to realize two of the most important things in the geography of this region: the broad southern entrance into the Gulf of St. Lawrence (subsequently called Cabot Strait), which separates Newfoundland on the north from Cape Breton Island on the south, and the broad entrance into the River St. Lawrence between Anticosti Island and the Gaspé Peninsula.

Yet, whilst staying in Gaspé Bay, he had a very important meeting with Amerindian natives of the Huron-Iroquois stock, who had come down the River St. Lawrence from the neighbourhood of Quebec, fishing for mackerel. These bold, friendly people welcomed the French heartily, greeting them with songs and dances. But when they saw Cartier erect a great cross on the land at the entrance to Gaspé Bay (a cross bearing a shield with the arms of France and the letters "Vive le Roi de France"), they were ill at ease. It is certain that not one word could be understood in language between the two parties, for there were as yet no interpreters; but the Amerindians were probably shrewd enough to perceive that Cartier was making some claim on the land, and they explained by signs that they considered all this country belonged to themselves. Nevertheless, Cartier persuaded two youths, the sons of one of the chiefs, to go back with him to France on his ship, to learn the French language, to see what France looked like, and to return afterwards as interpreters. The boys, though they were practically kidnapped at first, were soon reconciled to going, especially when they were dressed in French clothes!

When Cartier was on his way home he sailed in a north-easterly direction in such a way as to overlook the broad channel between the Gaspé Peninsula and Anticosti Island, but having rounded the easternmost extremity of

C 312

JACQUES CARTIER

that large island, he coasted along its northern shores until he caught sight of the opening of the Canadian channel to the west. He believed then that he had discovered the long-looked-for opening of the trans-continental passage, and sailed for France with his wonderful news.

On the 19th of May, 1535, Cartier started again from St. Malo with three ships, the biggest of which was only 120 tons, while the others were respectively 60 and 40 tons capacity. The crew consisted of about 112 persons, and in addition there were the two Indian youths who had been kidnapped on the previous voyage, and were now returning as interpreters. Instead, however, of reaching Newfoundland in twenty days, he spent five weeks crossing the Atlantic before he reached his rendezvous with the other ships at Blanc Sablon, on the south coast of Labrador; for the easy access to the Gulf of St. Lawrence through Cabot Strait (between Newfoundland and Cape Breton) was not yet realized. Once past Anticosti Island, the two Huron interpreters began to recognize the scenery.[1] They now explained to Cartier that he had entered the estuary of a vast river. This they said he had only to pursue in ships and boats and he would reach "Canada" (which was the name they gave to the district round about Quebec), and that beyond "Canada" no man had ever been known to reach the end of this great water; but, they added, it was fresh water, not salt, and this last piece of information much disheartened Cartier, who feared that he had not, after all, discovered the water route across North America to the Pacific Ocean. He therefore turned about and once more searched the opposite coast of Labrador most minutely, displaying, as he did so, a seaman-

[1] Anticosti Island received from Cartier the name of "the Island of the Assumption of the Blessed Virgin", in consequence of his having discovered it to be an island on the feast day of that name. It did not receive its present title until the late seventeenth century.

ship which was little else than marvellous, for it is a very dangerous coast, the seas are very stormy, and the look-out often hampered by a sudden rising of dense fog; there are islands and rocks (some of them almost hidden by the water) and sandbanks; but Cartier made this survey of southern Labrador without an accident.

At this period, some three hundred and seventy-five years ago, the northern coasts of the Gulf of St. Lawrence and of Anticosti Island swarmed with huge walruses, which were described by Cartier as sea horses that spent the night on land and the day in the water. They have long since been exterminated by the English and French seamen and settlers.

At last Cartier set sail for the south-west, intending to explore this wonderful river and to reach the kingdom of Canada. According to his understanding of the Amerindian interpreters, the waters of the St. Lawrence flowed through three great states: *Saguenay*, which was the mountainous Gaspé Peninsula and the opposite coast; *Canada*, Quebec and its neighbourhood; and *Hochelaga*, the region between Montreal and Lake Ontario. At the mouth of the Saguenay River, where Tadoussac is now situated, he encountered large numbers of white whales—the Beluga. These are really huge porpoises, allied to the narwhals, but without the narwhal's exaggerated tusk. When he reached the vicinity of the modern Quebec,[1] and his Amerindian interpreters found themselves at their actual home (for they were far away from home on a fishing expedition when he caught them in Gaspé Bay) there was great rejoicing; for they were able to tell their relations of the wonderful country to which they had been across the ocean. Cartier was delighted with the surroundings of "Canada" (Quebec), near which at that time was a large settlement (Stadacona) of Huron

[1] Then called "Canada". The word Quebec (pronounced *Kebek*) means the narrow part of a river.

Indians under a chief named Donnacona. He decided to lay up his ships here for the winter, and to pursue the rest of his western explorations in his boats.

But the Amerindians for some reason were not willing that he should go any farther, and attempted to scare him from his projects by arranging for three of their number to come down river in a canoe, dressed in dogs' skins, with their faces blackened, and with bisons' horns fastened to their heads. These devils pretended to take no notice of the French, but to die suddenly as they reached the shore, while the rest of the natives gave vent to howlings of despair and consternation. The three devils were pretending to have brought a message from a god to these Hurons of "Canada" that the country up river (Hochelaga) was so full of ice and snow that it would be death for anyone to go there.

However, this made little or no impression on Cartier; but he consented to leave a proportion of his party behind with the chief Donnacona as hostages, and then started up country in his boats with about seventy picked officers and men. On the 2nd of October, 1535, they reached the vicinity of the modern Montreal, the chief settlement of Hochelaga. The Huron town at the foot of the hills was circular in outline, surrounded by a stockade of three rows of upright tree trunks, which rose to its highest point in the middle, where the timbers of the inner and outward sides sloped to meet one another, the height of the central row being about 8 feet above the ground. All round the inside there was a platform or rampart on which were stored heavy stones to be hurled at any enemy who should attempt to scale the fence. The town was entered by only one doorway, and contained about fifty houses surrounding an open space whereon the townspeople made their bonfires. Each house was about 50 feet long by 12 to 15 feet wide. They were roofed with bark, and usually had attics which were storerooms for food. In the centre of each of these long houses there was a fireplace where the cooking for the whole of the house inhabitants was done. Each family had its own room, but each house probably contained five families. Almost the only furniture, except cooking pots, was mats on which the people sat and slept. The food of the people consisted, besides fish and the flesh of beavers and deer, of maize and beans. Cartier at once recognized the maize or Indian corn as the same grain ("a large millet") as that which he had seen in Brazil.

He gives a description of how they made the maize into bread (or rather "dampers", "ashcakes"); but as this is not altogether clear, it is better to combine it with Champlain's description, written a good many years later, but still at a time when the Hurons were unaffected by the white man's civilization. According to both Cartier and Champlain, the women pounded the corn to meal in a wooden mortar, and removed the bran by means of fans made of the bark of trees. From this meal they made bread, sometimes mixing with the meal the beans (*Phaseolus vulgaris*), which had been boiled and mashed. Or they would boil both Indian corn and beans into a thick soup, adding to the soup blueberries,[1] dried raspberries, or pieces of deer's fat. The meal derived from the corn and beans they would make into bread, baking it in the ashes.

Or they would take the pounded Indian corn without removing the bran, and put two or three handfuls of it into an earthen pot full of water, stirring it from time to time, when it boiled, so that it might not adhere to the pot. To this was added a small quantity of fish, fresh or dry, according to the season, to give a flavour to the *migane* or porridge. When the dried fish was

[1] The Canada Blueberry (*Vaccinium canadense*), called by the French *bluës* or *bluëts*. These bluës were collected and dried by the Amerindians, and made a sweet nutriment for eating in the winter.

used the porridge smelt very badly in the nostrils of Europeans, but worst of all when the porridge was mixed with dried venison, which was sometimes nearly putrid! If fish was put into this porridge it was boiled whole in the mealy water, then taken out without any attempt to remove the fins, scales, or entrails, and the whole of the boiled fish was pounded up and put back into the porridge. Sometimes a great birch-bark "kettle" would be filled with water, fish, and meat, and red-hot stones be dropped in till it boiled. Then with a spoon they would collect from the surface the fat and oil arising from the fish or meat. This they afterwards mixed with the meal of roasted Indian corn, stirring it with this fat till they had made a thick soup. Sometimes, however, they were content to eat the young corn-cobs freshly roasted, which as a matter of fact (with a little salt) is one of the most delicious things in the world. Or they would take ears of Indian corn and bury them in wet mud, leaving them thus for two or three months; then the cobs would be removed and the rotted grain eaten with meat and fish, though it was all muddy and smelt horribly. Cartier also noticed that these Huron Indians had melons and pumpkins, and described their wampum or shell money.[1]

From the eminence on which the Huron city stood, Cartier obtained a splendid view of rivers and moun-

[1] Cartier, in Hakluyt's translation, is made to say (I modernize the spelling): "They dig their grounds with certain pieces of wood as big as half a sword, on which ground groweth their corn, which they call 'offici'; it is as big as our small peason. . . . They have also great store of musk melons, pompions, gourds, cucumbers, peas, and beans of every colour, yet differing from ours."

Wampum, or shell money (which recalls the shell money of the Pacific Islands), consisted either of beads made from the interior parts of sea shells or land shells, or of strings of perforated sea shells. The most elaborate kind of wampum was that of the Amerindians of Canada and the eastern United States, the shell beads of which were generally white. The commoner wampum beads were black and violet. Wampum belts were made which illustrated events, dates, treaties of peace, &c., by a rude symbolism (figures of men and animals, upright lines, &c.), and these were worked neatly on string by employing different-coloured beads.

tains and magnificent forests, and called the place then and there, in his Norman French, Mont Réal, or Royal Eminence, a name which it will probably bear for all time, though the actual city of Montreal lies a few miles below.

Montreal was the limit of Cartier's explorations on this journey. He returned thence to "Canada" or Stadacona, where his men built a fort armed with artillery, and where his ships were anchored. Here he had to stay from the middle of November, 1535, to the middle of April, 1536, his ships being shut in by the ice. The experiences of the French during these five months were mostly unhappy. At first Cartier gave himself up to the collecting of information. He noticed for the first time the smoking of tobacco,[1] and collected information about the products and features of "Canada". The Indians told him of great lakes in the far west, one of which was so vast that no man had seen the end of it. They told him that anyone travelling up the Richelieu River (as it was called sixty years later) would eventually reach a land in the south where in the winter there was no ice or snow, and where fruit and nut trees grew in abundance. Cartier thought that they were talking to him of Florida, but their geographical information can scarcely have stretched so far; they probably referred to the milder regions of New Jersey and Virginia, which would be reached by following southwards the valley of the Hudson and keeping to the lowlands of the eastern United States.

[1] "There groweth also a certain kind of herb whereof in summer they make a great provision for all the year, making great account of it, and only men use it; and first they cause it to be dried in the sun, then wear it about their necks wrapped in a little beast's skin made like a bag, together with a hollow piece of stone or wood like a pipe. Then when they please they make powder of it and put it in one of the ends of the said cornet or pipe, and laying a coal of fire upon it at the other end, suck so long that they fill their bodies full of smoke, till that it cometh out of their mouth and nostrils, even as out of the tunnel of a chimney. They say that this doth keep them warm and in health: they never go without some of it about them. We ourselves have tried the same smoke, and having put it in our mouths, it seemed almost as hot as pepper." The foregoing is one of the earliest descriptions of tobacco smoking in any European language, the original words being in Cartier's Norman French.

As the winter set in with its customary Canadian severity the real trouble of the French began. They did not suffer from the cold, but they were dying of scurvy. This disease, from which the natives also suffered to some extent, was due to their eating nothing but salt or smoked provisions—forms of meat or fish. They lived, of course, shut up in the fort, and Cartier's fixed idea was to keep the Hurons from the knowledge of his misfortune, fearing lest, if they realized how the garrison was reduced, they might treacherously attack and massacre the rest; for in spite of the extravagant joy with which their arrival had been greeted, the Amerindians—notably the two interpreters who had been to France and returned—showed at intervals signs of disquiet and a longing to be rid of these mysterious white men, whose coming might involve the country in unknown misfortunes. In January and February, also, Donnacona and these two interpreters and many of the Huron men had been absent hunting in the forests, so that there was no one among the Amerindians to whom the French could turn for information regarding this strange disease. At last 25 out of the 112 who had left France were dead, and of the remainder only 10 men, including Cartier, were not grievously ill. Those who were living found it sometimes beyond their strength to bury the dead in the frozen ground, and simply placed their bodies in deep snow. Once or twice, when Cartier left the fort to go out to the ships, he met Domagaya, one of the two interpreters, and found that he also was suffering from this mysterious disease, though not nearly so badly as the French people. On the body of one young man who died of scurvy Cartier and his officers, shuddering, made investigations, opening the corpse and examining the organs to try and find the cause of death. This was on the afternoon of a day on which they had held a solemn service before a statue erected to the Virgin

Mary on the shore opposite to the ships. All who were fit to walk went in procession from the fort to the statue, singing penitential psalms and the Litany and celebrating Mass.

Some days after this religious service Cartier met the interpreter, Domagaya, and to his surprise found him perfectly well and strong. He asked him for an explanation, and was told that the medicine which cured this disease was made from the leaves and bark of a tree called ameda.[1] Cartier then ventured to say that one of his servants was sick of this unknown disease, and Domagaya sent for two women, who taught the French people how to make an extract from the balsam fir for drinking, and how to apply the same liquid to the inflamed skin. The effect on the crews was miraculous. In six days all the sick were well and strong.

Then came the sudden spring. Between April 15th and May 1st the ice on the river was all melted, and on the 6th May, 1536, Cartier started from the vicinity of Quebec to return to France. But before leaving he had managed to kidnap Donnacona, the chief of the Huron settlement, and six or seven other Amerindians, amongst them Tainyoanyi, one of the two interpreters who had already been to France. He seized these men, it appears, partly because he wanted hostages and had good reason to fear that the Indians meditated a treacherous attack on his ships before they could get away. He also wished for native witnesses at Court, when he reached France, to testify to the truth of his discoveries, and even more to convince the King of France that there was great profit to be obtained from giving effect to Cartier's explorations. The chief, Donnacona, was full of wonderful stories of the Saguenay region, and of the great lakes to the northwards of Quebec. Probably he was only alluding to the wealth of copper now known to exist in northern Canada, but to

[1] This tree was the balsam fir, *Abies balsamea.*

Cartier and the other Frenchmen it seemed as though he spoke of gold and silver, rubies, and other precious stones.

Donnacona's people howled and wept when their chief was seized; but Cartier obliged the chief to reassure them, and to say that the French had promised to bring him back after he had paid a visit to their great king, who would return him to his country with great presents. As a matter of fact, not one of these Indians rapt away by Cartier ever saw Canada again. But this was not the fault of Cartier, but of the distractions of the times which turned away the thoughts of King Francis I from American adventures. The Indians were well and kindly treated in France, but all of them died there before Cartier left St. Malo to return to Canada in 1541.

One advantage he derived from sailing away with these hostages was (no doubt) that they could give him geographical information of importance which materially shortened the return journey. For the first time he made use of the broad strait between Anticosti Island and Gaspé Peninsula, and, better still, entered the Atlantic, not by the dangerous northern route through the straits of Belle Isle, but by means of Cabot Strait, between Newfoundland and Cape Breton Island. Of these discoveries he availed himself on his third and last voyage in 1541.

When in that year he once more anchored his ships near Quebec he found the attitude of the Hurons changed. They enquired about their friends and relations who had been carried off five years before, and although they pretended to be reconciled to their fate when they heard (not altogether truly) that one or two were dead, and the others had become great lords in France and had married French women, they really felt a disappointment so bitter and a hostility so great that Cartier guessed their expressions of welcome to be false. However, he sent back to France two of the ships under his command and beached the other three, landed his stores, built two forts at Cap Rouge, above and below, and then started off with a few of his men and two boats to revisit the country of Hochelaga. Here he intended to examine the three rapids or "saults"—interruptions to the navigation of the St. Lawrence—which he had observed on his previous journey, and which were later named the La Chine Rapids (in the belief that they were obstacles on the river route to China). But these falls proved insuperable obstacles to his boats, and he gave up any further idea of westward exploration, returned to his forts and ships near Quebec, and there laid the foundations of a fortified town, which he called Charlesbourg Royal. Here he spent a very difficult winter, the Hurons in the neighbourhood becoming increasingly hostile, and at last, when the spring came, as he had received no relief from France, he took to his three ships, abandoned Charlesbourg Royal (having probably to do some fighting before he could get safely away) and thence sailed for France. Off the Avalon Peninsula of Newfoundland he met the other ships of the expedition which was to have occupied Canada for France. These were under the command of the Sieur de Roberval, a French nobleman, who had really been made head of the whole enterprise, with Cartier as a subordinate officer, but who, the year before, had allowed Cartier to go off to Canada and prepare the way, promising to follow immediately. The interview between Cartier and Roberval, near where the capital of Newfoundland (St. John's) now stands, was a stormy one. Roberval ordered Cartier to return at once to Charlesbourg and await his arrival. However, in the middle of the night which followed this interview, Cartier took advantage of a favourable wind and set sail for France, arriving soon afterwards at St. Malo.

But Roberval arrived at Charlesbourg (going the roundabout way through the straits of Belle Isle, for Cartier had told him nothing of the convenient passage through Cabot Strait), and there spent the winter of

1542–3, sending his ships back to France. This winter was one of horrors. Roberval was a headstrong, passionate man, perfectly reckless of human life. He maintained discipline by ferocious sentences, putting many of his men in irons, whipping others cruelly, women as well as men, and shooting those who seemed the most rebellious. Even the Indians were moved to pity, and wept at the sight of the woes of these unhappy French men and women under the control of a bloodthirsty tyrant, and many of them dying of scurvy, or miserably weak from that disease.[1]

However, when the weather was warm again, in June, 1543, Roberval started up the St. Lawrence River in boats to reach the wonderful country of Saguenay. Apparently he met with little success, and, being relieved by French ships in the late summer of 1543, he returned to France.

Thus the splendid work achieved by Cartier seemed to have come to nothing, for neither he nor Roberval revisited America. The French settlement near Quebec was aban-

[1] A story was subsequently told of Roberval's stern treatment which had a germ of truth in it, though it has since been the foundation of many a romance. On the journey out from France it is said that Roberval took with him his niece Marguérite, a high-born lady, who was accompanied by an old companion or nurse. Marguérite was travelling with her uncle because, unknown to him, she had a lover who had sailed with him on this expedition and whom she hoped to marry. As they crossed the Atlantic these facts leaked out, and Roberval resolved to bide his time and punish his niece for her deception. As they passed the coast of Southern Labrador Marguérite and her old nurse were seized and put into a boat, Roberval ordering his sailors to row them ashore to an island, and leave them to their fate. They were given four guns with ammunition and a small supply of provisions. But, as the boat was leaving the ship, Marguérite's lover threw himself into the sea and swam to the island. Here, according to the story which Marguérite is supposed to have told afterwards, they endeavoured to live by killing the wild animals and eating their flesh; but her lover-husband died, so also did her child soon after it was born, and then the old nurse, and the unhappy Marguérite was left alone with the wild beasts, especially the white Polar bears, who thronged round her hut. Nevertheless she kept them at bay with her arquebus, and managed somehow to support an existence, until after nineteen months' isolation the ascending smoke of her fire was seen by people on one of the many fishing vessels which, by this time, frequented the coasts of Newfoundland. She was taken off the island and restored to her home in France. The island to which this tradition more especially relates is now called Grand Meccatina.

doned, so far as the officers of the French king were concerned, and between 1545 and about 1583, if any other Frenchman or European visited Canada it was some private adventurer who traded with the natives in furs, or Basques from France and Spain who frequented the waters of the Gulf of St. Lawrence on account of the abundance of whales, walruses, and seals. In fact, at the close of the sixteenth century, the Spanish Basques had established themselves on shore at Tadoussac and other places, and seemed likely to colonize the country.

# CHAPTER III

## Elizabethan Pioneers in North America

Except that the ships of Bristol still no doubt continued to resort to the banks of Newfoundland for fishing, and that even the captains of these ships were occasionally elected admirals of the French, Basque, Portuguese, and English fishing fleets during the summer, the English, as a nation, took no part in claiming political dominion over North America after the voyage of Captain John Rut in 1527. This was the fault of Sebastian Cabot, the son of the man who founded British America, and who had returned to England long afterwards as the Grand Pilot appointed by Edward VI to further the discovery of a northern sea passage to China. Through him the attention of adventurers for a time was diverted from America to the "discovery" of Russia (as it has been called). The efforts of Sebastion Cabot were directed towards the revelation of a north-east passage by way of Arctic Russia to the Pacific, rather than past Newfoundland and Labrador and across Arctic America.

But as soon as Elizabeth came to the throne the sea adventurers of Britain, freed from any subservience to Spanish wishes, developed maritime intercourse between England, Morocco, and West Africa on the one hand, and Tropical and North America on the other. Once more the discovery of the North-west Passage across America to China came into favour. MARTIN FROBISHER[1]

[1] The name was also spelt Furbusher, and in other ways. He became Sir Martin Frobisher over the wars of the Armada, and died Lord High Admiral of England in 1592.

offered himself as a discoverer, and the Earl of Warwick found the means which provided him with two small sailing vessels of 25 and 20 tons each, besides a pinnace of 10 tons.[1] Queen Elizabeth confined herself, in the way of encouragement, to waving her lily hand from her palace of Greenwich as these three little boats dropped down the Thames on the 8th of June, 1576. She also sent them "an honourable message", which no doubt reached them at Tilbury.

But the pinnace was soon swallowed up in the high seas; the seamen in the vessel of 20 tons lost heart and turned their ship homewards. Frobisher alone, in his 25-ton bark, sailed on and on across the stormy Atlantic, past the south end of Greenland, and over the great gulf that separates Greenland from Labrador. He missed the entrance to Hudson's Bay, but reached a great "island" which he named Meta Incognita[2]. Here he gathered up stones and, as he believed, minerals, besides capturing at least one Eskimo, and then returned.

One of his stones was declared by the refiners of London to contain gold. There was at once—as we should say in modern slang—a boom for these Arctic regions. Queen Elizabeth took part in it, and on the 27th of May, 1577, a considerable fleet, under the command of Frobisher, sailed past the Orkneys for the south end of Greenland. It did not reach as far as Meta Incognita, but it brought back large heaps of earth and pieces of rock, probably from northern Labrador, which

[1] It may be of interest to set forth the kind of rations shipped in those Elizabethan times for the food of the sailors. According to Frobisher's accounts these consisted of salted beef, salt pork, salt fish, biscuit, meal for making bread, dried peas, oatmeal, rice, cheese, butter, beer, and wine, with brandy for emergencies. As regards beer, the men were to have a ration of 1 gallon a day each. Altogether it may be said that these rations were superior in variety—and no doubt in quality—to the food given to seamen in the British merchant marine in the nineteenth century.

[2] We now know Meta Incognita to be the southernmost peninsula of the vast Baffin Island.

almost certainly contained mica schist, and were therefore believed to be full of gold. The following year, 1578, Frobisher started on his third American voyage with a fleet of fifteen vessels, mainly financed by Queen Elizabeth, and manned to a great extent by the sons of the aristocracy, besides a hundred persons who were going out as colonists. For this region of ice and snow which was believed to be a mass of gold-bearing rocks! But the result was one of bitter disappointment. The captains were bewildered by the immense icebergs, "so vast that, as they melted, torrents poured from them in sparkling waterfalls". One iceberg toppled over on to a ship and crushed it, though most of the sailors were picked up in the sea and saved. In the thick mists the greater part of the fleet blundered into Hudson's Straits, yet did not realize that they had found a passage into the heart of Canada. At last, disgusted with this land of bare rocks, ice, and snow, they filled up the ships with cargoes of stones supposed to contain gold, and straggled back to England. No gold was extracted, however, from these cargoes, and much discouragement ensued.

Sir Humphrey Gilbert, one of the brilliant figures of Elizabeth's reign—scholar, poet, courageous adventurer, and man of chivalry—stimulated by the discoveries of Frobisher, obtained a patent or charter in 1578, and, after several unsuccessful attempts, led an expedition of small sailing ships to Newfoundland, where he entered St. John's Bay, and in the presence of the Basque, Portuguese, and Breton fishermen took formal possession of the country for Queen Elizabeth, raising a pillar on which the arms of England were engraved as a token. He then proceeded to grant lands to the fishermen to reassure them, and loaded his ships with rocks brought from the interior mountains and supposed to contain minerals. But in his further explorations of the southern coast of Newfoundland one of the ships was lost and nearly a hundred men intended as colonists were drowned.

Gilbert then determined to return to England in his small frigate of 10 tons named the *Squirrel*. He was accompanied by a larger vessel, the *Golden Hinde*, but refused to leave the men on the *Squirrel* to their fate. Consequently, between the Azores and the north coast of Spain, when the *Squirrel* was overwhelmed by the heavy seas, Sir Humphrey Gilbert perished together with all on board.

In spite, however, of the disappointing results of Gilbert's attempt to found a colony in Newfoundland, the importance of the cod fishery and the ivory tusks and oil of the walruses drew ever more and more ships from Bristol and Devonshire to the coasts of that great island and to the Gulf of St. Lawrence beyond. In 1592 the English adventurers got as far west as Anticosti Island (in a ship from Bristol), and in 1597 there is the first record of English ships (from London—the *Hopewell* and the *Chancewell*) sailing up the St. Lawrence River, perhaps as far west as Quebec.

In 1602, stimulated by Sir Walter Raleigh,[1] Bartholomew Gosnold sailed direct to the coast of North America south of the Newfoundland latitudes, and anchored his bark off the coast of Massachusetts on the 26th of March, 1602. Failing to find a good harbour here, he stood out for the south and definitely discovered and named Cape Cod, not far from the modern city of Boston. From Cape Cod he made his way to the Elizabeth Islands in Buzzard's Bay, and here he built a storehouse and fort, and may be said to have laid the foundations of the future colony of New England. He

[1] In 1584, Sir Walter Raleigh, the half-brother of Sir Humphrey Gilbert, financed an expedition to sail to the coast of North America in a more southerly direction. In this way was founded the (afterwards abandoned) colony of Roanoke, in North Carolina. It was to this region that Queen Elizabeth applied the title of Virginia, which some years afterwards was transferred to the first English colony on the James River.

brought back with him a cargo of sassafras root, which was then much esteemed as a valuable medicine and a remedy for almost all diseases.

Subsequent expeditions of English ships explored and mapped the coast of Maine, and took on board Amerindians for exhibition in England. Their adventures, together with those of the colonists farther south, led to the creation of chartered companies, and to the great British colonies of New England, New York, Virginia, the Carolinas, and Georgia, which were to become in time the United States of America—a vast field of adventure which we cannot follow farther in this book.

As regards Newfoundland, James I, in 1610, granted a patent to a Bristol merchant for the foundation there of a colony, and although this attempt, and another under Sir George Calvert (Lord Baltimore) in 1616, came almost to nothing through the attacks of the French and the dislike of the crews of the fishing vessels to permanent settlers who might interfere with the fishing industry, the English colonization of Newfoundland to some extent caught hold, so that in 1650 there were about two thousand colonists of English descent along the east and south-east coasts of the island. But settlement was prohibited within six miles of the shore, to please the fishermen, and this regulation checked for more than two hundred years the colonization of Newfoundland.

Nova Scotia as a British colony also came into being as another result of these adventurous British expeditions to North America in the reign of James I. Under the name of Acadie this region had been declared to be a portion of New France by De Monts and Champlain in 1604–14. But the English colonists in 1614 drove the French out of the peninsula of Nova Scotia on the plea that it was a part of the discoveries made by the Cabots on behalf of the British Crown. In 1621 James I gave a grant of all this territory to Sir William Alexander under the name of

Nova Scotia, and both Charles I and Cromwell encouraged settlement in this beautiful region. When Charles II ceded it to France in 1667 the English and Scottish colonists who were residing there, and the English settlers of New England, refused to recognize the effects of the Treaty of Bréda, and so harassed the French in the years which followed that in 1713 Nova Scotia was, together with Newfoundland, recognized as belonging to Great Britain. The French colonists were allowed to remain, but during the course of the eighteenth century they combined with the Amerindians (who liked the French and disliked the British) and made the position of the British colonists so precarious that they were finally expelled and obliged to transfer themselves to Louisiana and Canada. This was the departure of the Acadians so touchingly described by Longfellow.

The British had become tenacious of their rights over the east coast of Newfoundland, because from the middle of the seventeenth century onwards they were becoming increasingly interested in the whale fisheries and the fur trade of the lands bordering on Hudson's Bay, and would not tolerate any blocking of the sea route thither by the French.

In the explorations of Arctic America, Frobisher's expeditions had been succeeded by those of JOHN DAVIS, who in the course of three voyages, beginning in June, 1585, passed the entrance of Hudson's Straits and reached a point as far north as 72° 41′, a lofty granite island, which he named Sanderson's Hope. He saw beyond him a great sea, free, large, very salt, and blue, unobstructed by ice and of an unsearchable depth, and believed that he had completely discovered the eastern entrance of the North-West Passage.

HENRY HUDSON, the great English navigator, who had made two voyages (1607–8) for the English-Moscovy Company to discover a north-east passage to India, past

c 312

ICEBERGS AND POLAR BEARS

Siberia, commanded a third experiment in 1609 at the expense of the Dutch East India Company. He was to discover the North-West Passage. For this purpose he entered the river now named the Hudson, but soon found it was only a river; though he returned to Holland with such an encouraging account of the surrounding country that the Dutch a little later on, founded on the banks of the Hudson River their colony of New Amsterdam (afterwards the State of New York). In 1610 Hudson accepted a British commission to sail beyond where Davis and Frobisher had passed, and once more seek for the north-west passage to China. Instead he found the way into Hudson's Bay. Here his men, alarmed at the idea of being lost in these regions of ice and snow, mutinied against him, placed him and those who were faithful to him in a boat, and cast them off, themselves returning to England with the news of his discovery. Hudson was never heard of again, and, strange to say, the mutineers apparently received no punishment.

Between 1602 and 1668, English adventurers from London and Bristol, notable amongst whom were WILLIAM BAFFIN, LUKE FOX, and CAPTAIN JAMES, mapped the coasts of Hudson's Bay and Baffin's Bay and brought to the notice of merchants in England the abundance of whales in these Arctic waters, and of fur-bearing beasts and fur-trading Indians in the region of Hudson's Bay.

This last point was most forcibly presented to Charles II and his Government by a disappointed French Canadian, Pierre Esprit Radisson, whose adventures will later on be described. Radisson, conceiving himself to be badly treated by the French Governor of Canada, crossed over to England with his brother-in-law, Chouart, and the two were warmly taken up by Prince Rupert of Bavaria, the cousin of Charles II. They were sent out by Prince Rupert in command of an expedition financed by him and a number of London merchants, and in 1669 the

New England captain, Gillam, returned to England with Chouart and the first cargo of furs from Hudson's Bay. This cargo so completely met the expectations of those who had promoted the venture that it led in 1670 to the foundation of the Governor and Company of Adventurers of England trading into Hudson's Bay, a company chartered by Charles II and presided over by Prince Rupert, and an association which proved to be the germ of British North America, of the vast three-quarters of the present Dominion of Canada.

# CHAPTER IV

## Champlain and the Foundation of Canada

From the first voyage of Cartier onwards, Canada was called intermittently New France, and its possibilities were not lost sight of by a few intelligent Frenchmen on account of the fur trade. Amongst these was Amyard de Chastes, at one time Governor of Dieppe, who got into correspondence with the adventurers who had settled as fur traders at Tadoussac, prominent amongst whom was Du Pont-Gravé. De Chastes dispatched with Pont-Gravé a young man whose acquaintance he had just made, SAMUEL CHAMPLAIN.[1] This was the man who, more than any other, created French Canada.

Champlain had had already a most adventurous life. He was born about 1567, at Brouage, in the Saintonge, opposite to the Island of Héron, on the coast of western France. From his earliest years he had a passion for the sea, but he also served as a soldier for six years. His father had been a sea captain, and his uncle as an experienced navigator was commissioned by the King of Spain to transport by sea to that country the remainder of the Spanish soldiers who had been serving in Brittany. The uncle took his nephew with him. Young Champlain when in Spain managed to ingratiate himself so much with the Spanish authorities that he was actually commissioned as a captain to take a king's ship out to the West Indies. No sooner did he reach Spanish America

[1] Afterwards the Sieur de Champlain. The title of *Sieur* (from the Latin *Senior*) is the origin of the English "sir", and is about equivalent to an English baronetcy.

than he availed himself of the first chance to explore it. For two years he travelled over Cuba, and above all Mexico. He visited the narrowest part of Central America and conceived the possibility of making a trans-oceanic canal across the Panama isthmus.

When he got back to France he placed before Henry IV a report on Spanish Central America, together with a project for making a canal at Panama. Henry IV was so pleased with his work and enterprise that he gave him a pension and the title of Geographer to the King. Shortly afterwards he met Governor de Chastes at Dieppe, and was by him sent out to Canada. The ship which carried Champlain, PONT-GRAVÉ,[1] the SIEUR DE MONTS,[2] and other French adventurers (together with two Amerindian interpreters whom Pont-Gravé had brought from Canada to learn French) arrived at Tadoussac on May 24, 1603.

Champlain lost no time in commencing his explorations. Tadoussac was at the mouth of an important river, called by the French the Saguenay, a name which they also applied to the mysterious and wonderful country through which it flowed in the far north; a country rich in copper and possibly other precious metals. Champlain ascended the Saguenay River for sixty miles as far as the rapids of Chicoutima. The Amerindians whom he met here told him of Lake St. John, lying at a short distance to the west, and that beyond this lake and the many streams which entered it there lay a region of uplands strewn with other lakes and pools; and farther away still began the sloping of the land to the north till the traveller sighted a great arm of the salt sea, and found himself amongst tribes (probably the Eskimo) who ate raw flesh, and to the Indians appeared absolute

[1] Correctly written this was François Gravé, Sieur du Pont.

[2] The full name was Pierre du Guast, Sieur de Monts. Including de Champlain and de Poutrincourt, who will be described later, we have here the four great heroes who founded French Canada.

savages.[1] This was probably the first allusion, recorded by a European, to the existence of Hudson's Bay, that huge inlet of the sea, which is one of the leading features in the geography of British North America.

The Montagnais Indians round about Tadoussac received Champlain with great protestations of friendship, and at the headquarters of their principal chief or "Sagamore" celebrated this new friendship and alliance with a feast in a very large hut. The banquet, as usual, was preceded by a long address from the Sagamore in answer to the description of France, given by one of the Indian interpreters. The address was accompanied by the solemn smoking of tobacco, and at every pause in this grave oration the natives present shouted with one voice: "Ho! ho! ho!" The repast consisted of elk's meat (which struck the Frenchmen as being like beef), also the flesh of bear, seal, beaver, and wild fowl. There were eight or ten stone boilers or cauldrons full of meats in the middle of the great hut, separated each six feet from each other, and each one having its own fire. Every native used a porringer or vessel made of birch bark. When the meat was cooked a man in authority distributed it to each person. But Champlain thought the Indians ate in a very filthy manner. When their hands were covered with fat or grease they would rub them on their own heads or on the hair of their dogs. Before the meat was cooked each guest arose, took a dog, and hopped round the boilers from one end of the great hut to the other. Arriving in front of the chief, the Montagnais Indian feaster would throw his dog violently to the ground, exclaiming: "Ho! ho! ho!" after which he returned to his place.

At the close of the banquet every one danced, with the

[1] The real name for this remarkable people, the Eskimo, is, in Alaska and Arctic North America, *Innuit*, and in Labrador and Greenland, *Karalit*. Eskimo (in French, *Esquimaux*) is said to be a corruption of the Montagnais-Indian word, Eskimantsik, meaning "eaters of raw flesh".

skulls of their Iroquois enemies slung over their backs. As they danced they slapped their knees with their hands, and shouted: "Ho! ho! ho!" till they were out of breath.

The huts of these Indians were low and made like tents, being covered with the bark of the birch tree. An opening about a foot of the top was left uncovered to admit light and to allow the smoke to escape. Though low, the huts were sometimes quite large, and would accommodate ten families. These slept higgledy-piggledy on skins, with their dogs amongst them. The dogs in appearance were something like what we know as Eskimo dogs, and also rather resembled the Chinese chow, with broad heads and rather short muzzles, prick ears, and a tail inclined to curl over the back. "All these people have a very cheerful disposition, laughing often, yet at the same time they are somewhat phlegmatic. They talk very deliberately, as if desiring to make themselves well understood, and, stopping suddenly, they reflect for a long time, when they resume their discourse."

They were agile, well-proportioned people, who in the summertime went about nearly naked, but in the winter were covered with good furs of elk, otter, beaver, bear, seal, and deer. The colour of their skin was usually a pale olive, but the women for some reason made themselves much darker-skinned than the men by rubbing their bodies with pigments which turned them to a dark brown. At times they suffered very much from lack of food, being obliged then to frequent the shore of the river or gulf to obtain shellfish. When pressed very hard by famine they would eat their dogs (their only domestic animal) and even the leather of the skins with which they clothed themselves. In the autumn they were much given to fishing for eels, and they dried a good deal of eel flesh, to last them through the winter. During the height of the winter they hunted the beaver, and later on the elk. Though they ate wild roots and fruits whenever they could obtain them, they do not seem to have cultivated any grain or vegetables. In the early spring they were sometimes dying of hunger, and looked so thin and haggard that they were mere walking skeletons. They were then ready to eat carrion that was putrid, so that it is little wonder that they suffered much from scurvy.

Yet the rivers and the gulf abounded in fish, and as soon as the waters were unlocked by the melting of the ice in April, the surviving Indians rapidly grew fat and well, and of course the late summer and the autumn brought them nuts (hickory and other kinds of walnut, and hazel nuts), wild cherries, wild plums, raspberries, strawberries, gooseberries, blackberries, currants,[1] cranberries, and grapes.

Champlain observed amongst them for the first time the far-famed Amerindian snowshoes, which he compares very aptly for shape to a racquet used in tennis.

Champlain next visited the site of Stadacona, but there was no longer any settlement of Europeans at that place, nor were the native Amerindians the descendants of the Hurons that had received Jacques Cartier. For the first time the name Quebec (pronounced Kebek) is applied to this point where the great River St. Lawrence narrows before dividing to encircle the Isle of Orleans. In fact, Quebec meant in the Algonkin speech a place where a river narrows; for a tribe of the great Algonkin family, *the*

[1] The wild currants so often mentioned by the early explorers of Canada are often referred to as red, green, and blue. The blue currants are really the black currant, now so familiar to our kitchen gardens (*Ribes nigrum*). This, together with the red currant (*Ribes rubrum*), grows throughout North America, Siberia, and eastern Europe. The unripe fruit may have been the green currants alluded to by Champlain, or these may have been the white variety of our gardens. The two species of wild strawberry which figure so frequently in the stories of these early explorers are *Fragaria vesca* and *F. virginiana*. From the last-named is derived the cultivated strawberry of Europe. The wild strawberries of North America were larger than those of Europe. Champlain does not himself allude to gooseberries (unless they are his *groseilles vertes*), but later travellers do. Three or more kinds of gooseberry grow wild in Canada, but they are different from the European species. The blueberry so often mentioned by Champlain (bluëts or bluës) was *Vaccinium canadense.*

Algonkins, allied to the tribes of Maine and New Brunswick, had replaced the Hurons as the native inhabitants of this region.

On the shore of Quebec he noticed "diamonds" in some slate rocks—no doubt quartz crystals. Proceeding on up the River St. Lawrence he observed the extensive woods of fir and cypress (some kind of *Thuja* or *Juniper*), the undergrowth of vines, "wild pears", hazel nuts, cherries, red currants and green currants, and "certain little radishes of the size of a small nut, resembling truffles in taste, which are very good when roasted or boiled". As they advanced towards the interior the country became increasingly mountainous on the south (the green mountains of New Hampshire), and was more and more beautiful—"the pleasantest land yet seen". Landing on the south bank of the St. Lawrence, west of the entrance of the river of the Iroquois (the Richelieu), he found magnificent forests, which, besides the trees already mentioned, included oaks, chestnuts, maples, pines, walnut-like nut trees,[1] aspens, poplars, and beeches; with climbing hops and vines, strawberries trailing over the ground, and raspberry canes and currant bushes "growing in the thick grass". These splendid woods on the islands and banks of the broad river were full of game: elks,[2] wapiti deer, Virginian deer, bears, porcupines, hares, foxes, beavers, otters, and musk rats, besides many animals he could not recognize.

At last his little expedition in "a skiff and canoe" had to draw into the bank, warned by the noise that they were approaching a great fall of water—the La Chine or St. Louis Rapids. Champlain wrote: "I saw, to my astonishment, a torrent of water descending with an impetuosity

[1] Of the genera *Juglans* and *Carya*.

[2] The huge deer of the genus *Alces*. Elk is the old Scandinavian name. *Moose*, derived from the Kri language, is the Canadian term, "Elk" being misapplied to the wapiti (red) deer. Champlain calls the elk *orignac*, its name in Algonkin.

such as I have never before witnessed. . . . It descends as if in steps, and at each descent there is a remarkable boiling, owing to the force and swiftness with which the water traverses the fall, which is about a league in length. . . . The territory on the side of the fall where we went overland consists, so far as we saw it, of very open wood, where one can go with his armour without much difficulty."

From the Algonkin Indians in the neighbourhood of these St. Louis Rapids, and also from those living near Quebec, Champlain obtained a good deal of geographical information to add to his own observations. He was given an idea, more or less correct, of Lake Ontario, the Falls of Niagara, Lake Erie and Lake Huron, and perhaps also of Lake Superior, a sea so vast, said the Amerindians, that the sun set on its horizon. This sheet of water, Champlain calculated, must be 1200 miles distant to the west, and therefore identical with the "Mer du sud" (Pacific Ocean), which all North-American explorers for three centuries wished to reach.

After collecting much information about possible copper mines in the regions north and south of the Lower St. Lawrence, and of silver[1] in New Brunswick or Nova Scotia, and a terrible story which he more than half believed about a monster of prodigious size, the *Gougou*,[2] Champlain set sail for France at the end of August, 1603.

In April, 1604, Champlain accompanied the Sieur de Monts (who had succeeded the dead Amyard de Chastes as head of a chartered fur-trading association) in a fresh expedition to North America, together with a hundred and

[1] Or lead mixed with silver. The local natives used this ore, which was white when beaten, for their arrowheads.

[2] The Gougou dwelt on the small island of Miscon, to the east of the Bay of Chaleurs. It had the form of a woman but was about a hundred feet high. Its habit was to catch and devour men and women, whom it first placed in a pocket capacious enough to hold a small ship. Its roarings and hissings could be heard at times coming from the island of Miscon, where the Gougou lay concealed. Even a Frenchman, the Sieur Prévert, had heard these noises. Probably this islet had a whirlpool communicating with a cavern into which fishermen were sucked by the current.

twenty artisans and several noblemen. They were to occupy the lands of "Cadie" (Acadia, Nova Scotia), Canada, and other places in New France. De Monts thought Tadoussac and Quebec too cold in wintertime, and preferred the sunnier east coast regions. He aimed indeed at colonizing what is now New England.

On the way to Nova Scotia, the expedition was nearly wrecked on Sable Island, about one hundred and twenty miles south of Cape Breton Island, and noticed there the large red cattle run wild from the bulls and cows landed on Sable Island by the Portuguese some sixty years earlier. (The Portuguese of the fifteenth and sixteenth centuries deserved well of humanity for the generous way in which they left cattle, goats, pigs, and rabbits to run wild on desert islands and serve as provender for shipwrecked mariners like Robinson Crusoe.) Champlain also speaks of the "fine large black foxes" which he and other voyagers noticed on Sable Island. How they came there is a mystery, unless the island had once been part of the mainland.

This same Sable Island had been the scene of an extraordinary experiment at the end of the previous century. In 1598 the Marquis de la Roche, given a commission to colonize New France, sailed in a small ship for North America with sixty convicts from French prisons as colonists. He landed them on Sable Island, and went away to look for some good site for his colony. But then a storm arose, and his little ship was literally blown back to France. The convicts, abandoned thus, built themselves shelters out of the driftwood of wrecks; killed and ate the cattle and caught fish. They made themselves warm clothes out of the skins of the seals which frequented the island coast in thousands. But these convicts quarrelled and fought among themselves so fiercely that when at last a ship from Normandy came to take them away, there were only twelve left—twelve shaggy men with long tangled hair and beards;

and, a legend says, in addition a Franciscan monk who had been landed on the island with them as a kind of missionary or chaplain, and who had been so heartbroken at their bloody quarrels and horrible deeds that when the Norman ship arrived to take the castaways back to France, the Franciscan refused to go with them, believing himself to be dying and wishing to end his life undisturbed. So he was left behind. But after the ship had sailed away he slowly mended, grew well and strong, and cultivated eagerly his little garden. For food he ate the whelks, mussels, and oysters that were so abundant on the shore. Occasionally ships (then as now) were wrecked on Sable Island in stormy weather, and the good monk ministered to the mariners who reached the shore. Also he was visited, ever and again, by the Breton fishing boats, which brought him supplies of necessaries and the bread and wine for celebrating Mass. Long after his death his spirit was thought to haunt the desolate island.

Champlain and his companions passed on from Sable Island to the south-east coast of Nova Scotia, noticing as they landed here and there the abundance of rabbits[1] and sea birds, especially the Greak Auk, of which they killed numbers with sticks, cormorants (whose fishy eggs they ate with enjoyment), puffins, guillemots, gulls, terns, scissorbills, divers, ospreys, buzzards, and falcons; and no doubt the typical American white-tailed sea eagles, ravens, ducks, geese, curlews, herons, and cranes. Here and there they found the shore "completely covered with sea wolves"—seals, of course, probably the common seal and the grey seal. Of these they captured as many as they wanted, for the seals, like most of the birds, were quite unafraid of man.

They then explored the Bay of Fundy, and, after zigzagging about, decided to fix on the harbour of St. John's

[1] There are no real rabbits in America. This was probably the Polar Hare (*Lepus timidus glacialis*), or the common small varying hare (*L. americanus*).

(New Brunswick) as the site for their colony. The future capital of New France, therefore, was begun on La Sainte Croix (Dochet) Island, near the mouth of the wonderful tidal estuary of the Uigudi (Ouygoudy) River.

Here they passed the winter, but suffered so badly from scurvy[1] that, when in the spring of 1605 Du Pont Gravé arrived from Brittany with supplies, the remnant of the colony was removed to the opposite coast of Nova Scotia to Port Royal (afterwards named by the English Annapolis[2]). The French seem to have fallen in love with this place from the very first. Nevertheless here they suffered from scurvy during the winter as elsewhere. Before moving over here, however, Champlain, together with De Monts, had explored the west of New England south of New Brunswick as far as Plymouth, just south of Boston.

Off the coast of Maine (Richmond's Island) they encountered agricultural Amerindians of a new tribe, the Penobskot probably, who cultivated a form of rank narcotic tobacco (*Nicotiana rustica*), which they called *Petun*. (A variety of this has produced the handsome garden flower *Petunia*, whose Latin name is derived from this native word Petun.) They also grew maize or Indian corn, planting very carefully three or four seeds in little mounds three

[1] How awful was this "mal de terre" or scurvy amongst the French settlers may be seen from this description of Champlain: "There were produced in the mouths of those who had it great pieces of superfluous and drivelling flesh, which got the upper hand to such an extent that scarcely anything but liquid could be taken. Their teeth became very loose and could be pulled out with the fingers without its causing them pain. . . . Afterwards a violent pain seized their arms and legs, which remained swollen and very hard, all spotted as if with fleabites; and they could not walk on account of the contraction of the muscles. . . . They suffered intolerable pains in the loins, stomach, and bowels, and had a very bad cough and short breath. . . . Out of seventy-nine who composed our party, thirty-five died and twenty were on the point of death (when spring began in May)."

Scurvy is said to be a disease of the blood caused by a damp, cold, and impure atmosphere combined with absence of vegetable food and a diet of salted or semi-putrid meat or fish, such as was so often the winter food of Amerindians and of the early French pioneers in Canada. We have already noted Cartier's discovery of the balsam remedy.

[2] From Queen Anne.

feet apart one from the other, the soil in between being kept clear of weeds. The American farmers of to-day cannot adopt any better method.

The islands round about Portland (Maine) were matted all over with wild red currants, so that the eye could scarcely discern anything else. Attracted by this fruit, clouds of wild pigeons had assembled.[1] They manifested hardly any fear of the French, who captured large numbers of them in snares, or killed them with guns. The natives of southern Maine fled with dismay on sighting the French ships, for they had never before seen sailing vessels, but later on they timidly approached the French ships in a canoe, then landed and went through a wild dance on the shore to typify friendliness. Champlain took with him some drawing paper and a pencil or crayon, together with a quantity of knives and ship's biscuit. Landing alone, he attracted the natives towards him by offering them biscuits, and having gathered them round him (being of course as much unable to understand their speech as they were French), he proceeded to ask questions by means of certain drawings, chiefly the outlines of the coast. The savages at once seized his idea, and taking up his pencil drew on the paper an accurate outline of Massachusetts Bay, adding also rivers and islands unknown to the French. They went on by further intelligent signs to supply information. For instance, they placed six pebbles at equal distances to intimate that Massachusetts Bay was occupied by six tribes and governed by as many chiefs. By drawings of growing maize and other plants they intimated that all these people lived by agriculture.

Champlain thought Massachusetts (in his first voyage)

[1] The pigeons referred to by Champlain were probably the Passenger pigeon (*Ectopistes*) which at one time was extraordinarily abundant in parts of North America, though it has now been nearly killed out by man. It would arrive in flocks of millions on its migratory journeys in search of food.

a most attractive region in the summer, what with the blue water of the enclosed arms of the sea, the lofty forest trees, and the fields of Indian corn and other crops.

When these French explorers reached the harbour of Boston, the islands and mainland were swarming with the native population. The Amerindians were intensely interested in the arrival of the first sailing vessel they had ever seen. Although it was only a small barque, its size was greater than any canoe known to them. As it seemed to spread huge white wings and to glide silently through the water without the use of paddles or oars, it filled them with surprise and admiration. They manned all their canoes[1] and came out in a flotilla to express their honour and reverence for the wonderful white men. But when the French took their leave, it was equally obvious that the natives experienced a sense of relief, for they were disquieted as well as filled with admiration at the arrival of these wonderful beings from an unknown world.

Champlain describes the wigwams or native huts as being cone-shaped, heavily thatched with reeds, with an opening at the top of the roof for the smoke to escape. Inside the huts was a low bed raised a foot from the ground and made of short posts driven into the ground, with a surface made of boards split from trees. On these boards were laid either the dressed skins of deer or bear, or thick mattresses made of reeds or rushes. The beds were large enough for several people to lie on. Champlain describes the huts as being full of fleas, and likewise the persons of the nearly naked Indians, who carried these fleas out with them into the fields when they were working, so that the Frenchmen by stopping to talk to

[1] It is interesting to learn from his accurate notes that in Massachusetts (and from thence southwards) there were no more bark canoes, but that the canoes were "dug-outs"—trunks of tall trees burnt and chipped till they were hollowed into a narrow vessel of considerable length.

the natives became covered with fleas to such an extent that they were obliged to change their clothes.

In the fields were cultivated not only maize, but beans similar to the beans grown by the natives of Brazil, vegetable marrows or pumpkins, Jerusalem artichokes[1], radishes, and tobacco. The woods were filled with oaks, walnut trees[2], and the red "cedar" of North America, really a very large juniper, the foliage of which in the summertime often assumes a reddish colour, together with the trunk. This Virginian juniper or "red cedar" is now quite a common tree in England. In warm weather it exhales a delicious aromatic scent.

All these natives of the Massachusetts coast were described by Champlain as being almost naked in the summertime, wearing at most a small piece of leather round the waist, and a short robe of spun hemp which hung down over the shoulders. Their faces were painted red, black and yellow. The men pulled out any hairs which might come on the chin, and thus were beardless. They were armed with pikes, clubs, bows, and arrows. The pikes were probably made of wood with the ends hardened by being burnt to a point in the fire, and the arrow tips were made of the sharp termination of the tail of the great king-crab.[3]

[1] This tuber, which is a well-known and very useful vegetable in England, comes from the root of a species of sunflower (*Helianthus tuberosus*). It has nothing to do with the real artichoke, which is a huge and gorgeous thistle, and it has equally nothing to do with Jerusalem. The English people have always taken a special delight in mispronouncing and corrupting words in order to produce as much confusion as possible in their names for things. Jerusalem is a corruption of *Girasole*, which is the Italian name given to this sunflower with the edible roots, because its flower is supposed always to turn towards the sun. The Jerusalem artichoke was originally a native of North America.

[2] These walnut trees were afterwards known in modern American speech as hickories, butter-nuts, and pig-nuts, all of which are allied to, but distinct from, the European walnut.

[3] *Limulus polyphemus.* This extraordinary crustacean is one of the oldest of living animals in its history, as it is closely related to the Xiphosura and even the Trilobites of the Primary Epoch, which existed millions of years ago. In a rough way it is a kind of connecting link between the Crustacea, or crabs and lobsters, and the Scorpions and spiders.

These Massachusetts "Indians" described to Champlain a wonderful bird which at some seasons of the year they caught in snares and ate. This Champlain at once guessed was the wild turkey, now, of course, quite extinct in that region. This wild turkey of the eastern half of North America (including southern Canada) was quite a distinct form from the Mexican bird, which last is the origin of our domestic turkey.

In July, 1606, as De Monts had not returned from France, and the little colony at Port Royal was without supplies, they decided to leave two Frenchmen in charge of the local chief of the Mikmak Indians, and find their way along the coast to Cape Breton, where they might get a fishing vessel to take them back to France. But after travelling in an open boat—a chaloupe—round the coast of Nova Scotia they met another small boat off Cape Sable, under the charge of the secretary of De Monts, and learnt that Lieutenant-General DE POUTRINCOURT[1] (one of the great names amongst the pioneers of Canada, and the man who had really chosen Port Royal for the French headquarters at Nova Scotia) had already returned from France with fresh supplies. Consequently, Champlain and his companions returned to Port Royal, and all set to work with eagerness to develop the settlement. Champlain relates in his book how he created vegetable gardens, trout streams and ponds, and a reservoir of salt water for sea fish; but he was soon off again on a fresh journey of exploration, because De Monts was not satisfied with Nova Scotia on account of the cold in winter. Accordingly Champlain examined the whole coast round the Bay of Fundy, and down to Cape Cod, and the islands of Martha's Vineyard and Nantucket. But in this region, already visited in past times by French, Spanish, and English ships, they found

[1] Jean de Biencourt, the Sieur de Poutrincourt and Baron de Saint-Just, were his full titles.

the natives treacherous and hostile. An unprovoked attack was made on the French after they landed, and several of the seamen were killed with arrows.

On the 24th of May, 1607, a small barque of six or seven tons burden (fancy crossing the wide Atlantic from Brittany to Nova Scotia in a ship of that size at the present day!) arrived outside Port Royal from France, with an abrupt notification that De Monts' ten years' monopoly and charter were *cancelled* by Henry IV, and that all the colony was to be withdrawn and brought back to France. Henry IV took this action simply because De Monts attempted to make his monopoly a real one,[1] and stop the ships of fur traders who were trading with the Amerindians of Cape Breton without his licence. These fur traders of Normandy then complained bitterly that because De Monts was a Protestant he was allowed not only to have this monopoly, but to endanger the spiritual welfare of the savages by spreading his false doctrines! So King Henry IV, volatile and capricious, like most of the French kings, cancelled a charter which had led to such heroic and remarkable results.

The greater part of the little colony had to leave Port Royal and make its way in small boats along the Nova Scotia coasts till they reached Cape Breton Island. Here fishing vessels conveyed them back to Brittany. It was in this boat journeying along the coast of Nova Scotia that Champlain discovered Halifax Harbour, then called by the Indian name of Shebuktu. As they passed along this coast with its many islands, they feasted on ripe raspberries, which grew everywhere "in the greatest possible quantity".

Poutrincourt, however, had succeeded in taking back

[1] You will observe that neither the French nor the English sovereigns of the sixteenth and seventeenth centuries went to much personal expense over the creation of colonies. They simply gave a charter or a monopoly, which cost them nothing, but which made other people pay.

with him samples of the corn, wheat, rye, barley, and oats which had been so successfully grown on the island of Sainte Croix and at Port Royal, and also presented to that monarch five brent-geese[1] which he had reared up from eggs hatched under a hen. The king was so delighted at these presents that he once more veered about and gave to De Monts the monopoly of the fur trade for one more year, in order to enable him to renew his colonies in New France.

The Sieur de Monts was again appointed by Henry IV Lieutenant-General in New France. The latter engaged Champlain as his lieutenant, and also sent out Du Pont Gravé in command of the second vessel, as head of the trading operations. This time, on the advice of Champlain, the expedition made its way directly to the St. Lawrence River, stopping first at Tadoussac, where Du Pont Gravé proceeded to take very strong measures with the Basque seamen, who were infringing his monopoly by trading with the natives in furs. Apparently they were still allowed to continue their whale fishery.

Once more Champlain heard from the Montagnais Indians of the great Salt Sea to the north of Saguenay, in other words, the southern extension of Hudson's Bay; and in his book he notes that the English in these latter years "had gone thither to find their way to China". However, he kept his intent fixed on the establishment of a French colony along the St. Lawrence, and may be said to have founded the city of Quebec (the site of which was then covered with nut trees) on the 4th of July, 1608. Then his enterprise was near being wrecked by a base conspiracy got up between a surgeon and a number of French artisans, who believed that by seizing and killing Champlain, and then handing over the infant settlement to the Spanish

[1] *Branta canadensis*, a handsome black-and-brown goose with white markings, which the French pioneers in Canada styled "outarde" or "bustard", and whose eggs were considered very good eating.

Basques, they might enable these traders and fishermen with their good strong ships to overcome Du Pont Gravé, and seize the whole country. Naturally (they believed) the Basques would reward the conspirators, who would thus at a stroke become rich men. They none of them wished to go to France, but would live here independent of outside interference. A conspirator, however, revealed the plot to Champlain as he was planting one of the little gardens which he started as soon as he had been in a place a few days. He went about his business very discreetly, arrested all the leading conspirators, gave them a fair trial, had the ringleader executed by Pont Gravé, and sent three others back to France. After this he settled down at Quebec for the winter, taking care, however, in the month of October, to plant seeds and vines for coming up in the spring.

In the summer of 1609 Champlain, apparently with the idea of thus exploring the country south of the St. Lawrence, decided to accompany a party of Algonkins and Hurons from Georgian Bay and the neighbourhood of Montreal, who were bent on attacking the Iroquois confederacy in the Mohawk country at the headwaters of the Hudson River. He was accompanied by two French soldiers—Des Marais and La Routte—and by a few Montagnais Indians from Tadoussac.

The Hurons[1] were really of the same group (as regards language and descent) as the Iroquois (Irokwá), but in those days held aloof from the five other tribes who had formed a confederacy[2] and alliance under the name of

[1] Huron was a French name given to the westernmost group of the Iroquois family (see p. 159). The Huron group included the Waiandots, the Eries or Erigas, the Arendáronons, and the Atiwándoronk or "neutral" nation. The French sometimes called all these Huron tribes "the good Iroquois". Iroquois was probably pronounced "Irokwá", and seems to have been derived from a word like Irokosia, the name of the Adirondack mountain country.

[2] The confederacy was founded about 1450 by the great Hiawatha (of Longfellow's poem), himself an Onondaga from south of Lake Ontario, but backed by the Mohawks only, in the beginning of his work.

*Ongwehonwe*—"Superior Men". The Iroquois (Mohawks, Oneidas, Onondagas, Kayugas, and Senekas) dominated much of what is now New York State, and from the mountain country of the Adirondaks and Catskills descended on the St. Lawrence valley and the shores of Lakes Ontario and Huron to rob and massacre.

The route into the enemy's country lay along the Richelieu River and across Lake Champlain to its southern end, in sight of the majestic snow-crowned Adirondak Mountains. On the way the allies stopped at an island, held a kind of review, and explained their tactics to Champlain. They set no sentries and kept no strict watch at night, being too tired; but during the daytime the army advanced as follows: The main body marched in the centre along the warpath; a portion of the troops diverged on either side to hunt up food for the expedition; and a third section was told off for "intelligence" work, namely, they ran on ahead and roundabout to locate the enemy, looking out especially along the rivers for marks or signals showing whether friends or enemies had passed that way. These marks were devised by the chiefs of the different tribes, and were duly communicated to the war leaders of tribes in friendship or alliance, like our cipher codes; and equally they were changed from time to time to baffle the enemy. Neither hunters nor main body ever got in front of the advance guard, lest they should give an alarm. Thus they travelled until they got within two days or so of the enemies' headquarters; thenceforward they only marched by night, and hid in the woods by day, making no fires or noise, and subsisting only on cooked maize meal.

At intervals the soothsayers accompanying the army were consulted for signs and omens; and when the war-chiefs decided on their plan of campaign they summoned all the fighting men to a smooth place in a wood, cut sticks a foot long (as many as there were warriors), and each leader of a division "put the sticks in such order as seemed to him best, indicating to his followers the rank and order they were to observe in battle. The warriors watched carefully this proceeding, observing attentively the outline which their chief had made with the sticks. Then they would go away and set to placing themselves in such order as the sticks were in. This manœuvre they repeated several times, and at all their encampments, without needing a sergeant to maintain them in the proper order they were able to keep accurately the positions assigned to them" (Champlain).

The Hurons who were accompanying Champlain frequently questioned him as to his dreams, they themselves having a great belief in the value of dreams as omens and indications of future events. One day, when they were approaching the country of the Iroquois, Champlain actually did have a dream. In this he imagined that he saw the Iroquois enemies drowning in a lake near a mountain. Moved to pity in his dream he wished to help them, but his savage allies insisted that they must be allowed to die. When he awoke he told the Amerindians of his dream, and they were greatly impressed, as they regarded it as a good omen.

Near the modern town of Ticonderoga the Hurons and Algonkins of Georgian Bay and Ottawa met a party of Iroquois, probably of the Mohawk tribe. The Iroquois had built rapidly a stockade in which to retreat if things should go badly with them, but the battle at first began in the old heroic style with as much ceremony as a French duel. First the allies from the St. Lawrence asked the Iroquois what time it would suit them to begin fighting the next day; then the latter replied: "When the sun is well up, if you don't mind? We can see better then to kill you all." Accordingly in the bright morning the Hurons and Algonkins advanced against the circular stockade of the Iroquois, and the Iroquois marched out to fight in great pomp, their leaders wearing plumed headdresses. With this exception both parties fought quite naked, and armed only with bows and arrows.

"I marched twenty paces in advance of the rest" (wrote Champlain) "till I was within about thirty paces of the Iroquois. . . . I rested my musket against my cheek, and aimed directly at one of the three chiefs. With the same shot two fell to the ground, and one of their men was so wounded that he died some time afterwards. I had loaded my musket with four balls. When they saw I had shot so favourably for them, they (the Algonkins and Hurons) raised such loud cries that one could not have heard it thunder.

"Meantime the arrows flew on both sides. The Iroquois were greatly astonished that two men had been so quickly killed, though they were equipped with armour woven from copper thread and with wood, which was proof against their arrows."

Whilst Champlain was loading to fire again one of his two companions fired a shot from the woods, whereupon the Iroquois took to flight, abandoning their camp and fort. As they fled they threw off their armour of wooden boards and cotton cloth.

As to the way in which the Hurons tortured their Iroquois prisoners, Champlain writes of one instance.

"They commanded him (the prisoner) to sing, if he had courage, which he did, but it was a very sad song." The Hurons kindled a fire, and when it was well alight they each took a brand from the blaze, the end of which was red-hot, and with this burnt the bodies of their prisoners tied to stakes. Every now and then they stopped and threw water over them to restore them from fainting. Then they tore out their finger nails and applied fire to the extremities of the fingers. After that they tore the scalps off their heads, and poured over the raw and bleeding flesh a kind of hot gum. Then they pierced the arms of the prisoners near the wrists, and drew up their sinews with sticks inserted underneath, trying to tear them out by force, and, if failing, cutting them. One poor wretch "uttered such terrible cries that it excited my pity to see him treated in this manner, yet at other times he showed such firmness that one would have said he suffered scarcely any pain at all".

In this case Champlain, seeing that the man could not recover from his injuries, drew apart and shot him dead, "thus putting an end to all the tortures he would have suffered".

But the savage Hurons were not yet satisfied. They opened the corpse and threw its entrails into the lake. Then they cut off head, arms, and legs, and cut out the heart; this they minced up, and endeavoured to force the other prisoners to eat it.

With those of his allies who were Montagnais Indians from Tadoussac, Champlain returned to that place. As they neared the shore the Montagnais women undressed themselves, jumped into the river, and swam to the prows of the canoes, from which they took the heads of the slain Iroquois. These they hung about their necks as if they had been some costly chain, singing and dancing meanwhile.

However, in spite of these and other horrors, Champlain had "separated from his Upper Canadian allies with loud protestations of mutual friendship", promising to go again into their country and assist them with continued "fraternal" relations.

From this expedition Champlain learned much regarding the geography of eastern North America, and he brought back with him to France, to present to King Henry IV, two scarlet tanagers—one of the commonest and most beautiful birds of the eastern United States—a girdle of porcupine quills made from the Canadian porcupine, and the head of a gar-pike caught in Lake Champlain.[1]

On Champlain's return from France in 1610 (he and other Frenchmen and Englishmen of the time made surprisingly little fuss about crossing the North Atlantic in small sailing vessels, in spite of the storms of spring and autumn) he found the Iroquois question still agitating the minds of the Algonkins, Montagnais, and Hurons. Representatives of these tribes were ready to meet this great captain of the *Mistigosh* or *Matigosh*[2] (as they called the French), and implored him to keep his promise to take part in another attack on the dreaded enemy of the Adirondak heights. Apparently the Iroquois (Mohawks) this time had advanced to meet the attack, and were ensconced in a round fortress of logs built near the Richelieu River.[3] The Algonkins and their allies on this expedition were armed with clubs, swords, and shields, as well as bows and arrows. The swords of copper (?) were really knife blades attached to long sticks like billhooks. Before the barricade, as usual, both parties commenced the fight by hurling insults at each other till they were out of breath, and shouting "till one could not have heard it thunder". The circular log barricade, however, would never have

[1] Unconsciously, no doubt, he brought away with him to the King of France one of the most remarkable freshwater fish living on the North-American continent, for the gar-pike belongs, together with the sturgeon and its allies, to an ancient type of fish the representatives of which are found in rock formations as ancient as those of the Secondary and Early Tertiary periods. Champlain may be said to have discovered this remarkable gar-pike (*Lepidosteus osseus*), which is covered with bony scales "so strong that a poniard could not pierce them". The colour he describes as silver-grey. The head has a snout two feet and a half long, and the jaws possess double rows of sharp and dangerous teeth. These teeth were used by the natives as lancets with which to bleed themselves when they suffered from inflammation or headache. Champlain declares that the gar-pike often captures and eats water birds. It would swim in and among rushes or reeds and then raise its snout out of the water and keep perfectly still. Birds would mistake this snout for the stump of a tree and would attempt to alight on it; whereupon the fish would seize them by the legs and pull them down under the water.

[2] Spelt by Champlain with a "ch" instead of *sh*.

[3] Then called the Rivière des Iroquois.

been taken by the Algonkins and their allies but for the assistance of Champlain and three or four Frenchmen, who with their musketry fire at short range paralysed the Iroquois. Champlain and one other Frenchman were wounded with arrows in the neck and arm, but not seriously. The victory of the allies was followed by the usual torture of prisoners, which Champlain made a slight—only slight—attempt to prevent.

But results far more serious arose from these two skirmishes with the Iroquois in 1609 and 1610. The Confederacy of the Five Nations (afterwards six) realized that they had been attacked unprovoked by the dominant white men of the St. Lawrence, called by the Montagnais *Mistigosh*, and by the Iroquois *Adoresetūi* ("men of iron", from their armour). They became the bitter enemies of the French, and tendered help first to the Dutch to establish themselves in the valley of the Hudson, and secondly to the English. In the great Colonial wars of the early eighteenth century the Iroquois were invaluable allies to the British forces, Colonial and Imperial, and counted for much in the struggle which eventually cost France Nova Scotia, New Brunswick, Maine, the two Canadas, and Louisiana. On the other hand, the French alliance with the Hurons, Algonkins, and Montagnais, begun by this brotherhood-in-arms with Champlain, secured for France and the French such widespread liking among the tribes of Algonkin speech, and their allies and friends, that the two Canadas and much of the Middle West, together with Michigan, Wisconsin, and Illinois, became French in sympathy without any war of conquest. When the French dominion over North America fell, in 1759, with the capture of Quebec by Wolfe's army, tribes of Amerindians went on fighting for five years afterwards to uphold the banner and the rule of the beloved French king.

On Champlain's next visit to Canada, in 1610, he handed over to the Algonkin Indians a French youth named Étienne Brulé (see p. 88), to be taught the Algonkin language (the use of which was spread far and wide over north-east America), and, further, sent a Huron youth to France to be taught French. Between 1611 and 1616 he had explored much of the country between Montreal (the foundations of which city he may be said to have laid on May 29, 1611, for his stockaded camp is now in the centre of it) and Lakes Huron and Ontario, especially along the Ottawa River, that convenient short cut (as a water route) between the St. Lawrence at Sault St. Louis (Montreal) and Lakes Huron and Superior. With short portages you can get in canoes from Montreal to the waters of Hudson Bay, or to Lake Winnipeg and the base of the Rocky Mountains.

In exploring this "River of the Algonkins" (as he called it), Champlain was nearly drowned between two rocks, and much hurt, from over bravery and want of knowledge of how to deal with a canoe on troubled water; but on June 4, 1613, he stood on the site of the modern city of Ottawa—the capital of the vast Canadian Dominion—and gazed at the marvellous Rideau or Curtain Fall, where the Rideau River enters the Ottawa. But the air was resonant with the sound of falling water. Three miles above the falls of the Gatineau and the Rideau, the main Ottawa River descended with a roar and a whirl of white foam and rainbow-tinted mist into the chasm called the Chaudière or Kettle. On a later occasion he describes the way in which the Algonkins propitiated the Spirit of the Chasm:

"Continuing our way, we came to the Chaudière Falls, where the savages carried out their customary ceremony. After transporting their canoes to the foot of the fall they assemble in one spot, where one of them takes up a collection on a wooden platter, into which each person puts a bit of tobacco. The collection having been made, the plate is placed in the midst of the troop, and all dance about it, singing after their style. Then one of the captains makes an harangue, setting forth that for a long time they have been accustomed to make this offering, by which means they are ensured protection against their enemies, that otherwise misfortune would befall them from the evil spirit. This done, the maker of the harangue takes the plate and throws the tobacco into the midst of the cauldron (the chasm of foaming water), whereupon they all together raise a loud cry. These poor people are so superstitious, that they would not believe it possible for them to make a prosperous journey without observing this ceremony at this place; for sometimes their enemies (Iroquois) await them at this portage, not venturing to go any farther on account of the difficulty of the journey. Consequently they are occasionally surprised and killed by the Iroquois at this place (the south bank of the Ottawa)."

Above the Chaudière Champlain met the Algonkin chief, Tessouat, and thus described the burial places of his tribe:

"On visiting the island I observed their cemeteries, and was struck with wonder as I saw sepulchres of a shape like shrines, made of pieces of wood fixed in the ground at a distance of about three feet from each other, and intersecting at the upper end. On the intersections above they place a large piece of wood, and in front another upright piece on which is carved roughly, as would be expected, the figure of the male or female interred. If it is a man, they add a shield, a sword attached to a handle after their manner, a mace, and bow and arrows. If it is a chief, there is a plume on his head, and some other *matachia* or embellishment. If it is a child, they give it a bow and arrow, if a woman or girl, a boiler, an earthen vessel, a wooden spoon, and an oar. The entire sepulchre is six or seven feet long at most, and four wide; others are smaller. They are painted yellow and red, with various ornaments as neatly done as the carving. The deceased is buried with his dress of beaver or other skins which he wore when living, and they lay by his side all his possessions, as hatchets, knives, boilers, and awls, so that these things may serve him in the land whither he goes; for they believe in the immortality of the soul, as I have elsewhere observed. These carved sepulchres are only made for the warriors, for in respect to others they add no more than in the case of women, who are considered a useless class, accordingly but little is added in their case."

In the summer of 1615 Champlain, returning from France, made his way up the Ottawa River, and, by a short portage, to Lake Nipissing, thence down French River to the waters of Lake Huron. On the banks of the French River he met a detachment of the Ottawa tribe (of the Algonkin family). These people he styled the *Cheveux Relevés*, because the men's hair was gathered up and dressed more carefully and becomingly on the top of the head than (he says) could at that time be done by a hairdresser in France. This arrangement of the hair gave the men a very handsome appearance, but here their toilet ended, for they wore no clothes whatever (in the summertime), making up for this simplicity by painting their faces in different colours, piercing their ears and nostrils and decorating them with shell beads, and tattooing their bodies and limbs with elaborate patterns.

These Ottawas carried a club, a long bow and arrows, and a round shield of dressed leather, made (wrote Champlain) "from the skin of an animal like the buffalo".[1] The chief of the party explained many things to the white man by drawing with a piece of charcoal

[1] This was the first intimation probably that any European sent home for publication regarding the existence of the bison in North America, though the Spanish explorers nearly a hundred years before Champlain must have met with it in travelling through Louisiana, Texas, and northern Mexico. The bison is not known ever to have existed near Hudson Bay, or in Canada proper (basin of the St. Lawrence). South of Canada it penetrated to Pennsylvania and the Susquehanna River, but not farther eastward.

on the white bark of the birch tree. He gave him to understand that the present occupation of his band of warriors was the gathering of blueberries, which would be dried in the sun, and could then be preserved for eating during the winter.

From French River, Champlain passed southwards to the homeland of the Hurons, which lay to the east of what Champlain called "the Fresh Water Sea" (Lake Huron). This country he describes in enthusiastic terms. The Hurons, like the other Iroquois tribes (and unlike the hunting races to the north of them), were agriculturists, and cultivated pumpkins, sunflowers,[1] beans and Indian corn.

The Hurons persuaded Champlain to go with them to attack the Iroquois tribe of the Senekas (Entuhónorons) on the south shores of Lake Ontario. On the way thither he noticed the abundance of stags and bears, and, near the lake, of cranes, white and purple-brown.[2]

On the southern shores of the lake[3] were large numbers

[1] The Amerindians of the Lake regions made much use of the sunflowers of the region (*Helianthus multiflorus*). Besides this species of sunflower already mentioned, which furnishes tubers from its roots (the "Jerusalem" artichoke) others were valued for their seeds, and some or all of these are probably the originals of the cultivated sunflower in European gardens. The largest of these was called *Soleille* by the French Canadians. It grew in the cultivated fields of the Amerindians to seven or eight feet in height, with an enormous flower. The seeds were carefully collected and boiled. Their oil was collected then from the water and was used to grease the hair. This same Huron country (the Simcoe country of modern times) was remarkable for its wild fruits. There was the Canada plum (*Prunus americana*), the wild black cherry (*Prunus serotina*), the red cherries (*P. pennsylvanica*), the choke cherry (*P. virginiana*), wild apples (*Pyrus coronaria*), wild pears (a small berry-like pear called "poire" by the French: *Pyrus canadensis*), and the may-apple (*Podophyllum peltatum*). Champlain describes this may-apple as of the form and colour of a small lemon with a similar taste, but having an interior which is very good and almost like that of figs. The may-apples grow on a plant which is two and a half feet high, with not more than three or four leaves like those of the fig tree, and only two fruits on each plant.

[2] The cranes of Canada—so often alluded to by the French explorers as "Grues"—are of two species, *Grus canadensis*, with its plumage of a purple-grey, and *Grus americanus*, which is pure white (see p. 139).

[3] Lakes Ontario and Huron were probably first actually reached by Father Le Caron, a Recollet missionary who came out with Champlain in 1615 (see p. 90), and by Étienne Brulé, Champlain's interpreter.

of chestnut trees, "whose fruit was still in the burr. The chestnuts are small but of a good flavour." The southern country was covered with forests, with very few clearings. After crossing the Oneida River the Hurons captured eleven of the Senekas, four women, one girl, three boys, and three men. The people had left the stockade in which their relations were living to go and fish by the lake shore. One of the Huron chiefs—the celebrated Iroquet, who had been so much associated with Champlain from the time of his arrival—proceeded at once to cut off the finger of one of these women prisoners. Whereupon Champlain, firmer than in years gone by, interposed and reprimanded him, pointing out that it was not the act of a warrior such as he declared himself to be, to conduct himself with cruelty towards women "who had no defence but their tears, so that one should treat them with humanity on account of their helplessness and weakness". Champlain went on to say that this act was base and brutal, and that if he committed any more of such cruelties he, Champlain, "would have no heart to assist or favour them in the war". To this Iroquet replied that their enemies treated them in the same manner, but that since this was displeasing to the Frenchmen he would not do anything more to women, but he would not promise to refrain from torturing the men.

However, in the subsequent fighting which occurred when they reached the six-sided stockade of the Senekas (a strong fortification which faced a large pond on one side, and was surrounded by a moat everywhere else except at the entrance), the Hurons and Algonkins showed a great lack of discipline. Champlain and the few Frenchmen with him, by using their arquebuses, drove the enemy back into the fort, but not without having some of their Indian allies wounded or killed. Champlain proposed to the Hurons that they should erect what was styled in French a *cavalier*—a kind of box, with high, loopholed sides, which was erected on a tall scaffolding of stout timbers. This was to be carried by the Hurons to within a pike's length of the stockade. Four French arquebusiers then scrambled up into the *cavalier* and fired through the loopholes into the huts of the Seneka town. Meantime the Hurons were to set fire, if possible, to the wooden stockade. They managed the whole business so stupidly that the fire produced no effect, the flames being blown in the opposite direction to that which was desired. The brave Senekas threw water on to the blazing sticks and put out the fire. Champlain was wounded by an arrow in the leg and knee. The reinforcement of the five hundred Hurons expected by the allies did not turn up. The Hurons with Champlain lost heart, and insisted on retreating. Only the dread of the French firearms prevented the retreat being converted into a complete disaster. Whenever the Senekas came near enough to get speech with the French they asked them "why they interfered with native quarrels".

Champlain being unable to walk, the Hurons made a kind of basket, similar to that in which they carried their wounded. In this he was so crowded into a heap, and bound and pinioned, that it was as impossible for him to move "as it would be for an infant in his swaddling clothes". This treatment caused him considerable pain after he had been carried for some days; in fact he suffered agonies while fastened in this way on to the back of a savage.

He was afterwards obliged to pass the winter of 1615–6 in the Huron country. At that time it swarmed with game. Amongst birds, there were swans, white cranes, brent-geese, ducks, teal, the redbreasted thrush (which the Americans call "robin"), brown larks (*Anthus*), snipe, and other birds too numerous to mention, which Champlain seems to have brought down with his fowling-piece in sufficient quantities to feed the whole party whilst waiting for the capture of deer on a large scale.

Meanwhile, many of the Indians were catching fish, "trout and pike of prodigious size". When they desired to secure a large number of deer, they would make an enclosure in a fir forest in the form of the two converging sides of a triangle, with an open base. The two sides of these traps were made of great stakes of wood closely pressed together, from 8 to 9 feet high; and each of the sides was 1000 yards long. At the point of the triangle there was a little enclosure. The Hurons were so expeditious in this work that in less than ten days these long fences and the "pound" or enclosure at their convergence were finished. They then started before daybreak and scattered themselves in the woods at a considerable distance behind the commencement of these fences, each man separated from his fellow by about 80 yards. Every Huron carried two pieces of wood, one like a drumstick and the other like a flat, resonant board. They struck the flat piece of wood with the drumstick and it made a loud clanging sound. The deer who swarmed in the forest, hearing this noise, fled before the savages, who drové them steadily towards the converging fences. As they closed up, the Hurons imitated very cleverly the yapping of wolves. This frightened the deer still more, so that they huddled at last into the final enclosure, where they were so tightly packed that they were completely at the men's mercy. "I assure you," writes Champlain, "there is a singular pleasure in this chase, which takes place every two days, and has been so successful that in thirty-eight days one hundred and twenty deer were captured. These were made good use of, the fat being kept for the winter to be used as we do butter, and some of the flesh to be taken to their homes for their festivities."

Champlain himself, in the winter of 1615, pursuing one day a remarkable bird "which was the size of a hen, had a beak like a parrot and was entirely yellow, except for a red head and blue wings, and which had the flight of the partridge"—a bird I cannot identify—lost his way in the woods. For two days he wandered in the wilderness, sustaining himself by shooting birds and roasting them. But at last he found his way back to a river which he recognized, and reached the camp of the Hurons, who were extremely delighted at his return. Had they not found him, or had he not come back of himself, they told him that they could never again have visited the French for fear of being held responsible for his death.

By the month of December of this year (1615) the rivers, lakes, and ponds were all frozen. Hitherto, Champlain had had to walk when he could not travel in a canoe, and carry a load of twenty pounds, while the Indians carried a hundred pounds each. But now the water was frozen the Hurons set to work and made their sledges. These were constructed of two pieces of board, manufactured from the trunks of trees by the patient use of a stone axe and by the application of fire. These boards were about 6 inches wide, and 6 or 7 feet long, curved upwards at the forward end and bound together by cross pieces. The sides were bordered with strips of wood, which served as brackets to which was fastened the strap that bound the baggage upon the sledge. The load was dragged by a rope or strap of leather passing round the breast of the Indian, and attached to the end of the sledge. The sledge was so narrow that it could be drawn easily without impediment wherever an Indian could thread his way over the snow through the pathless forests.

The rest of the winter and early spring Champlain spent alone, or in company with Father Joseph Le Caron (one of the Recollet missionaries), visiting the Algonkin and Huron tribes in the region east of Lake Huron. He has left this description of the modern country of Simcoe, the home, three hundred years ago, of the long-vanished

Hurons[1]; and gives us the following particulars of their home life. The Huron country was a pleasant land, most of it cleared of forest. It contained eighteen villages, six of which were enclosed and fortified by palisades of wood in triple rows, bound together, on the top of which were galleries provided with stores of stones, and birch-bark buckets of water; the stones to throw at an enemy, and the water to extinguish any fire which might be put to the palisades. These eighteen villages contained about two thousand warriors, and about thirty thousand people in all. The houses were in the shape of tunnels, and were thatched with the bark of trees. Each lodge or house would be about 120 feet long, more or less, and 36 feet wide, with a 10-foot passage-way through the middle from one end to the other. On either side of the tunnel were placed benches 4 feet high, on which the people slept in summer in order to avoid the annoyance of the fleas which swarmed in these habitations. In winter time they slept on the ground on mats near the fire. In the summer the cabins were filled with stocks of wood to dry and be ready for burning in winter. At the end of each of these long houses was a space in which the Indian corn was preserved in great casks made of the bark of trees. Inside the long houses pieces of wood were suspended from the roof, on to which were fastened the clothes, provisions, and other things of the inmates, to keep them from the attacks of the mice which swarmed in these villages. Each hut might be inhabited by twenty-four families, who would maintain twelve fires. The smoke, having no proper means of egress except at either end of the long dwelling, and through the chinks of the roof, so injured their eyes during the winter season that many people lost their sight as they grew old.

"Their life", writes Champlain, "is a miserable one

[1] They were almost completely exterminated by the Iroquois confederacy between thirty and forty years after Champlain's visit.

SAMUEL DE CHAMPLAIN

c 812

ALEXANDER HENRY THE ELDER

in comparison with our own, but they are happy amongst themselves, not having experienced anything better, nor imagining that anything more excellent could be found."

These Amerindians ordinarily ate two meals a day, and although Champlain and his men fasted all through Lent, "in order to influence them by our example", that was one of the practices they did *not* copy from the French.

The Hurons of this period painted their faces black and red, mixing the colours with oil made from sunflower seed, or with bears' fat. The hair was carefully combed and oiled, and sometimes dyed a reddish colour; it might be worn long or short, or only on one side of the head. The women usually dressed theirs in one long plait. Sometimes it was done up into a knot at the back of the head, bound with eelskin. The men were usually dressed in deerskin breeches, with gaiters of soft leather. The shoes ("Moccasins") were made of the skin of deer, bears, or beavers. In addition to this the men in cold weather wore a great cloak. The edges of these cloaks would often be decorated with bands of brown and red colour alternating with strips of a whitish-blue, and ornamented with bands of porcupine quills. These, which were originally white or grey in colour, had been previously dyed a fine scarlet with colouring matter from the root of the bed-straw (*Galium tinctorum*). The women were loaded with necklaces of violet or white shell beads, bracelets, ear-rings, and great strings of beads falling below the waist. Sometimes they would have plates of leather studded with shell beads and hanging over the back.

In 1616 Champlain returned to France, but visited Quebec in 1617 and 1618. During the years spent at Quebec, which followed his explorations of 1616, he was greatly impeded in his work of consolidating Canada as a French colony by the religious strife between the

Catholics and Huguenots, and the narrow-minded greed of the Chartered company of fur-trading merchants for whom he worked. But in 1620 he came back to Canada as Lieutenant-Governor (bringing his wife with him), and after attending to the settlement of a violent commercial dispute between fur-trading companies he tried to compose the quarrel between the Iroquois and the Algonkins, and brought about a truce which lasted till 1627.

In 1628 came the first English attack on Canada. A French fleet was defeated and captured in the Gulf of St. Lawrence, and in the following year Champlain, having been obliged to surrender Quebec (he had only sixteen soldiers as a garrison, owing to lack of food), voyaged to England more or less as a prisoner of state in the summer of 1629. He found, on arriving there, that the cession of Quebec was null and void, peace having been concluded between Britain and France two months before the cession. Charles I remained true to his compact with Louis XIII, and Quebec and Nova Scotia were restored to French keeping. In 1633 Champlain returned to Canada as Governor, bringing with him a considerable number of French colonists. *It is from 1633 that the real French colonization of Canada begins*: hitherto there had been only one family of settlers in the fixed sense of the word; the other Frenchmen were fur traders, soldiers, and missionaries. But Champlain only lived two years after his triumphant return, and died at Quebec on Christmas Day, 1635.

His character has been so well summed up by Dr. S. E. Dawson, in his admirable book on the *Story of the St. Lawrence Basin*, that I cannot do better than quote his words:

"Champlain was as much at home in the brilliant court of France as in a wigwam on a Canadian lake, as patient and politic with a wild band of savages on Lake Huron as with a crowd of grasping traders in St. Malo or Dieppe. Always calm, always unselfish, always depending on God, in whom he believed and trusted, and thinking of France, which he loved, this single-hearted man resolutely followed the path of his duty under all circumstances; never looking for ease or asking for profit, loved by the wild people of the forest, respected by the courtiers of the king, and trusted by the close-fisted merchants of the maritime cities of France."

# CHAPTER V

## After Champlain: from Montreal to the Mississippi

A very remarkable series of further explorations were carried out as the indirect result of Champlain's work. In 1610 he had allowed a French boy of about eighteen years of age, named ÉTIENNE BRULÉ, to volunteer to go away with the Algonkins, in order to learn their language. Brulé was taken in hand by Iroquet,[1] a chief of the "Little Algonkins", whose people were then occupying the lands on either side of the Ottawa River, including the site of the now great city of Ottawa. After four years of roaming with the Indians, Brulé was dispatched by Champlain with an escort of twelve Algonkins to the headwaters of the Suskuehanna, far to the south of Lake Ontario, in order to warn the Andastes[2] tribe of military operations to be undertaken by the allied French, Hurons, and Algonkins against the Iroquois. This enabled Brulé to explore Lake Ontario and to descend the River Suskuehanna as far south as Chesapeake Bay, a truly extraordinary journey at the period. This region of northern Virginia had just been surveyed by the English, and was soon to be the site of the first English colony in North America.[3]

[1] Mentioned on p. 80.

[2] The Andastes were akin to the Iroquois, but did not belong to their confederacy; they lived in Pennsylvania.

[3] The inaccurate statement has frequently been written about Newfoundland being "the first British American colony". Newfoundland was reached by the ship in which John Cabot sailed on his 1497 voyage of discovery, and a few years after-

In attempting to return to the valley of the St. Lawrence in 1616, with his Andaste guides, Brulé lost his way, and to avoid starvation surrendered himself to the Seneka Indians (the westernmost clan of the Iroquois) against whom the recent warlike operations of the French were being directed. Discovering his nationality, the Senekas decided to torture him before burning him to death at the stake. As they tore off his clothes they found that he was wearing an *Agnus Dei* medal next his skin. Brulé told them to be careful, as it was a medicine of great power which would certainly kill them. By a coincidence, at that very moment a terrific thunderstorm burst from a sky which until recently had been all sunshine. The Senekas were so scared by the thunder and lightning that they believed Brulé to be a person of supernatural powers. They therefore released him, strove to heal such slight wounds as he had incurred, and carried him off to their principal town, where he became a great favourite. After a while they gave him guides to take him north into the country of the Hurons.

His further adventures led him to discover Lake Superior and the way thither through the Sault Ste. Marie, and to reach a place probably not far from the south coast of Hudson Bay, in which there was a copper mine. Then he explored the Montagnais country north of Quebec, and even at one time (in 1629) entered the service of the English, who had captured Quebec and Tadoussac from the French. When the English left this region Brulé travelled again to the west and joined the Hurons once more.

wards its shores were sought by the English in common with the French and the Portuguese, and later on the Spaniards and Basques, for the cod fishery. But no definite British settlement, such as subsequently grew into an actual colony, was founded in Newfoundland until the year 1624; the island was not recognized as definitely British till 1713, and no governor was appointed till 1728. The first permanent English colonial settlement in America was founded at Jamestown, Virginia, in 1607; and in the Bermudas and Barbados (West Indies) soon afterwards.

His licentious conduct amongst his Indian friends seems to have roused them to such a pitch of anger that in 1632 they murdered him, then boiled and ate his body. But immediately afterwards misfortune seemed to fall on the place. The Hurons were terrified at what they had done, and thought they heard or saw in the sky the spirits of the white relations of Brulé—some said the sister, some the uncle—threatening their town (Toanche), which they soon afterwards burnt and deserted.

In 1615 Champlain, returning from France, had brought out with him friars of the Récollet order.[1] These were the pioneer missionaries of Canada, prominent amongst whom was FATHER LE CARON, and these Récollets traversed the countries in the basin of the St. Lawrence between Lake Huron and Cape Breton Island, preaching Christianity to the Amerindians as well as ministering to the French colonists and fur traders. One of these Récollet missionaries died of cold and hunger in attempting to cross New Brunswick from the St. Lawrence to the Bay of Fundy, and another—Nicholas Viel—was the first martyr in Canada in the spread of Christianity, for when travelling down the Ottawa River to Montreal he was thrown by the pagan Hurons (together with one of his converts) into the waters of a rapid since christened Sault le Récollet. Another Récollet, Father d'Aillon, prompted by Brulé, explored the richly fertile, beautiful country known then as the territory of the Neutral nation, that group of Huron-Iroquois Amerindians who strove to keep aloof from the fierce struggles between the Algonkins and Hurons on the one hand and the eastern Iroquois clans

[1] The Récollet (properly Recollect) friars were a strict branch of the Franciscan order that were sometimes called the Observantines. They were also known as "Recollects" (pronounced in French *récollet*) because they were required to be constantly keeping guard over their thoughts. This development of the Franciscan order of preaching missionary friars was originally a Spanish one, founded early in the sixteenth century, and becoming well established in the Spanish Netherlands. Many of them were Flemings or Walloons.

on the other. This region, which lies between the Lakes Ontario, Erie, and Huron, is the most attractive portion of western Canada. Lying in the southernmost parts of the Dominion, and nearly surrounded by sheets of open water, it has a far milder climate than the rest of eastern Canada.

In 1626 the Jesuit order supplanted the Récollets, and commenced a campaign both of Christian propaganda and of geographical exploration which has scarcely finished in the Canada of to-day.

In 1627 the war between the Iroquois Confederacy and the Huron and Algonkin tribes recommenced, and this, together with the British capture of Quebec and other portions of Canada, put a stop for several years to the work of exploration. This was not resumed on an advanced scale till 1634, when Champlain, unable himself, from failing health, to carry out his original commission of seeking a direct passage to China and India across the North-American continent, dispatched a Norman Frenchman named JEAN NICOLLET to find a way to the Western Sea. Nicollet, as a very young man, had lived for years amongst the Amerindian tribes, especially amongst the Nipissings near the lake of that name. Being charged, amongst other things, with the task of making peace between the Hurons and the tribes dwelling to the west of the great lakes, Nicollet discovered Lake Michigan. He was so convinced of the possibility of arriving at the Pacific Ocean, and thence making his way to China, that in the luggage which he carried in his birch-bark canoe was a dress of ceremony made of Chinese damask silk embroidered richly with birds and flowers. He was on his way to discover the Winnebago Indians, or "Men of the Sea", of whom Champlain had heard from the Hurons, with whom they were at war. But the great water from which they derived their name was not in this instance a sea, but the Mississippi River.

The Winnebago Indians were totally distinct from the Algonkins or the Iroquois, and belonged to the Dakota stock, from which the great Siou confederation[1] was also derived.

Nicollet advanced to meet the Winnebagos clad in his Chinese robe and with a pistol in each hand. As he drew near he discharged his pistols, and the women and children fled in terror, for all believed him to be a supernatural being, a spirit wielding thunder and lightning. However, when they recovered from their terror the Winnebagos gave him a hearty welcome, and got up such lavish feasts in his honour, that one chief alone cooked 120 beavers at a single banquet.

Nicollet certainly reached the water-parting between the systems of the St. Lawrence and the Mississippi, and under that name—Misi-sipi—"great water"—he heard through the Algonkin Indians of a mighty river lying three days' journey westward from his last camp. Winnebago (from which root is also derived the names of the Lakes Winnipeg and Winnipegosis much farther to the north-west) meant "salt" or "foul" water. Both terms might therefore be applied to the sea, and also to the lakes and rivers which, in the minds of the Amerindians, were equally vast in length or breadth.

From 1648 to 1653 the whole of the Canada known to the French settlers and explorers was convulsed by the devastating warfare carried on by the Iroquois, who during that period destroyed the greater part of the Algonkin and Huron clans. The neutral nation of Lake Erie (the Erigas) was scattered, and between the shores of Lakes Michigan and Huron and Montreal the country was practically depopulated, except for the handfuls of French settlers and traders who trembled behind their fortifications. Then, to the relief and astonishment of the French, one of the Iroquois clans—the Onondaga—

[1] See p. 160.

proposed terms of peace, probably because they had no more enemies to fight of their own colour, and wished to trade with the French.

The fur trade of the Quebec province had attracted an increasing number of French people (men bringing their wives) to such settlements as Tadoussac and Three Rivers. Amongst these were the parents of PIERRE ESPRIT RADISSON. This young man went hunting near Three Rivers station and was captured in the woods by Mohawks (Iroquois) who carried him off to one of their towns and intended to burn him alive. Having bound him at a stake, they proceeded to tear out some of his finger nails and shoot arrows at the less vital parts of his body. But a Mohawk woman was looking on and was filled with pity at the sufferings of this handsome boy. She announced her intention of adopting him as a member of her family, and by sheer force of will she compelled the men to release him. After staying for some time amongst the Mohawks he escaped, but was again captured just as he was nearing Three Rivers. Once more he was spared from torture at the intercession of his adopted relations. He then made an even bolder bid for freedom, and fled to the south, up the valley of the Richelieu and the Hudson, and thus reached the most advanced inland post of Dutch America—then called Orange, now Albany—on the Hudson River. From this point he was conveyed to Holland, and from Holland he returned to Canada.

Soon after his return he joined two Jesuit fathers who were to visit a mission station of the Jesuits amongst the Onondagas (Iroquois) on a lakelet about thirty miles south-east of the present city of Rochester. The Iroquois (whose language Radisson had learnt to speak) received them with apparent friendliness, and there they passed the winter. But in the spring Radisson found out that the Onondaga Iroquois were intending to massacre the whole of the mission. Instructed by him, the Jesuits pretended to have no suspicions of the coming attack, but all the while they were secretly building canoes at their fort. As soon as they were ready for flight, and the sun of April had completely melted the ice in the River Oswego, the French missionaries invited the Onondagas to a great feast, no doubt making out that it was part of the Easter festivities sanctioned by the Church. They pointed out to their guests that from religious motives as well as those of politeness it was essential that the *whole* of the food provided should be eaten, "nothing was to be left on the plate". They set before their savage guests an enormous banquet of maize puddings, roast pigs, roast ducks, game birds, and fish of many kinds, even terrapins, or fresh-water turtles. The Iroquois ate and ate until even *their* appetites were satisfied. Then they began to cry off; but the missionaries politely insisted, and even told them that in failing to eat they were neglecting their religious duties. To help them in this respect they played hymn and psalm tunes on musical instruments. At last the Onondagas were gorged to repletion, and sank into a stertorous slumber at sunset. Whilst they slept; the Jesuits, their converts, and Radisson got into the already prepared canoes and paddled quickly down the Oswego River far beyond pursuit.

Radisson next joined his brother-in-law, Medard Chouart, and after narrowly escaping massacre by the Iroquois (once more on the warpath along the Ottawa River) reached the northern part of Lake Huron, and Green Bay on the north-west of Lake Michigan. From Green Bay they travelled up the Fox River and across a portage to the Wisconsin, which flows into the Mississippi. Down this river they sped (meeting people of the great Siou confederation and Kri (Cree) Indians, these last an Algonkin nation roaming in the summertime as far north as Hudson's Bay, until at length they reached the actual waters of the Mississippi, first of all white men. Returning then to Lake Michigan, the shores of which seemed to them an earthly paradise with a climate finer than Italy, they journeyed northwards into Lake Huron, and thence north-westwards through the narrow passages of St. Mary's River into Lake Superior. The southern coast of Lake Superior was followed to its westernmost point, where they made a camp, and from which they explored during the winter (in snowshoes) the Wisconsin country and collected information regarding the Mississippi and its great western affluent the Missouri. The Mississippi, they declared, led to Mexico, while the other great forked river in the far west was a pathway, perhaps, to the Southern Sea (Pacific).

The Jesuits, on the other hand, were convinced that Hudson's Bay (or the "Bay of the North") was at no great distance from Lake Superior (which was true) and that it must communicate to the north-west with the Pacific Ocean or the sea that led to China.

In 1661, without the leave of the French Governor of Canada, who wanted them to take two servants of his own with them and to give him half the profits of the venture, Chouart and Radisson hurried away to the west, picked up large bodies of natives who were returning to the regions north of Lake Huron, with them fought their way through the ambushed Iroquois, and once more navigated the waters of Lake Superior. Once again they started for the Mississippi basin and explored the country of Minnesota, coming thus into contact with native tribes which lived on the flesh of the bison. In Minnesota they met a second time the Kri or Kinistino Indians of north-central Canada, and joined one of their camps in the spring of 1662, somewhere to the west of Lake Superior. With Kri guides they started away to the north and north-east, no doubt by way of the Lake of the Woods, the English River, Lake St. Joseph, and the Albany River, thus reaching the salt sea at James Bay, the southernmost extension of Hudson Bay. Or they may have proceeded by an even shorter route, though with longer portages for canoes, through Lake Nipigon to the Albany.

The summer of 1662 they passed on the islands and shores of James Bay hunting "buffalo"[1] with the Indians. Then, in 1663, travelling back along the same route they had followed in the previous year, they regained Lake Superior, and so passed by the north of Lake Huron to the Ottawa River and the St. Lawrence. But on their return to Three Rivers they were arrested by the French Governor, D'Avaugour, who condemned them to imprisonment and severe fines. The courts of France gave them no redress, and in their furious anger Chouart and Radisson went over to the English, offered their services to England, and so brought about the creation of the Hudson Bay Company.

Radisson's journey from England to Hudson Bay has been treated of in an earlier chapter: it is preferable to follow out to its finish the great, western impulse of the French, which led them to neglect for a time the doings of the British on the east coast of North America and in the sub-Arctic regions of Hudson Bay.

From 1660 onwards the Jesuit missionaries again took up vigorously that work of Christianizing the Amerindians which had been so completely checked by the frightful ravages of the Iroquois between 1648 and 1654.

By 1669 the Jesuits had three permanent stations in western Canada. The first was the mission station at Sault Ste. Marie, the second was the station of Ste. Esprit, on Lake Superior (not far from the modern town of Ashland), and the third was the station of St. François Xavier at the mouth of the Fox River, on Green Bay, Lake Michigan.

As regards some of the sufferings which these missionaries had to go through when travelling across Canada

[1] More probably musk oxen.

in the winter, I quote the following from *The Relations of the Jesuits* (p. 35):—

"I [Father de Crépieul] set out on the 16th of January, 1674, from the vicinity of Lake St. John, near the Saguenay River, with an Algonkin captain and two Frenchmen. We started after Mass, and walked five long leagues on snowshoes with much trouble, because the snow was soft and made our snowshoes very heavy. At the end of five leagues, we found ourselves on a lake four or five leagues long all frozen over, on which the wind caused great quantities of snow to drift, obscuring the air and preventing us from seeing where we are going. After walking another league and a half with great difficulty our strength began to fail. The wind, cold, and snow were so intolerable that they compelled us to retrace our steps a little, to cut some branches of fir which might in default of bark serve to build a cabin. After this we tried to light a fire, but were unable to do so. We were thus reduced to a most pitiful condition. The cold was beginning to seize us to an extraordinary degree, the darkness was great, and the wind blew fearfully. In order to keep ourselves from dying with cold, we resumed our march on the lake in spite of our fatigue, without knowing whither we were going, and all were greatly impeded with the wind and snow. After walking a league and a half we had to succumb in spite of ourselves and stop where we were. The danger we ran of dying from cold caused me to remember the charitable Father de Noue, who in a similar occasion was found dead in the snow, kneeling and with clasped hands. . . . We therefore remained awake during the rest of the night. . . . On the following morning two Frenchmen arrived from Father Albanel's cabin very opportunely, and kindled a great fire on the snow. . . . After this we resumed our journey on the same lake, and at last reached the spot where Father Albanel was. . . . A serious injury, caused by the fall of a heavy load upon his loins, prevented him from moving, and still more, from performing a missionary's duties."

One of the Jesuit fathers, Allouez, in founding the station of St. François Xavier on Green Bay, Lake Michigan, had gained further information about the wonderful Mississippi, which he called "Messi Sipi". He also thoroughly explored Lake Nipigon, to the north of Lake Superior. In 1669 two missionaries, named Dollier de Casson and Galinée, started from the seminary of St. Sulpice (Montreal) to reach the great tribes of the far west, supposed to be eager to learn of Christianity and known to be much more tractable than the Iroquois. These two missionaries, in their expedition of seven canoes and twenty-one Amerindians, were accompanied by a remarkable young man commonly known as La Salle, but whose real name was Robert Cavalier.[1]

Before leaving Lake Ontario, they actually passed the mouth of the Niagara River and heard the falls, but had not sufficient curiosity to leave their canoes and walk a short distance to see them. The wonderful cascades of Niagara, where the St. Lawrence leaving Lake Erie plunges 328 feet down into Lake Ontario (which is not much above sea level), remained nearly undiscovered and undescribed until the year 1678, when they were visited by Father Hennepin. Near the western end of Lake Ontario the two Sulpician missionaries met another Frenchman, Jolliet, who had come down to Lake Superior by way of the Detroit passage, which is really the portion of the St. Lawrence connecting Lake Huron with Lake Erie. Jolliet told the missionary de Casson of a great tribe in the far west, the Pottawatomies, who had asked for missionaries, and who were of Algonkin stock. La Salle, on the other hand, was determined to make for the rumoured Ohio River, which lay somewhere to the south-west of Lake Erie.

[1] La Salle was the name of his property in France.

The two Sulpicians wintered in "the earthly paradise" to the north of Lake Erie, passing a delightful six months there in the amazing abundance of game and fish. They then met with various disasters to their canoes, and consequently gave up their western journey, passing northwards through Detroit and Lake St. Clair into Lake Huron, and thence to the Jesuit mission station of the Sault Ste. Marie. Here they were received rather coldly, as being rivals in the mission field and in exploration. They in their turn accused the Jesuits of thinking mainly, if not entirely, of the foundation of French colonies, and very little of evangelizing the natives.

JOLLIET, a Canadian by birth,[1] was dispatched by the Viceroy of Canada in 1672 to explore the far west. Two years—1670—previously the French Government had for the first time adopted a really definite policy about Canada, and had taken formal possession of the Lake region and of all the territories lying between the lakes and the Mississippi. A great assembly of Indians was held at Sault Ste. Marie, near the east end of Lake Superior; and here a representative of the French Government, accompanied by numerous missionaries and by Jolliet, read a proclamation of the sovereignty of King Louis XIV of France and Navarre. Below a tall cross was erected a great shield bearing the arms of France. Father Allouez addressed the Indians in the Algonkin language, and told them of the all-powerful Louis XIV, who "had ten thousand commanders and captains, each as great as the Governor of Quebec". He reminded them how the troops of this king had beaten the unconquerable Iroquois, of how he possessed innumerable soldiers and uncountable ships; that at times the ground of France shook with the discharge of cannon, while the blaze of musketry was like the lightning. He pictured the king covered with the blood of his enemies and riding in the middle of his cavalry, and

[1] Born at Quebec in 1645.

ordering so many of his enemies to be slain that no account could be kept of the number of their scalps, whilst their blood flowed in rivers. The Amerindians being what they were, addicted to warfare, and only recognizing the right of the strongest, it may be that this gospel of force was not quite so shocking and unchristian as it reads to us nearly 250 years afterwards, though it jars very much as coming from the lips of a missionary of Christianity. However, it must be remembered that but for the valour of the French soldiers in the awful period between 1648 and 1666 (when the Mohawks received a thorough and well-deserved thrashing) many of the tribes addressed on this occasion by the Jesuit missionaries would have been completely exterminated; the Iroquois would have depopulated much of north-eastern America. It is obvious, indeed, from our study of the conditions of life amongst the Amerindians, that one reason why the New World was so poorly populated at the time of its discovery by Europeans was the wars of extermination between tribe and tribe; for America between the Arctic regions and Tierra del Fuego is marvellously well supplied with natural food products—game, fish, fruits, nuts, roots, and grain—much more so than any area of similar extent in the Old World.

Jolliet was to be accompanied on his westward expedition by Father JACQUES MARQUETTE,[1] a Jesuit missionary who had become well acquainted with the tribes visiting Lake Superior, and had learnt the Siou dialect of the Illinois people. On May 17, 1673, Jolliet and Marquette started from the Straits of Michili-Makinak with only two bark canoes and five Amerindians. They coasted along the north coast of Lake Michigan, passed

[1] Father Jacques Marquette was born in the province of Champagne, eastern France. He came to Canada when he was twenty-nine years old, having already been prepared by the Jesuits for priesthood and missionary work since his seventeenth year. He spent nine years in Canada, and died at the age of thirty-eight. He has left an enduring memory for goodness, courage, and purity of life.

into Green Bay, and thence up the River Fox. They were assisted by the Maskutins, or Fire Indians, and were given Miami guides. Thence the natives assisted them to transport their canoes and baggage over the very short distance that separates the upper waters of the Fox River from the Wisconsin River, and down the Wisconsin they glided till they reached the great Mississippi. The Governor of Quebec, who had sent Jolliet on this mission, believed that the Great River of the west would lead them to the Gulf of California, which was then called the Vermilion Sea by the Spaniards, because it resembled in shape and colour the Red Sea.

"On the 17th of June (1673)", writes Father Marquette, "we safely entered the Mississippi with a joy that I cannot express. Its current is slow and gentle, the width very unequal. On its banks there are hardly any woods or mountains. The islands are most beautiful, and they are covered with fine trees. We saw deer and cattle (bison), geese, and swans. From time to time we came upon monstrous fish, one of which struck our canoe with such violence that I thought it was a great tree. On another occasion we saw on the water a monster with the head of a tiger, a sharp nose like that of a wild cat, with whiskers and straight erect ears. The head was grey, and the neck quite black (possibly a lynx). . . . We found that turkeys had taken the place of game, and the *pisikiou*, or wild cattle, that of the other animals."

Father Marquette, of course, by his wild cattle means the bison, of which he proceeds to give an excellent description. He adds: "They are very fierce, and not a year passes without their killing some savages. When attacked, they catch a man on their horns if they can, toss him in the air, throw him on the ground, then trample him under foot and kill him. If a person fires at them from a distance with either a bow or a gun, he must immediately after the shot throw himself down and hide in the grass, for if they perceive him who has fired they run at him and atttack him."

Soon after entering the Mississippi, Marquette noticed some rocks which by their height and length inspired awe. "We saw upon one of them two painted monsters which at first made us afraid, and upon which the boldest savages dare not long rest their eyes. They are as large as a calf; they have horns on their heads like those of deer, a horrible look, red eyes, a beard like a tiger's, a face somewhat like a man's, a body covered with scales, and so long a tail that it winds all round the body and ends like that of a fish. Green, red, and black are the three colours composing the picture. Moreover, these two monsters are so well painted that we cannot believe that any savage is their author, for good painters in France would find it difficult to paint so well, and, besides, they are so high up on the rock that it is difficult to reach that place conveniently to paint them."[1]

As the Jolliet expedition paddled down the Mississippi—ever so easily and swiftly—a marvellous panorama unfolded itself before the Frenchmen's fascinated gaze. Immense herds of bison occasionally appeared on the river banks, flocks of turkeys flew up from the glades and roosted in the trees and on the river bank. Everywhere the natives seemed friendly, and Father Marquette was usually able to communicate with them through his knowledge of the Illinois Algonkin dialect, which the Siou understood.

On their first meeting with the Mississippi Indians, the French explorers were not only offered the natives' pipes to smoke in token of peace, but an old man amongst the latter uttered these words to Jolliet: "How beautiful the

[1] These remarkable rock pictures were situated immediately above the present city of Alton, Illinois. In 1812 they still remained in a good state of preservation, but the thoughtless Americans had gradually destroyed them by 1867 in quarrying the rock for building stone.

c 312

INDIANS HUNTING BISON

sun is, O Frenchman, when thou comest to visit us. Our village awaits thee, and thou shalt enter all our cabins in peace." . . . "There was a crowd of people," writes Marquette; "they devoured us with their eyes, but nevertheless preserved profound silence. We could, however, hear these words addressed to us from time to time in a low voice: 'How good it is, my brothers, that you should visit us'.

" . . . The council was followed by a great feast, consisting of four dishes, which had to be partaken of in accordance with all their fashions. The first course was a great wooden platter full of sagamité, that is to say, meal of Indian corn boiled in water, and seasoned with fat. The Master of the Ceremonies filled a spoon with sagamité three or four times, and put it to my mouth as if I were a little child. He did the same to Monsieur Jollyet. As a second course he caused a second platter to be brought, on which were three fish. He took some pieces of them, removed the bones therefrom, and, after blowing upon them to cool them, he put them in our mouths as one would give food to a bird. For the third course, they brought a large dog that had just been killed, but, when they learned that we did not eat this meat, they removed it from before us. Finally, the fourth course was a piece of wild ox, the fattest morsels of which were placed in our mouths. . . . We thus pushed forward and no longer saw so many prairies, because both shores of the river are bordered with lofty trees. The cotton wood, elm and bass wood are admirable for their height and thickness. There are great numbers of wild cattle whom we hear bellowing. We killed a little parroquet, with a red and yellow head and green body. . . . We have got down to near the 33° of latitude. . . . We heard from afar savages who were inciting one another to attack us by their continual yelling. They were armed with bows and arrows, hatchets, clubs, and shields. . . . Part of them embarked in great wooden canoes, some to ascend, others to descend the river in order to surround us on all sides. . . . Some young men threw themselves into the water and seized my canoe, but the current compelled them to return to land. One of them hurled his club, which passed over without striking us. In vain I showed the calumet (pipe of peace), and made them signs that we were not coming to war against them. The alarm continued; they were already preparing to pierce us with arrows from all sides when God suddenly touched the hearts of the old men who were standing at the water's edge, who checked the ardour of their young men. . . . Whereon we landed, not without fear on our part. First we had to speak by signs, because none of them understood the six languages which I spoke. At last we found an old man who could speak a little Illinois. We informed them that we were going to the sea.

"The next day was spent in feasting on Indian corn and dogs' flesh. The people here had an abundance of Indian corn, which they sowed at all seasons. They cook it in great earthen jars which are very well made, and also have plates of baked earth. The men go naked and wear their hair short; they pierce their noses, from which, as well as from their ears, hang beads. . . . Their cabins are made of bark, and are long and wide. They sleep at the two ends, which are raised two feet above the ground. They know nothing of the beaver, and their wealth consists in the skins of wild cattle. They never see snow in their country, and recognize the winter only through the rains."

The expedition had passed the confluence of the Missouri and that of the Ohio, and had finally reached the place where the Arkansas River enters the Mississippi. Here the Frenchmen gathered from the natives that the sea was only ten days distant, and this sea they knew (for Jolliet was able to take astrononiical observations and to make a rough survey) could only be the Gulf of Mexico. Jolliet feared if he prosecuted his journey any farther, he and his people would fall into the hands of the Spaniards and be imprisoned, if not killed. Therefore, at this point on the Lower Mississippi, the expedition turned back. Its return journey was a weary business, for the current was against the canoes as they were propelled northwards up the Great River. But Jolliet learnt from the natives of a better homeward route, that of following the Illinois River upstream until the expedition came within a very short distance of Lake Michigan, near where Chicago now stands. Tbe canoes were carried over a low ridge of ground, launched again in the Chicago River, and so passed into Lake Michigan. (There is, in fact, at this point the remains of an ancient water connection between Lake Michigan and the Illinois River, and a canal now connects the two systems.) Jolliet, in describing this region, realized that by cutting a canal through two miles of prairie it would be possible to go "in a small ship" from Lake Erie or Lake Superior "to Florida".

Father Marquette remained at his new mission on the Fox River (he died two years afterwards on the shores of the Straits of Michili-makinak). Jolliet, on returning by way of the Ottawa River to Quebec, was nearly drowned in the La Chine Rapids (Montreal), and all his papers and maps were lost. The natives with him also perished, but he struggled to shore with difficulty, and went on his way to Quebec to report his wonderful discoveries to the Governor, Frontenac. Fortunately Father Marquette had also kept a journal and had made maps, and these reaching the superior of his mission arrived in time to confirm Jolliet's statements.

Jolliet married at Quebec, and proceeded to explore and develop the regions along the north coast of the Gulf of St. Lawrence, travelling in this work as far as Hudson's

Bay. He was given by the French Government the Island of Anticosti as a reward for his achievements, but the work and capital which he put into the development of this long-neglected island came to nothing; for it was captured by the English, and Jolliet died a poor man whilst attempting to explore the coast of Labrador.

As to ROBERT CAVALIER DE LA SALLE, he had, after all, discovered the Ohio, and had descended that river as far as the site of the present town of Louisville. Then he interested the Governor (Frontenac) of Canada in his enterprises. A fort, called Fort Frontenac, was built at what is now Kingston, at the point where the St. Lawrence leaves Lake Ontario. La Salle returned to France, and obtained the grant of the lordship of this fort and the surrounding country on conditions of maintaining the whole cost of the establishment, and making a settlement of colonists. Another visit to France in 1677–8 secured him further support and capital, and he returned from France with a companion, Henry de Tonty.

La Salle, with de Tonty, started from Fort Frontenac in September, 1678, so intensely anxious to commence his discoveries that he disregarded the difficulties of the winter season. On his way to Niagara he paid a visit to the Iroquois to conciliate them, and cleverly got from them permission to build a vessel on Lake Erie and also to erect a blacksmith's forge, near where Niagara now stands. The blacksmith's forge grew rapidly into a fort before the Indians were aware of what was being done. By August, 1679, he had built and launched (in spite of extraordinary calamities and misfortunes) on the Upper Niagara River the first sailing boat which ever appeared on the four great upper lakes of the St. Lawrence basin.

In this ship he sailed through Lake Erie and past Detroit into Lake Huron, and thence to Green Bay (Lake Michigan), stopping at intervals amongst the canoes of the amazed natives, who for the first time heard the sound of cannon, for he had armed his vessel with guns. At Green Bay he collected a large quantity of furs, which had been obtained in trade by the men he had sent on in advance. He loaded up his sailing boat, the *Griffon*, and sent her on a voyage back to the east to transport this splendid load of furs to the merchants with whom he had become deeply indebted. Unhappily the *Griffon* foundered in a storm on Lake Michigan, and was never heard of again. Meantime La Salle, with de Tonty and Father HENNEPIN, the discoverer of Niagara, had travelled in canoes to the south-east end of Lake Michigan, had passed up the Joseph River, and thence by portage into the Kankaki, which flows into the Illinois. This river he descended till he stopped near the site of the modern Peoria. Below this place he built a fort—for it was winter time—and although the natives were not very friendly he collected enough information from them to satisfy himself that he could easily pass down the Illinois to the Mississippi.

He sent one of the Frenchmen, Michel Accault, together with Father Hennepin, to explore the Illinois down to the Mississippi; de Tonty he placed in charge of the fort with a small garrison; and then himself, on the last day of February, 1680, started to walk overland from Lake Michigan to Detroit. Eventually, by means of a canoe, which he constructed himself, he regained Fort Frontenac and Montreal. When he returned to Fort Crèvecœur, on the Illinois River,[1] it was to meet with the signs of a horrible disaster. The Iroquois in his absence had descended

[1] He had named this place "Heartbreak" because when building it he had learnt of the loss of his sailing ship *Griffon*, with the splendid supply of furs which was to have paid off his debts, with all his reserve supplies and his men. This was not the limit of his troubles; for, after the overland journey of appalling hardships through a country of melting ice, flood, swamp, and hostile Iroquois—the Iroquois being furious with La Salle for having outwitted them in the building of this fort, and seeking him everywhere to destroy him—when he got to Montreal it was only to learn that a ship, coming from France with further supplies for his great journey had been wrecked at the mouth of the St. Lawrence!

on the place with a great war party. They had massacred the Illinois people dwelling in a big settlement near the fort, and the remains of their mutilated bodies were scattered all over the place. Their town had been burnt; the fort was empty and abandoned. There were no traces of the Frenchmen, however, amongst the skulls and skeletons lying around him; for the skulls retained sufficient hair to show that they belonged to Amerindians. Nevertheless, he deposited his new stock of goods and most of his men in the ruins of the Fort Crèvecœur, and descended the River Illinois to the Mississippi. But he was obliged to turn back. On the west bank of the river were the scared Illinois Indians, on the east the raging Iroquois. Whenever La Salle could safely visit a deserted camp he would examine the remains of the tortured men tied to stakes to see if amongst them there was a Frenchman.

But de Tonty was not dead. After incredible adventures he had escaped the raids of the Iroquois and had reached the Straits of Michili-makinak, between Lakes Michigan and Huron, and there met La Salle, who was once more on his way to Montreal.

Again de La Salle and de Tonty, in the winter of 1681, returned to the south end of Lake Michigan, and made their way over the snow to the Illinois River. On the 6th February, 1682, they left the junction of the Illinois and the Mississippi to trace that great river to its outlet in the sea. La Salle reached the delta on the 6th April, 1682, having on the way taken possession of the country in the name of the King of France. Accault and Father Hennepin had meantime paddled up the Northern Mississippi as far as its junction with the Wisconsin. At this place their party was surrounded and captured by a large band of Siou warriors.

The Frenchmen were at first in danger of being killed, as the Sious refused to smoke with them the pipe of peace.

But being much less bloodthirsty than the Iroquois, they soon calmed down and treated their captives with a certain rough friendliness. All their goods were taken from them, even the vestments worn by Father Hennepin. But they were well supplied with food such as the country produced—bison, beef, fish, wild turkeys, and the grain of the wild rice, which made such excellent flour. They were gradually conveyed by the Siou[1] to a large settlement of that tribe on the shore of Mille Lacs, a sheet of water not far distant from the westernmost extremity of Lake Superior. Whilst staying at this Siou town Hennepin conversed with Indians from the far north and north-west, and from what they told him came to the conclusion that there was no continuous waterway or "Strait of Anian" across the North-American continent, but that the land extended to the north-west till it finally joined the north-eastern part of Asia—a guess that was not very far wrong. But he also surmised that there were rivers in the far west which led to an ocean—the Pacific—across which ships might go to Japan and China without passing to the southward of the Equator.

Whilst moving up and down the northern Mississippi, bison-hunting with the Indians, the Frenchmen were met near the site of St. Paul by one of the great French pioneers of the seventeenth century, the Sieur DANIEL DE GREYSOLON DU L'HUT. This remarkable man, who was an officer of the French army, had already planted the French arms at the Amerindian settlement of Mille Lacs in 1679, and had established himself as a powerful authority at the west end of Lake Superior. He had also summoned a great council of Amerindian tribes—the Siou from the Upper Mississippi, the Assiniboins from the Lake of the Woods (between Lake Superior and Lake Winnipeg), and the Kri Indians from Lake Nipigon.

[1] The real name of the Siou, as far as we can arrive at it through the records of the French pioneers, was Issati or Naduessiu.

He had further discovered, in 1679, the water route of the St. Croix River from near Lake Superior to the Mississippi.

Du L'Hut soon persuaded the Siou to let his fellow countrymen return with him to Lake Superior. Accault remained behind with the Siou, delighted with their wild, roving life, and no doubt married an Indian wife and became the father of some of those bold half-breeds who played such a great part in the subsequent history of innermost Canada. But Father Hennepin returned to Montreal, and made his way eventually to France, where he fell into great disgrace and was unfrocked. He had richly merited this treatment, for after he heard of the death of La Salle he impudently claimed the discovery of the whole course of the Mississippi River for himself, and for a long time was believed. He will certainly go down in history as the man who discovered and described Niagara Falls (in 1678), and he also assisted greatly to clear up the geography of the time by the information he collected from the Amerindians as to the vast extent of the North-American continent; but he was a boastful, unscrupulous man.

Du L'Hut, who came to the rescue of Accault and Hennepin, was of noble family, and a member of the king's bodyguard. He decided, however, to seek his fortune in Canada, and obtained a commission as captain. It was his cousin, Henri de Tonty, who had accompanied La Salle. After returning to France to fight in the wars then going on, he came back to Canada with a younger brother, Claude. He had in him the spirit of great adventurers, and longed to visit the unknown countries of the upper Mississippi. In the early part of these journeys he rescued his fellow countrymen from the keeping of the Sious in the manner described. After that he spent *thirty* years travelling and trading about North America, from the northern Mississippi into what we should now call Manitoba, and from the vicinity of Lake Winnipeg to Hudson Bay. He brought the great Amerindian nation of the Dakotas into direct relations with the French. He was absolutely fearless, and in no period of Canadian history has France been more splendidly represented in the personality of any of her officers than she was by Daniel de Greysolon du L'Hut. His was a tiresome name for English scribes and speakers. It was therefore written by them "Duluth" and pronounced Dălăth (instead of "Dülüt"). It is the name given to the township near the southernmost extremity of Lake Superior.

When the journeys of du L'Hut came to an end—he died at Montreal in 1710—and after the era of great French explorations in North America drew to a close, the French power was beginning to be eclipsed by that of the British, who were building up the foundations of a colony on the shores of Hudson's Bay, and were taking steps to acquire Newfoundland and to colonize New Brunswick and Nova Scotia.

Nevertheless, in 1720, the King of France, or rather the regent acting for the king, decided that a serious attempt must be made to discover the Western Sea, or Pacific Ocean, from the French posts which had been established in what is now known as Manitoba. The French had already discovered the Missouri, and had heard from several Indian tribes that it was possible to cross the Rocky Mountains and descend by other rivers to the waters of a great ocean, the coasts of which were visited by Spaniards. Several expeditions were sent out, more or less under the control of Jesuits, but did not accomplish much.

The really great discoveries which link the "Great North-West" for all time in history with France and French names were initiated by PIERRE GAULTIER DE LA VÉRENDRYE, who was born in 1685 at the town of Three

Rivers, in Lower Canada, where his father was Governor. He entered the army at the age of twelve, and took part in the French campaigns in Flanders, winning the rank of lieutenant at the battle of Malplaquet, where he received nine wounds and was left for dead on the field. He then returned to Canada, not having the necessary means with which to support the position of a lieutenant; and then, as France seemed to have entered upon a period of protracted peace, he determined to become an explorer. In 1728, when he was commandant of the trading post of Nipigon, to the north of Lake Superior, he heard from an Indian that there was a great lake beyond Lake Superior, out of which flowed a river towards the west, which ultimately led to a great salt lake where the water ebbed and flowed. As a matter of fact, these stories simply referred to Lake Winnipeg, but the importance of them lay in the fact that they acted as a powerful incentive to La Vérendrye to push his explorations westwards, and perhaps discover a route to the Pacific Ocean.[1]

La Vérendrye afterwards went to Quebec, where he discussed his plans for Western exploration with the Governor of New France, the Marquis de Beauharnais, who was a distant connection of the Beauharnais family from which sprang the first husband of the Empress Joséphine, the grandfather of Napoleon III.

This Governor entered into his scheme with enthusiasm, though he could obtain little or no money from the ministers of Lous XVI. But a way out of the difficulty was found by the Governor giving La Vérendrye the monopoly of the fur trade in the far North-West.[2]

[1] The water of Lake Winnipeg—whatever it may be now—was frequently stated by Amerindians in earlier days to be "stinking water", or salt, brackish water, disagreeable to drink, and this lake exhibits a curious phenomenon of a regular rise and fall, reminding the observer of a tide, a phenomenon by no means confined to Lake Winnipeg, but occurring on sheets of water of much smaller extent.

[2] What we should call to-day a "concession".

This monopoly enabled La Vérendrye to obtain the funds for his expenditure from the merchants of Montreal, and in the summer of 1731 he started out on his explorations, accompanied by three of his sons, his nephew, fifty soldiers and French Canadian canoe men, and a Jesuit missionary. For a guide they had the Indian, Oshagash, who had first told La Vérendrye of the western river and the salt water. After many delays, necessitated by the need for trading in furs to satisfy the merchants of Montreal, La Vérendrye and his expedition skated on snowshoes down the ice of the Winnipeg River and reached the shores of Lake Winnipeg. They were probably the first white men to arrive there. La Vérendrye established forts and posts along his route from Lake Nipigon, but his expedition had not been a commercial success. There was a deficit of £1700 between the amount realized in furs and the cost of the equipment and wages of the French and French Canadians. De Beauharnais made a fresh appeal to the French Court; he urged that the expenditure to convey La Vérendrye's expedition to the Pacific Ocean would not be a large one—perhaps only £1500.

But the French Court was obdurate; it would not furnish a penny. Thus La Vérendrye, in all probability, was prevented from forestalling the British explorers of sixty and seventy years later, besides the expeditions of Captain Cook and Captain Vancouver, which secured for Great Britain a foothold on the Pacific seaboard of British Columbia.

La Vérendrye in his fort on Lake Winnipeg was in a desperate position. He made a hasty journey back to Montreal and even Quebec, to beat up funds and to pacify the capitalists of his fur-trading monopoly. He painted in glowing colours the prospects of cutting off the trade of the Hudson's Bay Company and the building up of an immense commerce in valuable furs, and these men agreed once again to furnish the funds for the extension of the expedition. On his return he took back with him his youngest son, Louis, a boy of eighteen. Whilst he had been absent from Fort St. Charles (a post which he had built on the Lake of the Woods, in communication by water with the Winnipeg River), on Lake Winnipeg, that place was visited by a party of Siou Indians. They found the fort occupied in the absence of the French by a number of Kri or "Knistino" Indians in French service. These Kris were frightened at the arrival of the Sious and fired guns at them. "Who fired on us?" demanded these haughty Indians from Dakota, and the Kris replied, "The French". Then the Sious withdrew, but vowed to be completely revenged on the treacherous white man.

When La Vérendrye reached Fort St. Charles its little garrison was almost at the point of starvation. He had travelled himself ahead of his party, and the immense stock of supplies and provisions he was bringing up country were a long way behind him when he reached the fort. He therefore sent back his son Jean, together with the most active of his Canadian voyageurs and the Jesuit missionary, in order that they might meet the heavily laden canoes and hurry them up country as fast as possible. But this party was met by the Sious on Rainy River, who massacred them to a man. They were afterwards found lying in a circle on the beach, decapitated and mutilated. The heads of most of them were wrapped ironically in beaver skins, and La Vérendrye's son, Jean, was horribly cut and slashed, and his mutilated, naked body decorated with garters and bracelets of porcupine quills.

Meantime, during his absence in Lower Canada, two of his sons in charge of Fort Maurepas, on Lake Winnipeg, had been very active. They had discovered the great size of this lake, and also the entrance of the Red

River on the south. They then proceeded to explore both the Red River and its western tributary the Assiniboin. On the Assiniboin was afterwards built the post of Fort La Reine, and from this place in 1738 La Vérendrye started with two of his sons, several other Frenchmen, a few Canadian voyageurs, and twenty-five Assiniboin Indians. Leaving the Assiniboin River, they crossed the North Dakota prairies on foot. Owing to the timidity of his Indian guides, La Vérendrye was not led direct to the Missouri River, the "Great River of the West", but along a zigzag route which permitted his guides to reinforce their numbers at Assiniboin villages, and every now and then join in a bison hunt. All the party were on foot, horses not then having reached the Assiniboin tribe. But on the 28th of November, 1738, they drew near to the Missouri and were met by a chief of the great Mandan tribe, who was accompanied by thirty of his warriors, and who presented La Vérendrye with young maize cobs and leaves of native tobacco, these being regarded as emblems of peace and friendship.

The Mandan tribe differed materially in its habits and customs from the Indians to the north, who supported themselves mainly, if not entirely, by hunting, who cared very little for agriculture, and moved continually like nomads over great stretches of country, living chiefly in tents or temporary villages. The Mandans, on the other hand, were a people who practised agriculture, and had permanent and well-constructed towns. In fact, their civilization and demeanour made such an impression on the Assiniboin and other northern tribes that they had been considered a sort of "white people", somewhat akin to Europeans, and La Vérendrye was a little disappointed to find them only Amerindians in race and colour.

The six hundred Assiniboins who had gathered about La Vérendrye's expedition proved to be a great trouble to him, as they were constantly picking quarrels with the Mandans, who were very dishonest. Accordingly, La Vérendrye arranged with the Mandans to frighten them away by pretending that the Siou Indians were on the warpath. The six hundred Assiniboins bolted, but took with them La Vérendrye's interpreter, so that he was henceforth obliged to communicate with the Mandans by means of signs and gestures. This and other reasons decided him to return—even though it was the depth of winter, to Fort La Reine, but not before he had given the head chief of the Mandans a flag and a leaden plate which (unknown to the Mandans) meant taking possession of their country in the name of the French king.

The journey back to Fort La Reine, over the plains of the Assiniboin, was a terrible experience. The party had to travel in the teeth of an almost unceasing north-east wind which was freezingly cold. Night after night they were obliged to dig deep holes in the snow for their sleeping places. La Vérendrye nearly died of agonizing pain and fatigue during this journey, and was a long time recovering from its effects.

As they continued to receive friendly messages from the Mandans, inviting them to make further discoveries, LA VÉRENDRYE'S sons, PIERRE and FRANCOIS, set out in the spring of 1742, and, after some checks and disappointments, managed with a single Mandan guide to reach Broad Lands on the Little Missouri River, where they noticed the earths of different colours, blue, green, red, black, white, and yellow, which are so characteristic of this region. They reached the village of the Crow Indians, passed through a portion of the friendly tribe, the Cheyennes (the name was probably pronounced Shian) and got into the country which was constantly being ravaged by the Snake Indians, or Shoshones. Here, on the 1st of January, 1743, when the mists of morning cleared away, they saw upon the horizon the outline of huge mountains. As they travelled westwards or south-westwards, day after day, the jagged blue wall resolved itself into towering snow-capped peaks, glittering in the sun and provoking the appellation of "the Mountains of Bright Stones", a name probably given to the Rocky Mountains by the Amerindians, but used in all the earlier French and English maps until the end of the eighteenth century.[1]

On the 12th of January they reached the very foot of the mountains, the slopes of which they saw were thickly covered with magnificent forests of pine and fir—forests, that have since suffered to an appalling extent from annual bush fires, which so far the United States Government seems unable to check. Here they were to meet with a bitter disappointment. They were travelling with a very large war party of the Bow Indians for the purpose, if need be, of attacking and routing the Shoshones; but a Shoshone camp at the base of the mountains was found to be deserted, and the Bow Indians jumped to the conclusion that the Shoshones had turned back through the forest unseen, and were now making with all speed for the principal war camp of the Bow Indians, where they would massacre the women and children. They would listen to no remonstrances from the two Frenchmen, who perforce had also to travel back, either alone or with the Bow Indians, in the direction of their war camp, where the idea of a Shoshone attack was found to be baseless. Eventually, the two La Vérendrye brothers were obliged to make their way to the Missouri River, and abandon any idea of finding a way to the Western Ocean across the Rocky Mountains.

The French pioneers had already heard of the Spaniards

[1] The term Rocky Mountains was probably first officially applied by the American expedition, under Lewis and Clarke, sent out by the United States Government in 1804 to take possession of the coast of Oregon, but it was used twenty or thirty years earlier by British explorers of Western Canada.

in California, and the possibility of getting into touch with them. They had now discovered, first of all Europeans, the Rocky Mountains—that great snowy range of North America which extends from Robson Peak on the eastern borders of British Columbia to Baldy Peak in New Mexico.

Afterwards the La Vérendryes directed their attention more to the opportunities of reaching the Far West through the streams that flowed into the system of Lake Winnipeg, and in this way discovered, in or about 1743, the great River Saskatchewan. This river La Vérendrye's sons followed up till they reached the junction between the North and the South Rivers, and then they probably learnt a good deal more of the Southern Saskatchewan, on which they may have built one or two posts. La Vérendrye himself thought that this would prove to be the best route by which the French could reach the Western Sea.

By this time the French Government was becoming alive to the importance of these discoveries, and it conferred a decoration on La Vérendrye, and allowed him to hope that he might be furnished with means for further exploration. But he died soon afterwards, at the close of 1749, and after his death his sons were treated with gross ingratitude and neglect. The self-seeking Governor of New France endeavoured to secure the fur trade for his own friends, and sent an officer with a terribly long name—Captain Jacques Répentigny Le Gardeur de Saint Pierre—to continue the exploration towards the Pacific. From 1750 to 1763 the French occupation of this region of the two Saskatchewan Rivers was extended till in all probability the French got within sight of the northern Rocky Mountains in the vicinity of Calgary. Then came the English conquest of Canada to stop all further enterprise in this direction, and the story was next to be taken up by English, Scottish, and Canadian explorers.

It will be men with English and Scottish names,

mainly, who will henceforth complete the work begun and established so magnificently by Cartier, Brulé, Nicollet, Jolliet, La Salle, du L'Hut, and La Vérendrye, though the French Canadians will also play a notable part, together with "Americans". from New England.

# CHAPTER VI

## The Geographical Conditions of the Canadian Dominion

Before we continue to follow the adventures of the pioneers of British North America, I think—even if it seems wearisome and discursive—my readers would better understand this story if I placed before them a general description of what is now the Dominion of Canada, more particularly as it was seen and discovered by the earliest European explorers.

The most prominent feature on the east, and that which was nearest to Europe, was the large island of NEWFOUNDLAND, 42,000 square miles in extent, that is to say, nearly as large as England without Wales. It seems to bar the way of the direct sea access by the Gulf of St. Lawrence to the very heart of North America; and, until the Straits of Belle Isle and of Cabot were discovered, did certainly arrest the voyages of the earliest pioneers. Newfoundland, as you can see on the map, has been cut into and carved by the forces of nature until it has a most fantastic outline. Long peninsulas of hills alternate with deep, narrow gulfs, and about the south-east and east coasts there are innumerable islets, most of which in the days of the early discoverers were the haunt of millions of sea birds who resorted there for breeding purposes. The heart of Newfoundland, so to speak, is an elevated country with hills and mountains rising to a little over 2000 feet. A great deal of the country is, or was, dense forests, chiefly consisting of fir trees. As numerous almost as the sea birds were the seals and walruses which frequented the Newfoundland coasts. Inland there were very large numbers of reindeer, generally styled nowadays by the French-Canadian name of *Caribou*[1]. Besides reindeer there were wolves, apparently of a smaller size than those of the mainland. There were also lynxes and foxes, besides polar bears, martens, squirrels, &c. The human inhabitants of Newfoundland, whom I shall describe in the next chapter, were known subsequently by the name of Beothuk, or Beothik, a nickname of no particular meaning. They had evidently been separated for many centuries from contact with the Amerindians of the mainland, though they may have been visited occasionally on the north by the Eskimo. They had in fact been so long separated from the other Amerindians of North America that they were strikingly different from them in their habits, customs, and language.

The climate of Newfoundland is not nearly so cold as that of the mainland, nor so hot in summer, but it is spoilt at times by fogs and sea mists which conceal the landscape for days together. In the wintertime, and quite late in the spring, quantities of ice hang about the shores of the islands, and when the warm weather comes, these accumulations of ice slip away into the Atlantic in the form of icebergs and are most dangerous to shipping.

To the south-east of Newfoundland the sea is very shallow for hundreds of miles, the remains no doubt of a great extension of North America in the direction of Europe which had sunk below the surface ages ago. In this shallow water—the "Banks" of Newfoundland—fish, especially codfish, swarmed in millions, and still continue to swarm with little, if any, diminution from the constant toll of the fishing fleets. Another creature found in great

[1] The first Frenchmen visiting North America, and seeing the caribou without their horns, thought they were a kind of wild ass. The reindeer of Newfoundland is a subspecies peculiar to this island.

abundance on these coasts is the true lobster,[1] which filled as important a part in the diet of the Beothuk natives, before the European occupation, as the salmon did in the dietary of the British Columbian tribes.

The next most striking feature in the geography of Eastern North America is NOVA SCOTIA. As you look at it on the map this province seems to be a long peninsula connected with the mainland by the narrow isthmus of Chignecto; but its northernmost portion—Cape Breton—really consists of two big and two little islands, only separated from Nova Scotia by a very narrow strait—the Gut of Canso. On the north of Nova Scotia lies the large Prince Edward Island, and north of this again the small group of the Magdalen Islands, discovered by Cartier, the resort of herds of immense walruses at one time. Due west of Nova Scotia the country, first flat (like Nova Scotia itself) and at one time covered with magnificent forests, rises into a very hilly region which culminates on the north in the Shikshok Mountains of the Gaspé Peninsula (nearly 4000 feet in height) and the White Mountains (over 6000 feet) and the Adirondak Mountains (over 5000 feet). The White, the Green, and the Adirondak Mountains lie just within the limits of the United States.

North of the Gaspé Peninsula, in the great Gulf of St. Lawrence, is Anticosti Island, which rises on the south in a series of terraces until it reaches an altitude of about 2000 feet. This island, which is well wooded, was said to have swarmed with reindeer at one time, and perhaps other forms of deer also, and to have possessed grizzly bears which fed on the deer, besides Polar bears visiting it in the winter.

[1] *Homarus americanus.* The lobster of Newfoundland and the coasts of North-east America is closely related to the common lobster of British waters. These true lobsters resemble the freshwater crayfish in having their foremost pair of legs modified into large, unequal-sized claws. The European rock-lobster of the Mediterranean and French coasts (the *langouste* of the French) has no large claws.

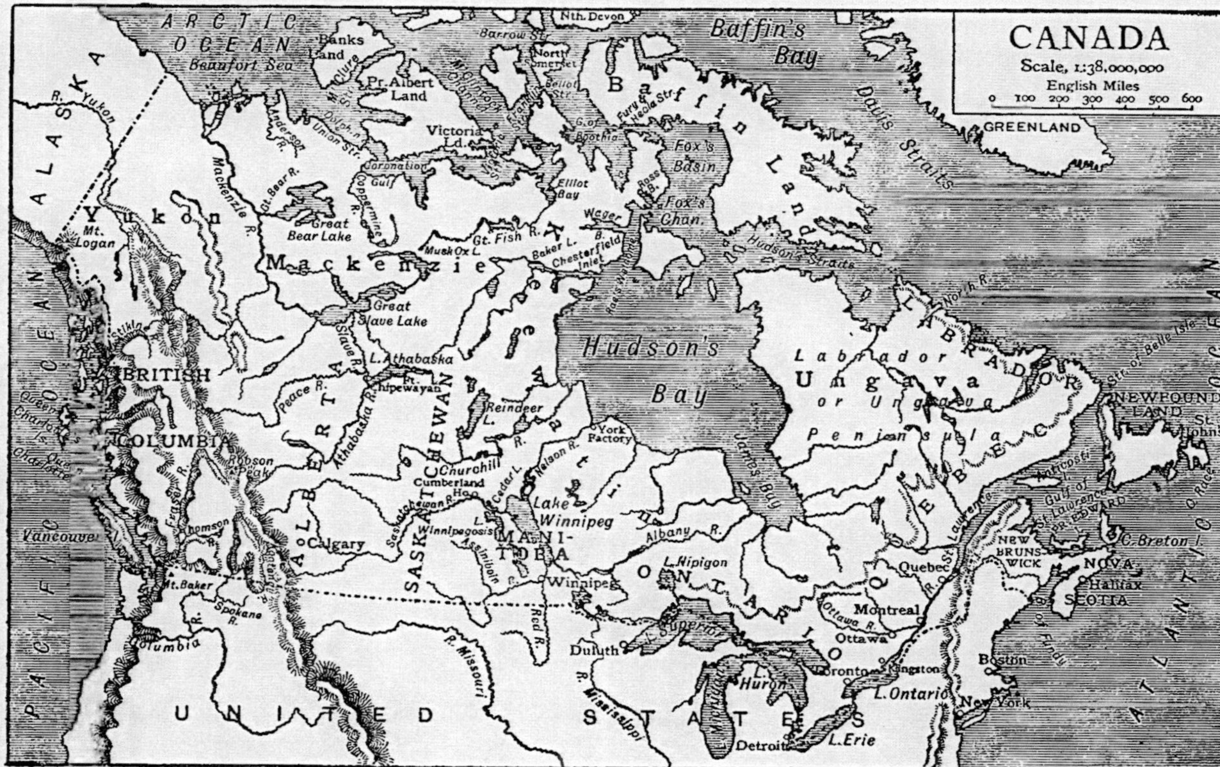
CANADA
Scale, 1:38,000,000
English Miles
0 100 200 300 400 500 600
GREENLAND
Baffin's Bay
Davis Straits
ARCTIC OCEAN
Beaufort Sea
Banks Land
Pr. Albert Land
Victoria Ld.
Nth. Devon
Barrow Str.
North Somerset
Baffin Land
Fox's Basin
Fox's Chan.
Hudson's Straits
Hudson's Bay
James Bay
ALASKA
Yukon
Mt. Logan
Mackenzie
Mackenzie R.
Great Bear Lake
Great Slave Lake
Coppermine R.
Coronation Gulf
Keewatin
Chesterfield Inlet
York Factory
L. Athabaska
Peace R.
BRITISH COLUMBIA
Robson Peak
ALBERTA
Calgary
SASKATCHEWAN
Churchill
Cumberland Hse.
MANITOBA
Lake Winnipeg
Winnipeg
ONTARIO
L. Nipigon
Albany R.
Labrador
Ungava or Ungava Peninsula
QUEBEC
NEWFOUNDLAND
St. Johns
Str. of Belle Isle
C. Race
C. Breton I.
NOVA SCOTIA
Halifax
NEW BRUNSWICK
Quebec
Montreal
Ottawa
Toronto
Kingston
L. Ontario
L. Erie
L. Huron
L. Superior
Duluth
Detroit
Boston
New York
Vancouver
Mt. Baker
Spokane R.
Columbia
R. Missouri
R. Mississippi
Red R.
UNITED STATES
PACIFIC OCEAN
ATLANTIC OCEAN

Newfoundland is separated from the mainland of LABRADOR on the north by the Strait of Belle Isle, and from Cape Breton Island on the south by Cabot Strait. Labrador is an immense region on the continent, where the coast (except for the deep inlet of Melville Lake) soon rises into an elevated plateau 2000 feet in height, which is strewn with almost uncountable lakes, out of which rivers flow north, south, east, and west. On the north-east corner of Labrador there are mountains from 3000 to 4000 feet, overlooking the sea. The whole of this vast Labrador or Ungava Peninsula, which is bounded on the south by the River and Gulf of St. Lawrence, and on the north by Hudson's Bay and Hudson's Straits, is an inhospitable land, at no time with much population.

"The winter of Labrador is long and severe; one would need to have blood like brandy, a skin of brass, and an eye of glass not to suffer from the rigours of a Labrador winter. In the summer the frequent fogs render the air damp, and the constant breezes from the immense fields of ice floating in the gulf keep the land very cool, and make any alteration in the winter dress almost unnecessary" (James M'Kenzie). Labrador and the lands farther north on the continent of North America are separated from Greenland on the east by the broad straits—a great branch of the Atlantic—named after Davis and Baffin, who first explored them. Passing up Davis Strait, along the coast of Labrador to beyond 60° N. lat., the voyager comes to Hudson's Straits, which, if followed up first to the northwards and then to the south-west, would lead him into the great expanse of Hudson's Bay, one of the most important features in the geography of North America.

HUDSON'S BAY, which is a great inland sea with an area of about 315,000 square miles, has a southern loop or extension called James Bay, the shores of which are not at a very great distance either from Lake Superior to the south-west, or from the source of the River Saguenay on the south. The Saguenay flows into the Lower St. Lawrence River. It is therefore not surprising that as soon as the French began to settle in Lower Canada they heard of a vast northern inland sea of salt water—Hudson's Bay. But the people who discovered and surveyed Hudson's Bay during the seventeenth, eighteenth, and nineteenth centuries were always on the search for a passage out of its waters into the Arctic Sea; which would enable them to get right round America into the Pacific Ocean.

In Arctic North America Nature really seems to have been preparing during millions of years a grim joke with which to baffle exploring humanity! It is easy enough to pass from Davis Straits into Hudson's Bay, but to get out of Hudson's Bay in the direction of the Arctic Ocean is like getting out of a very cleverly arranged maze. There are innumerable false exits, which have disappointed one Arctic explorer after another. When they had discovered that Hudson's Bay to the south was only like a great bottle, and had no outlet, they explored its northern waters; and when they found Chesterfield Inlet on the north-west, which leads into Baker Lake, they thought perhaps here was the passage through into the Arctic Sea. But no; that was no good. To the north of Chesterfield Inlet was a broad channel called Roe's Welcome, which led into Wager Bay and through frozen straits into Fox's Channel, and this again into Ross Bay. Here only a very narrow isthmus separates Hudson's Bay from the Arctic Sea; but still it is an isthmus of solid land. Turning to the north-east and north there are the broad waters of Fox's Channel leading into Fox's Basin; but the north-west corner of this inland sea was so blocked with ice and islands that it was not until the year 1822 that the *real* northern outlet of Hudson's Bay was discovered by Captain EDWARD PARRY to be the narrow Fury and Hecla Straits (the discovery was not completed until 1839 by the Hudson's Bay Company's explorers T. SIMPSON and W. DEASE).

Here you have found the way out into the Gulf of Boothia, which communicates in the north with Barrow Strait and Baffin's Bay. But across the supposed peninsula of Boothia there were discovered, in 1847, by Dr. JOHN RAE (also an officer of the Hudson's Bay Company) the narrow Bellot Straits, which lead into Franklin Straits and so into M'Clintock Channel and the Arctic Ocean. After this you might theoretically (if the ice permitted it) sail or steam your ship through Victoria Straits and Coronation Gulf till you got into Beaufort Sea (part of the open Arctic Ocean), or, by turning round Prince Albert Land, pass through the Prince of Wales' Straits or M'Clure Straits into the same Beaufort Sea.

The North-West Passage across the Arctic extremity of North America, therefore, *did* exist after all, and the directest route would be up Davis Straits, through Hudson's Straits into Fox's Basin, then through the Fury and Hecla Straits into the Gulf of Boothia, then through the Bellot Straits and Franklin Straits (past Victorialand and Kemp Peninsula) and out through the Dolphin and Union Straits into the Arctic Ocean, and so on round the north coast of Alaska, past Bering's Straits into Bering Sea and the Pacific. But of course the accumulations of ice completely block continuous navigation.

The huge jagged island of BAFFIN'S LAND differs from much of Arctic America in that it has high land rising into mountains. This is so completely covered with ice that it is of little interest under present circumstances to the world of civilization, though the large herds of musk oxen which it once supported were of much use to Arctic explorers as a food supply in winter. The coasts are inhabited by a few thousand Eskimo, and Davis Straits and Baffin's Bay possess a certain amount of commercial importance owing to the whale fisheries which are carried on there by the British, the Danes, the Americans, and the Eskimo. In fact the importance of these whale fisheries have of late made the Americans of the United States a little inclined to challenge the British possession of these great Arctic islands. North Devon, North Somerset, Prince of Wales' Land, Melville Island, Banks Land, Prince Albert Land, &c. &c., are names of other great Arctic islands completely within the grip of the ice. The nature of their interior is almost unknown. They are at present of use to no form of man unless it be to a few wandering Eskimo, who come to their coasts in the summer to kill seals.

The great NORTH-WEST TERRITORIES of the Canadian Dominion extend from the American frontier of Alaska (which is the 141° of w. long.) to the Ungava Peninsula, which abuts on Labrador. Where this vast region slopes to the Arctic Ocean and Hudson's Bay it is rather low and flat, except between Alaska and the Mackenzie River, and between the Mackenzie and the watershed of Hudson's Bay. The principal river system in the far North-West is that of the great Mackenzie River, which flows into the Arctic Ocean (Beaufort Sea) through an immense delta, and is one of the longest rivers in the world. The southernmost sources of the Mackenzie (such as the Peace River and the Athabaska River) rise in the Rocky Mountains to the east of British Columbia. These waters are stored for a time in Lake Athabaska, and then under the name of Slave River flow northwards into the Great Slave Lake, and out of this, under the name of Mackenzie River, into Beaufort Sea, through an immense delta. The Great Bear Lake is also a feeder of the Mackenzie.

Two other Arctic rivers at one time thought to be of great importance as means of communication with the Arctic Ocean, are the Great Fish River, which flows into Elliot Bay, and the Coppermine River, which enters Coronation Gulf. The other northward-flowing rivers (passing through innumerable lakes and lakelets) enter Hudson's Bay.

West of the great Mackenzie River rises the northernmost extension of the Rocky Mountains. All this easternmost part of Alaska, which is under British control, is a region of great elevation, something like parts of Central Asia. The streams which rise here unite in the great Yukon River, and this has its outlet in Bering's Sea. Some points of the great mountains within the limits of British territory in this direction reach to nearly 20,000 feet (Mount Logan).

But the climate of the northern parts of the Canadian Dominion differs very greatly in the west as compared to the east. For instance, the northern parts of Labrador are cruelly Arctic, hopelessly frozen, though they are in the same latitude as St. Petersburg (the capital of European Russia) and as the splendidly forested northern parts of British Columbia. Eastern Labrador is a region in which explorers have frequently perished from cold and starvation. Although in the lofty parts of the Yukon country (three hundred and fifty miles north of treeless Labrador) the winter is intensely cold, and the ground is frozen for a considerable depth downwards, all the year round, there are still great forests; and a white and Amerindian population find it possible to live there all the year round, while animal life is extremely abundant. On the other hand, a good deal of the territory between Mackenzie River and Hudson's Bay is almost uninhabitable, except during the summertime, owing to the depth of the snow and the bare rocky nature of the ground.

The treeless area north of Lake Athabaska (the "barren lands" of the Canadian Dominion) seems to consist of nothing but slabs of rock and loose stones. Yet this region is far from being without vegetation. The rock is often covered with a thin or thick sod of lichen ("reindeer moss", in some districts three feet deep) intermixed with the roots of the wishakapakka herb (*Ledum palustre*, from which Labrador tea is made), of cranberries, gooseberries, heather (with white bell flowers), and a dwarf birch. This last, in sheltered places where a little vegetable soil has been formed, grows into a low scrubby bush. As to the gooseberries—here and farther south—Hearne describes them as "thriving best on the stony or rocky ground, open and much exposed to the sun". They spread along the ground like vines. The small red fruit is always most plentiful and fine on the under side of the branches, probably owing to the reflected heat of the stones. In the bleaker places a hard, black, crumply lichen—the "Tripe de roche" of the French Canadians (*Gyrophoreus*) grows on the rocks and stones, and is of great service to the Amerindians, as it furnishes them with a temporary subsistence when no animal food can be procured. This lichen, when boiled, turns to a gummy consistence something like sago. Hearne describes it as being remarkably good when used to thicken broth; but some other pioneers complained that it made them and their Indians seriously ill. Another lichen, "reindeer moss" (*Cladina*), is also eaten by men as well as deer. The *muskegs*, or bogs and marshes, produce in the summertime a very rapid growth of grass (as well as breeding swarms of mosquitoes!), and thus furnish food for the geese and swans which throng them between June and October.

In the summertime all these northern territories of Canada—from the basin of Lake Winnipeg, with its white pelicans, to the Arctic circle—swarm with birds, wild swans, geese, ducks, plovers, grouse, cranes, eagles, owls of several kinds—especially the great snowy eagle-owl—red-breasted thrushes, black and white snow-buntings, scarlet grosbeaks (the female green and grey), crested jays, and ravens "of a beautiful glossy black, richly tinged with purple" but smaller in size than those of Europe.

This is also the country for bears. Some grizzlies still linger here. Their range at one time extended to near the Arctic circle. In Alaska (British as well as United States) there is an enormous chocolate-coloured bear, the biggest in the world. The Polar bear, usually creamy white along the seacoast, is stated to range inland during the summer over the "barren grounds", and to develop either a permanent local variety or a seasonal change of coat, which is greyish-brown or blue-grey.

The black bear in northern Canada is said to give birth at times to cubs which are cinnamon-brown in colour.

"In the early summer the black bears swim up and down the northern rivers with their mouths open, swallowing the immense number of water insects which have come into being at that season." Hearne goes on to state that bears which have subsisted on this food for some days, when cut open emit a stench that is intolerable, and which taints their flesh to a sickening degree. The insects on which they feed are mostly of two kinds: one a sort of grasshopper with a hard black skin, and the other a soft, brown, sluggish fly. "This last is the most numerous. In some of the lakes such quantities are forced into the bays when the wind blows hard, that they are pressed together in dead multitudes and remain a great nuisance. I have several times, in my inland voyages from York Fort (Hudson's Bay), found it scarcely possible to land in some of those bays for the intolerable stench of those insects, which in some places were lying in putrid masses to the depth of two or three feet." It is more than probable that the bears occasionally feed on these dead insects. After the middle of July, when they take to a diet of berries, they are excellent eating, and continue to be so to the end of the winter.

The Arctic foxes of this region when young are sooty black all over, and gradually change to a light ash-grey in colour, with a dark, almost blue, tint on the head, legs, and back. In winter they usually become white all over, with or without a black tip to the tail; but it is recorded by some travellers that not all the foxes of the *Canis lagopus* species turn white; some keep their dark-grey colour all the year round. The common fox (*C. vulpes fulvus*) in Northern Canada is sometimes black, with white-tipped hairs. Wolves in these far northern regions do not seem to have been so abundant as farther south.

The deer tribe are represented (north of the Athabaska region) by the reindeer and the elk (called by the Canadians "Moose"). The wapiti or red deer (for which the common Amerindian name in the north was *Waskesiu*) seldom ranged farther north than the vicinity of Lake Winnipeg. The reindeer of the "barren ground" subspecies extended to the Arctic seacoast, and were at one time especially abundant in Labrador. Here they were so tame, down to a hundred years ago, that fishermen were often known to shoot many of them from the windows of their huts near the seashore. This type (*Rangifer tarandus arcticus*) might possibly be domesticated; not so the larger and much wilder Caribou woodland reindeer of the more southern and western parts of the Dominion, which dislikes the neighbourhood of man. The elk or moose, east of the Rocky Mountains, was not found northward of about 50° to 55°; but west of that range extended over all British Columbia and Alaska, in which latter country it grows to a giant size and develops enormous antlers.

Hearne says of the elk in northern Canada: "In summer, when they frequent the margins of rivers and lakes, they are often killed by the Indians in the water while they are crossing rivers or swimming from the mainland to islands, &c. When pursued in this manner, they are the most inoffensive of all animals, never making any resistance; and the young ones are so simple that I remember to have seen an Indian paddle his canoe up to one of them and take it by the poll without the least opposition; the poor, harmless animal seeming at the same time as contented alongside the canoe as if swimming by the side of its dam, and looking up in our faces with the same fearless innocence that a house lamb would; making use of its fore foot almost every instant to clear its eyes of mosquitoes, which at that time were remarkably numerous. . . . The moose are also the easiest to tame and domesticate of any of the deer kind. I have repeatedly seen them at Churchill as tame as sheep, and even more so; for they would follow their keeper any distance from home, and at his call return with him without the least trouble, or ever offering to deviate from the path."

The most northern range of the elk would seem to be the region round Lake Athabaska.

The musk ox (*Ovibos*) is perhaps the most remarkable beast of Arctic Canada.[1] Samuel Hearne is my principal source for the following notes as to its habits and appearance: The number of bulls is very few in proportion to the cows, for it is rare to see more than two or three full-grown bulls with the largest herd; and from the number

[1] The musk ox, which is not an ox, but a creature about midway in structure and affinities between cattle on the one hand and sheep and goats on the other, is a large beast comparatively, being the size of a small ox, but appearing very much larger than it is on account of the extremely thick coat of hair and wool. Both sexes have horns, and the horns, after meeting in the middle and making more or less of a boss over the forehead, droop down at the sides of the cheeks and then turn up with sharp points. The musk ox once ranged right across the northern world, from England and Scandinavia, through Germany, Russia, and Siberia, to Alaska and North America. Many thousands of years ago, during one of the Glacial periods, it inhabited southern England. At the present day it is extinct everywhere, excepting in the eastern parts of Arctic America, not going west of the Mackenzie River nor south of Labrador. It is also found in Greenland.

of the males that are found dead, the Indians are of opinion that they kill each other in contending for the females. In the rutting season they are so jealous of the cows that they run at either man or beast who offers to approach them, and have been observed to run and bellow even at ravens and other large birds which chanced to alight near them. They delight in the most stony and mountainous parts of the "barren ground", but are seldom found at any great distance from the woods. Though they are a beast of great magnitude, and apparently of a very unwieldy inactive structure, yet they climb the rocks with ease and agility, and are nearly as surefooted as a goat. Like it, too, they will feed on anything; and though they seem fondest of grass, yet in winter, when grass cannot be had in sufficient quantity, they will eat moss or any other herbage they can find, as also the tops of willows and the tender branches of the pine tree.

"The musk ox, when full grown, is as large as the generality of English black cattle; but their legs, though thick, are not so long, nor is their tail longer than that of a bear; and, like the tail of that animal, it always bends downward and inward, so that it is entirely hid by the long hair of the rump and hind quarters. The hunch on their shoulders is not large, being little more in proportion than that of a deer. Their hair is in some parts very long, particularly on the belly, sides, and hind quarters; but the longest hair about them, particularly the bulls, is under the throat, extending from the chin to the lower part of the chest between the fore legs. It there hangs down like a horse's mane inverted, and is fully as long, which gives the animal a most formidable appearance. It is of the hair from this part that the Eskimo make their mosquito wigs (face screens or masks). In winter the musk oxen are provided with a thick fine wool or fur that grows at the root of the long hair, and shields them from the intense cold to which they are exposed during that season; but as the summer advances this fur loosens from the skin, and by frequently rolling themselves on the ground it works out to the end of the hair, and in time drops off, leaving little for their summer clothing except the long hair. This season is so short in these high latitudes, that the new fleece begins to appear almost as soon as the old one drops off, so that by the time the cold becomes severe they are again provided with a winter dress."

According to Hearne, the flesh of the musk ox does not resemble that of the bison, but is more like the meat of the moose or wapiti. The fat is of a clear white, "slightly tinged with a light azure". The calves and young heifers are good eating, but the flesh of the bulls both smells and tastes so strongly of musk as to be very disagreeable; "even the knife that cuts the flesh of an old bull will smell so strongly of musk that nothing but scouring the blade quite bright can remove it, and the handle will retain the scent for a long time".

Bisons of the "wood" variety are (or were) found far up the heights of the Rocky Mountains and in the regions south-west of the Great Slave Lake. These "wood buffaloes" delight in mountain valleys, and never resort to the plains. And higher than anything, of course, range the great white mountain goat-antelopes (*Oreamnus montanus*) from northern Alaska to the Columbia River.

The north and the north-west were, of course, pre-eminently the great fur-trading regions, though all parts of the vast Dominion have at one time or another yielded furs for commerce with the white man. The principal fur-bearing smaller mammals of the north and north-west were wolves, foxes, lynxes, gluttons (wolverene), otters, martens (sables) and black fishing martens, mink (a kind of polecat), ermine-stoats, weasels, polar hares (*Lepus timidus*), beavers, musquash, lemming, gopher or pouched ground-squirrels, and the common red squirrel of North

America. The grey squirrel and striped chipmunk are only found in southern Canada.

The musquash (*Fiber zibethicus*) is such a characteristic animal of northern Canada that it is worth while to give Hearne's description of it (I would mention it is really a huge *vole*, and no relation of the beaver):—

"The musk rat or musquash builds a dwelling near the banks of ponds or swamps to shelter it from the bitter cold of the winter, but never on land, always on the ice, as soon as it is firm enough, taking care to keep a hole open to admit it to dive for its food, which chiefly consists of the roots of grass or arums. It sometimes happens in very cold winters that the holes communicating with their dwellings under the water are so blocked by ice that they cannot break through them. When this is the case, and they have no provisions left in the house, they begin to eat one another. At last there may be only one rat left out of a whole lodge. They occasionally eat fish, but in general feed very cleanly, and when fat are good eating. They are easily tamed and soon grow fond of their owner. They are very cleanly and playful, and 'smell exceedingly pleasant of musk', but their resemblance to the rat is so great that few are partial to them, though of course they are much larger in size, and have webbed hind feet and a flat scaly tail. In Canadian regions farther south the musquash no longer builds on the ice, but in swamps, where it raises heaps of mud like islands in the surrounding water. On the top of these mounds they build their nests, and on the top of the musquash nest, or 'lodge', wild geese frequently lay their eggs and bring forth their young brood without any fear of being molested by foxes."

The YUKON territories of the Dominion, and above all the State of BRITISH COLUMBIA, constitute a very distinct region from the rest of British North America, not only in their tribes of Amerindians but in their fauna, flora, and climate. British Columbia is one of the most beautiful and richly endowed countries in the world. Here, in spite of northern latitudes, the warm airs coming up from the Pacific Ocean act somewhat in the same way as the Gulf Stream on north-west Europe, and favour the growth of magnificent forests.

All this north-western part of British Columbia is very mountainous, and the rocks are rich in minerals, especially gold in the Fraser and Columbia Rivers, far north in the upper valley of the Yukon, and copper and coal in Vancouver Island.

The rainfall in British Columbia is considerable, and the flora—trees, plants, ferns—richer than anywhere else in North America, with many resemblances to the trees and plants of Japan and northern China. In British Columbia more than in any other part of the world are found the noblest developments of the pines, firs, and junipers (*Coniferæ*).

The coast rivers swarm with salmon, and perhaps because of the abundance of sea fish close in shore there have been developed in the course of ages those remarkable aquatic mammals, the sea lions or fur seals (*Otaria*), whose relationship to the true seals is a very distant one. On the Alaskan coasts and islands is *Otaria ursina*, the creature which provides the sealskin fur of commerce. There is also the much larger sea lion (*Otaria stelleri*), on the coasts of British Columbia and Vancouver Island. Alexander Henry, jun., gives some interesting facts about this remarkable beast.

"The natives at Oak Point, during the time Mr. Keith was there, killed five very large sea lions by spearing them at night. Two canoes being lashed together, they approach very softly, and throw their spears, which are fastened by a long, strong cord, with a barb so fixed in a socket that, when it strikes the animal and pierces the flesh, it is detached from the shaft of the spear, but remains fastened to the cord. This is instantly made fast between the canoes; the animal dives and swims down river, dragging the canoes with such velocity that they may be in danger of filling, and require great skill in steering. In this manner they are carried down some miles before the animal becomes exhausted with loss of blood, makes for the shore, and lies on the beach, where they dispatch it and cut it up. The price of a sea lion among the natives is one slave and an assortment of other articles. Mr. Keith bought the flesh of one of these animals, and we had some roasted; it resembles bear's meat. The hair is like that of a horse, in summer of a chestnut colour. The natives, and also the Russians, are particularly fond of marine animals, such as whales, &c.; they drink the oil like milk."

Another notable water beast of the British Columbia coast was the sea otter (*Enhydris*), described on p. 305. Such an immense value was set on its fur that it is now nearly extinct within British limits.

The huge chocolate-coloured bear of the Yukon valley has already been mentioned; also the very large, blackish-brown wild dog (*Canis pambasileus*), which from one or two passages in the writings of Canadian pioneers may also be found as far south as the British Columbian Rocky Mountains. In the Yukon country the elk (which was formerly very common in British Columbia) grows to gigantic proportions with longer and larger antlers than elsewhere. In the forested mountains of British Columbia (as well as farther north) are the wood bison, the white mountain goat, grizzly bears, black bears, two kinds of lynx, the wapiti red deer, and the large bighorn sheep.

These (*Ovis montana*) sheep are of a grey or leaden colour; the rump and the inner side of the legs are white; the hoofs black, about one inch long. "The hair is rather soft, and at the roots is mixed with exceedingly fine white wool, which seems to grow only in certain patches. The neck is relatively much thicker than that of other animals of the same size; the legs and hoofs are also strongly built, like the neck." The horns of the female are comparatively small, flat, and have only a small bend backward; they are of a dirty-yellowish white, marked with closely connected annulations to the very tip. The legs are brown, as are also the ends of the hairs about the neck; the hoofs are black. "A ewe will weigh about 100 lb. when in full flesh, with only the entrails taken out. The head bears every resemblance to that of our European sheep." The colour of the males is nearly the same as that of the females, only rather browner; they are much larger and more strongly built, with a pair of enormous horns, which incline backward. As they grow they bend downward, and in the course of time form a complete curve and project forward. At the root the horns are nearly three inches square, the flat sides opposite; they are marked with closely connected ridges and end in a tapering flat point.

When the horns grow to a great length, forming a complete curve, the tips project on both sides of the head so as to prevent the ram from feeding. This, with their great weight, causes the sheep to dwindle to a mere skeleton and die. The bighorn sheep feed much in the caverns of the Rocky Mountains, eating a kind of moss and grass growing on the floors of these caves, and also a peculiar soft, sweet-tasting "clay", of which the natives also are fond.

The southern part of British Columbia contains the mule deer of western North America (*Mazama macrotis*), and a very strange rodent, the sewellel or mountain beaver (*Haplodon*), a creature distantly allied to squirrels, marmots, and beavers, but restricted in its distribution to a few parts of California, Oregon, and British Columbia. Amongst the birds noteworthy in the landscape are the white-headed sea eagles and Californian condors (*Pseudogryphus californianus*). Humming-birds range through British Columbia and Vancouver Island between mid-April and October.

In the regions about the upper Kootenay River (Eastern British Columbia), before the railway was constructed, there were wild horses, descended, no doubt, from those which had escaped from the Spaniards in New Mexico and California. They went in large herds, and in the winter when the snow was deep the natives would try to catch them by running them down with relays of fresh horses, or driving them up the mountains into the deepest snow or some narrow pass. A noose would then be thrown about the exhausted animal, which would be instantly mounted by an Indian and broken immediately to the saddle. Some of these wild horses were exceedingly swift, well-proportioned, and handsome in shape, but they seldom proved as docile as those born in captivity. When in a wild condition they would snort so loudly through the nostrils on descrying an enemy that they could be heard at a distance of five hundred yards.

The provinces of Alberta, Saskatchewan and Manitoba —the MIDDLE WEST—represent mainly the great prairie region of the Canadian Dominion. Nearly all the streams here flow from the eastern side of the Rocky Mountains and direct their course to the basin of Lake Winnipeg and to Hudson's Bay. A few turn south-west to the Missouri and Mississippi. The landscapes here remind one more of the middle part of the United States. The climate is severe in winter but very warm and dry in summer. In the extreme south, within the basin of the upper Missouri, the "prickly pear" (*Opuntia*) cactus grows in sheltered places, and suggests affinities with distant Colorado and California.

These great plains and river courses of the middle West were, until about fifty years ago, one of the world's great natural parks or zoological gardens. Large numbers of wapiti deer, of the smaller Virginian deer,[1] and of the

[1] *Mazama americana*, similar to, but quite distinct from, the larger mule deer of British Columbia.

prongbuck "antelope"[1] thronged the grassy flats, and elk browsed on the foliage of the thickets along the river banks. Grizzly bears and black bears,[2] large grey wolves, the small coyote wolf, the pretty little kit fox and large red fox preyed on these herbivores, as did also pumas and lynxes. Marmots and prairie hares (*Lepus campestris*)—often called rabbits by the pioneers, who also named the marmots "wood-chucks"—frolicked in the herbage, and formed the principal prey of the numerous rattlesnakes. By the shores of streams and lakes stood rows of stately cranes: the whooping crane, of large size, pure white, with black quill feathers, the crown of the head crimson scarlet and the long legs black; and the purple-brown crane, somewhat smaller in size. On hot, calm days in the region of Lake Winnipeg the cranes soar to an amazing height, flying in circles, till by degrees they are almost out of sight. Yet their loud note sounds so distinct and near that the spectator might fancy they were close to him.

The air at this season is full of great birds—eagles, buzzards, hawks, and falcons—soaring in circles to look out for prey among the flocks of wild swans, white geese, bernicle geese and brent geese, duck and teal, which cover the backwaters and the marshes and shallow lagoons. Turkey buzzards, coming up from the south, act as scavengers during the summer months. Immense flocks of passenger pigeons, buntings, grosbeaks, attack the ripening fruits and the wild rice of the swamps. Grouse in uncountable numbers inhabit the drier tablelands and open moors.[3]

[1] The prongbuck (*Antilocapra americana*) is not a true antelope, though in outward appearance it resembles a large gazelle. It was called "cabri" by the French Canadians.

[2] "Bears make prodigious ravages in the brush and willows; the plum trees, and every tree that bears fruit share the same fate. The tops of the oaks are also very roughly handled, broken, and torn down, to get the acorns. The havoc they commit is astonishing. . . . "—Alex. Henry, jun.

[3] Nowhere in the world are there so many kinds of grouse as in North America. In the more northern regions are several species of ptarmigan or snow partridges

But—a hundred years ago and more—the dominant features in the fauna of the Middle West was the bison. Between the Athabaska and Saskatchewan Rivers on the north, the Rocky Mountains on the west, and Lake Superior on the east the bison passed backwards and forwards over the great plains and prairies in millions, when white explorers first penetrated these lands. They moved in herds which concealed the ground from sight for miles. Here are some word pictures selected from the writings of the pioneers between 1770 and 1810:

"The buffaloes chiefly delight in wide open plains, which in those parts produce very long coarse grass, or rather a kind of small flags and rushes, upon which they feed; but when pursued they always take to the woods. They are of such an amazing strength, that when they fly through the woods from a pursuer, they frequently brush down trees as thick as a man's arm; and be the snow ever so deep, such is their strength and agility, that they are enabled to plunge through it faster than the swiftest Indian can run in snowshoes. To this I have been an eyewitness many times, and once had the vanity to think that I could have kept pace with them; but though I was at that time celebrated for being particularly fleet of foot in snowshoes, I soon found that I was no match for the buffaloes, notwithstanding they were then plunging through such deep snow, that their bellies made

(*Lagopus*), which turn white in winter, and the spruce partridges (*Canachites*); in the more genial climate of the great plains of eastern Canada and in the Far West the ruffled grouse and hazel grouse (*Bonasa*), the sage cocks (*Centrocercus*), the prairie hens (*Tympanuchus*), and the blue or pine grouse (*Dendrapagus*).

"To snare grouse requires no other process than making a few little hedges across a creek, or a few short hedges projecting at right angles from the side of an island of willows, which those birds are found to frequent. Several openings must be left in each hedge, to admit the birds to pass through, and in each of them a snare must be set; so that when the grouse are hopping along the edge of the willows to feed, which is their usual custom, some of them soon get into the snares, where they are confined till they are taken out. I have caught from three to ten grouse in a day by this simple contrivance, which requires no further attendance than going round them night and morning" (Hearne).

c 312

INDIANS LYING IN WAIT FOR MOOSE

a trench in it as large as if many sacks had been hauled through it. Of all the large beasts in those parts the buffalo is easiest to kill, and the moose are the most difficult; neither are the (red) deer very easy to come at, except in windy weather: indeed it requires much practice and a great deal of patience to slay any of them, as they will by no means suffer a direct approach, unless the hunter be entirely sheltered by woods or willows.

"The flesh of the buffalo is exceedingly good eating, and so entirely free from any disagreeable smell or taste, that it resembles beef as nearly as possible."

"The spots of wood along the Park River are ravaged by buffaloes (bison); none but the large trees are standing, the bark of which is rubbed perfectly smooth, and heaps of hair and wool lie at the bottom of the trees . . . and even the grass is not permitted to grow. . . . The ground is trampled more by these cattle than about the gate of a farmyard."

"The Kris informed me they had seen a calf as white as snow in a herd of buffalo. White buffalo are very scarce. They are of inestimable value among the nations of the Missouri. . . . There were also some of a dirty-grey colour, but these are very rare."

"I brought home two buffalo calves alive; they no sooner lost sight of the herd than they followed my horse like dogs, directly into the fort. On chasing a herd at this season the calves follow it until they are fatigued, when they throw themselves down in high grass and lie still, hiding their heads if possible. But seeing only a man and his horse they remain quiet and allow themselves to be taken. Having been a little handled, they follow like dogs."

In the spring, when the ice melted, innumerable buffaloes were killed through attempting to cross the rivers on the melting ice. They would drift by an observer (such as Alexander Henry, jun.) in entire herds of drowned corpses. Vast numbers perished. They formed one continuous line on the current for two days and two nights.

"By this time the river was crowded with them, swimming across, bellowing and grunting terribly. The bulls really looked fierce; all had their tails up, and each appeared eager to land first. The scene would have struck terror to one unaccustomed to such innumerable herds. From out in the plains, as far as the eye could reach, to the middle of the river, they were rushing toward us, and soon began to land about ten yards off. I shot one dead on the spot, my ball having broken his neck; my hunter and guide only wounded theirs. This discharge suddenly halted those on the south side, and turned those that were still in the water."

In the autumn:—"Plains burned in every direction and blind buffalo seen every moment wandering about. The poor beasts have all the hair singed off; even the skin in many places is shrivelled up and terribly burned, and their eyes are swollen and closed fast. It was really pitiful to see them staggering about, sometimes running afoul of a large stone, at other times tumbling down hill and falling into creeks not yet frozen over. In one spot we found a whole herd lying dead."

Throughout British North America, from the Yukon to Newfoundland, and from Labrador to Vancouver's Island, the rivers and freshwater lakes swarm with fish, and fish that in most cases is exceedingly good to eat. Salmon are most strikingly abundant in the rivers of British Columbia and Newfoundland, but they also ascend most of the rivers flowing into the Atlantic and Hudson's Bay. In the great lakes of Canada and of the middle west there are trout and white fish (*Coregonus*), pike, bass, chub, barbel, and five species of sturgeon. In the rivers and lakes of the far north-west is found the blackfish (*Dallia*).

Hearne writes of Lake Athabasca that it swarms with fish, such as pike, trout, perch, barbel, and other kinds not easily identified. Apparently there is also a form of gar-pike found here (see p. 74); this is described as having scales of a very large and stiff kind, and being a beautiful bright silver in colour. The size of these gar-pike range from two feet to four feet in length. Their flesh was delicately white and soft, but so foul and rank in taste that even the Indians would not eat it. The trout in Lake Athabaska seem to have been enormous, weighing from 35 to 40 pounds, while pike were of about the same weight.

The Amerindian tribes and the early European explorers lived mainly on fish, which was a palatable and easily obtained food. Yet it must be admitted that they had a splendid array of large and small game from which to take their toll.

Nor was the whole Dominion, from west to east and up to the Arctic zone, wanting in wild vegetable produce fit for man's consumption. The sugar maple (*Acer saccharinum*) and its ally the *Negundo* maple provided a delicious syrup; the bark of certain poplars and the bast of the sugar pine were chewed for their well-flavoured sweetness; the wild rice of the marshes will be further described in the next chapter. The wild fruits included delicious strawberries, cherries, gooseberries, currants, black currants, grapes (in the south only), blackberries of many kinds, whortleberries, cranberries, pears of the service tree (*Pyrus canadensis*[1]), and raspberries of various types—red, yellow, and black. Southern Canada and Nova Scotia contained various nut trees of the walnut order (hickories, butter-nuts, &c.), and hazel nuts were found everywhere except in the north.

We have left undescribed what is still politically the most important part of the whole of British North

[1] Sometimes called *Amelanchier canadensis*.

America—UPPER and LOWER CANADA. These regions lie within the basin of the great St. Lawrence River, beyond all doubt the most important waterway of North America, more important even than the Mississippi. The main origin of the St. Lawrence in the west is Lake Superior, the largest sea of fresh water in the world, which is connected with Lake Nipigon on the north. The waters of Lake Superior are carried over the Sault Ste. Marie rapids into Lake Huron and find a huge backwater in Lake Michigan.[1] Out of Lake Huron again they flow past Detroit into Lake Erie. From Duluth, at the westernmost extremity of Lake Superior, to Buffalo, on the easternmost point of Lake Erie, including all Lake Michigan and Lake Huron, with its bays and channels, a steamer can pass with just the one difficulty (easily surmounted) of the rapids at Sault Ste. Marie between Lake Superior and Lake Huron. But after you have left Lake Erie on the east you find yourself in the Niagara River, which at the Niagara Falls plunges several hundred feet downwards into Lake Ontario. From Lake Ontario to the sea along the St. Lawrence there is uninterrupted navigation, though there are rapids that require careful steering both with steamers and boats. Quebec marks the place where the St. Lawrence River suddenly broadens from a river into a tidal gulf of brackish or salt water. Ocean steamers from all over the world can come (except during the height of the winter, when the water freezes) to Quebec. But for the ice in wintertime Quebec would be *the* great seaport of eastern Canada.

"If pitiless rock is commonly understood by an 'iron-bound shore', then the coasts of the River St. Lawrence along the northern side of the Gulf may truly be so styled,

[1] The south shore of Lake Superior, the whole of Lake Michigan, the west shore of Lake Huron, and the south coasts of Lake Erie and Lake Ontario are within the territories of the United States.

as nothing scarcely is to be seen for hundreds of leagues but bare rocky mountains, capes and cliffs in various shapes and figures, some of which are dotted with a few spruce firs, while others present their bald pates deprived of covering by the unmerciful hand of time" (James M'Kenzie).

The winters of the Quebec province are extremely cold, but the summer and autumn are warm and sunny. The best winter climate, possibly, in all Canada (though not as good as that of Vancouver Island, British Columbia) is to be found in the small peninsula region, on the shores of Lakes Erie and Huron, between Toronto and Detroit. This is the district which the Jesuit missionaries described as "an earthly paradise" even during the winter-time.

The following extracts, mostly from the journals of Alex. Henry, jun., give a good idea of the difference in climate and temperature between the western and the central parts of the Canadian Dominion.

The late spring of northern Canada (Lake Nipigon, 50° N. lat.):—About May 15, the tops of the poplars begin to appear green, with fresh buds; the hills are changing their hue from a dry straw colour to a delightful verdure, and fragrant odours greet us.

"Early in March, 1800, in the Assiniboin country (Manitoba, about 29° N. lat.) the snow was entirely gone, for this winter had been an abnormally mild one for central Canada. The birds soon realized the openness of the season, for, on the 7th of March, turkey-buzzards began to arrive from the south, and cormorants, ducks, swans, and other spring birds; indeed, by the 24th of March not only had the snow quite melted, but the meadows had grown so dry with the hot sun that some accidents set them on fire. By April the 11th the weather had become excessively hot, and immense flocks of the traveller-pigeon (*Ectopistes*) flew northwards over the country."

In somewhat similar latitudes (50°) the spring bursts on the Pacific coast region of British Columbia towards the end of February. "The tall raspberry bushes were in blossom with a beautiful red flower, which appeared more forward than the leaf (*Rubus spectabilis*). The elder had sprouts an inch long, the alder was also beginning to sprout, and willows were budding."

Although nowhere in Upper and Lower Canada (or in the maritime provinces of New Brunswick and Nova Scotia) are the forests so splendid as in parts of British Columbia, yet nevertheless when this region was first discovered the magnificence of its woodlands greatly impressed even the explorers of the sixteenth and seventeenth centuries, who were not as much given to praise of landscape beauty as are we of later times. These Canadian forests include oaks, elms, pines and firs, chestnuts and beeches, birch trees and sycamores, maples and poplars, willows, alders, and hazelnuts (these last sometimes growing into tall trees with thick trunks). The trees and low-growing plants are partly like those of the north-eastern United States, and partly resemble those of northern and central Europe.

Nowadays, owing to two centuries of incessant killing, the beasts and birds of Upper and Lower Canada are not nearly so abundant as they were a hundred years ago. When Canada proper was first discovered, the wapiti red deer was still found in the basin of the St. Lawrence; it has long since been extinct. There are, however, still lingering, reindeer in the north, and elk in the forests of the east. There are also Virginian deer (*Mazama*), but there is no bison (and, so far as we know, never has been). There is no prongbuck, and many other creatures characteristic of the United States and British Columbia are not found in Upper and Lower Canada or in the maritime provinces. The tree porcupine (*Erethizon dorsatus*), which the Canadians call "Urson", or "Little Bear" is found still in the well-wooded regions of eastern and southern Canada, as well as in British Columbia and Alaska. In southern Canada there is the wood hare (*Lepus sylvaticus*), and in the east and north the varying hare (*L. americanus*) which turns white in winter.

Perhaps the most characteristic animal of this region was and is still the beaver, though the beaver is found all over British North America as far north as the Saskatchewan province and westwards into British Columbia.

It is curious that the Indians of central Canada had a belief (recorded by French and English pioneers) that occasionally in the dusk, or at night, they have seen an enormously large beaver in the water, so large that at first sight they have taken it for a moose. Travellers who have related this have surmised that the Indian perhaps saw a bear swimming, or a female moose, and in the dim light mistook it for a giant beaver. But as we know that there were once giant beavers (*Trogontherium*) as large as a bear, existing in England, it is just possible there may have been a gigantic type of beaver lingering in Canada before the opening up of the country by Europeans.

The beaver of North America is a very similar animal to the beaver which used to exist wild in Wales, England, France, Germany, and central Europe, and which still lingers in some parts of the Rhine valley, Poland, Russia, and Siberia; but the American form is classified as a separate species—*Castor canadensis*.

Beavers were sometimes exterminated or diminished in numbers by an epidemic disease, which, according to JAMES TANNER[1], destroyed vast quantities of them.

"I found them dead or dying in the water, on the ice, and on the land; sometimes I found one that, having

[1] A remarkable eighteenth-century pioneer who joined the Indians when a boy and lived as one of them.

cut a tree half down, had died at its roots; sometimes one who had drawn a stick of timber halfway to his lodge was lying dead by his burthen. Many of them which I opened were red and bloody about the heart. Those in large rivers and running water suffered less; almost all of those that lived in ponds and stagnant water, died. Since that year the beaver have never been so plentiful in the country of Red River and Hudson's Bay as they used formerly to be."

The great attraction which Canada offered to France and England as a field of adventure lay in its wonderful supply of furs. The beaver skins were perhaps the commonest article of export, and were generally regarded as a unit of value, such as a shilling might be. Other skins were valued at "so many beavers," or the smaller ones at half or a quarter of a beaver each. Besides beaver skins, which were used for making hats, as well as capes and coats, the following furs and skins were formerly, or are still, exported from Canada. "Buffalo" robes—the carefully rubbed-down hides of the bison, rendered, by shaving and rubbing, so thin and supple that they could be easily folded; reindeer and musk-ox skins treated in the same way; marten or sable skins; mink (a kind of polecat); ermine (the white winter dress of the stoat); the fishing marten, or pekan; otter skins; black bear and white polar bear skins; raccoon, musk-wash, squirrel, suslik, and marmot skins, and the soft white fur of the polar hare; the white skins of the Arctic fox, the skins of the blue fox, black fox, and red fox;[1] wolf skins, and the furs of the wolverene or glutton, and of the skunk—a handsome black-and-white creature of the weasel family, which emits a most disgusting smell

[1] The blue fox is the Arctic fox (*Canis lagopus*) in its summer dress; the black fox is a beautiful variety or sub-species of the common fox (*C. vulpes*); so also is the red or "cross" fox. There is also common throughout the Canadian Dominion the pretty little kit fox (*Canis velox*).

from a gland in its body. (The skunk only comes from the south-central parts of the Canadian Dominion). At one time a good many swans' skins were exported for the sake of the down between the feathers, also the skins of grebes.

A general fact that must not be forgotten in studying the adventures of the pioneers of Canada was the means which Nature and savage man had provided or invented for quickly traversing in all directions this enormous area of nearly half North America. These means consisted (1) of the distribution of salt and fresh water in such a way that by means of ocean-sailing ships explorers coming from the east could enter through straits and bays of the sea into the heart of Canada; and (2) the facility, on quitting the seashore, of passing up navigable rivers in boats or canoes into big lakes, and from these lakes into other rivers leading to other lakes. Moreover, the different river systems approached so closely to one another that even the Amerindians and the Eskimo, long before the white man, had realized that they had only to pick up their light canoes and carry them a few miles, to launch them on fresh waters which might provide hundreds or even thousands of miles of continuous travel. These are the celebrated "portages" of Canadian history, from the French word *porter*, to carry, transport. Sometimes the portages were made still easier for loaded canoes by a road being cleared through the scrub and over the rocks, and wooden rollers placed across it. Strong men could then easily haul a loaded canoe over these wooden rollers until it could be launched again in the water. Often these portages were made to circumvent dangerous rapids or waterfalls. The Indians and the French Canadians soon learnt how to steer canoes down rushes of water—rapids—which we should think very dangerous on an English river; but of course many of the rivers were obstructed at intervals by descents of water which no canoe could traverse up or down, and in these cases a path was cut from one smooth part of the river to another, and the canoe carried or hauled overland.

In this way the great French and British explorers found it possible to travel by water from the Atlantic to the Pacific Ocean across a width of land of something like 2500 miles. The only serious walking that had to be done was the crossing somewhere or other of the Rocky Mountains, where the streams, of course, were far too precipitate in descent to be navigable. In the hot, dusty plains of Assiniboia and the upper Missouri region the Amerindians had introduced horses, obtained indirectly from Spanish Mexico, and these were of great service to the white pioneers, especially in their pursuit of the bison.

So much for the summer season, when the rivers were full and overflowing, and the ground consisted of bare rock, sand, or soil covered with vegetation; the abundance of navigable streams and the suitability of the country to horses rendered very little walking necessary for those who wished to traverse the Canadian Dominion from end to end.

But the winter changed these conditions, the rivers became coated with thick ice, and the ground was covered, except in steep places, with an unvarying mantle of snow. Yet transport became just as easy as in the summertime, though perhaps a trifle more fatiguing. Men and women put on snowshoes shaped like tennis rackets, and flew over the hard snow quicker than a canoe could travel, dragging after them small sledges on which their luggage was packed; or, if they had not much luggage, carrying it slung round the shoulders and scurrying away on their snowshoes even swifter for the weight they carried; or they travelled over the smooth ice of the rivers and lakes.

Winter travellers, however, were sometimes troubled with a disorder known as the snowshoe evil. This arose from the placing of an unusual strain on the tendons of the leg, occasioned by the weight of the snowshoe. It often resulted in severe inflammation of the lower leg. The local remedy was a drastic one: it was to place a piece of lighted touchwood on the most inflamed part, and to leave it there till the flesh was burnt to the nerve!

In the north and the regions round Hudson's Bay, and also in the far west—British Columbia and Alaska—there were dogs, more or less of the Eskimo breed, trained by Eskimo or by Amerindians to drag the sledges. In the months of December and January it is true that the daylight in Arctic Canada (north of Lake Athapaska) became so short that the sun at its greatest altitude only appeared for two or three hours a short distance above the horizon. But there were compensations. The brilliancy of the Aurora Borealis, even without the assistance of the moon and the stars, made some amends for that deficiency, for it was frequently so light all night that travellers could see to read a very small print (Samuel Hearne). The importance of these "Northern lights" must not be overlooked in forming an opinion on the habitability of the far north in the "dark" winter months. The display was frequent and brilliant.

The Athapaskan Indians called this phenomenon *Ed-thin*, that is to say, "reindeer". When the Aurora Borealis was particularly bright in the sky they would say that deer were plentiful in that part of the heavens. Their fancy in this respect was not quite so silly as one might think. They had learnt from experience that the Aurora Borealis was in some way connected with electricity, and experience had equally shown them that the skin of the reindeer, if briskly stroked by the hand on a dark night, would emit as many electric sparks as the back of a cat. On the other hand, the Amerindians in the southern and more temperate regions thought the Aurora Borealis was a vast concourse of "spirits of the happy day" dancing in the clouds.

Thus there were no climatic reasons why, both in summer and in winter, immense distances should not be quickly covered in Canada between the Rocky Mountains and the Atlantic Ocean. This is how a mere hundred of white pioneers opened up Canada to the knowledge of the civilized world far quicker than the same area could have been discovered in Africa or Asia. Sometimes, for about a month, between the melting of the snow and ice and the steady flowing of the rivers in the late spring, or between the uncertain autumn of November and the confirmed winter of December, there might be an interval of a few weeks in which journeys had to be made on foot under conditions of great hardship, through mud, swamp, and over sharp stones or slippery rocks.

"The plains are covered with water from the melting of the snow so suddenly, and our men suffer much, as they are continually on the march, looking after Indians in every creek and little river. The water is commonly knee deep, in some places up to the middle, and in the morning is usually covered with ice, which makes it tedious and even dangerous travelling. Some of our men lose the use of their legs while still in the prime of life", wrote one eighteenth-century pioneer, in the Canadian spring.

Severe as were the winter conditions of climate, the explorers were just as willing to travel through the winter as the summer, because in the winter they were spared the awful plague of mosquitoes and midges which still renders summer and early-autumn travel throughout the whole of Canada, from the United States borders on the south to the Arctic Ocean on the north, a severe trial, and even an unbearable degree of physical suffering.

# CHAPTER VII

## The Amerindians and Eskimo: the Aborigines of British North America

I have already attempted to describe in the first chapter the ancient peopling of America from north-eastern Asia, but it might be useful if I gave here some description of the Eskimo and Amerindian tribes of the Canadian Dominion at the time of its gradual discovery by Europeans, especially during the great explorations of the eighteenth and early nineteenth centuries.

It is evident that the ESKIMO—who are quite distinct from the Amerindians in physical type, language, customs, and industries—have been for thousands of years the only inhabitants of Arctic America. When the Norsemen came to the New World they seem to have met with Eskimo as far south as New England, but in more recent times the Eskimo have only been found inhabiting the extreme north and north-east: in Greenland, on the Labrador coast, on Baffin's Land, and along the Arctic coast of the North-American continent, between the Coppermine River and the westernmost extremity of Alaska, as well as on the opposite islands and promontories of Asia.

Their name for themselves as a people is usually "Innuit" (in Greenland, "Karalit"). Eskimo is a corruption of *Eskimantsik*, a northern Algonkin word meaning "eaters of raw flesh". Although their geographical range extends over a distance of about three thousand five hundred miles—from north-easternmost Asia to the east coast of Greenland—the difference in their dialects is little more than that between French and Italian; whereas the difference between the speech of one Amerindian tribe and another—even where they belong to the same language group—is very great—not less than that between German and Latin, or English and French, or even between Russian and Hindustani. This fact—of the widespread Eskimo language—makes some authorities suppose that the presence of the Eskimo in Arctic America cannot be such a very ancient event as, from other evidence, one might believe. Perhaps the bold travelling habits of the Eskimo—which makes them range over vast distances of ice and snow when hunting seals, walruses, whales, musk ox, or reindeer—enables them to keep in touch with their far-away relations.

The canoes or *kayaks* in which they travel (first described by the Norsemen in the tenth century) are made out of the hide of the seal or walrus. The leather is stretched over a framework constructed from driftwood or whales' bones. There is a hole in the middle for the man or woman to insert their legs. This hole they fill up with their bodies. If the canoe capsizes, the Eskimo cannot fall out, but bobs up immediately. He and the canoe are really "one-and-indivisible" when he is navigating the seas and lakes, plying deftly a large paddle.

In regard to food they were certainly not particular or squeamish. They loved best of all whales' blubber, or to drink the fishy-tasting oil from bodies of whales, seals, or walruses. Besides the meat of Polar bears and of any fur animals they could catch, or the musky beef of the musk ox, they devoured eagerly sea birds' eggs, Iceland moss, and even the parasitic insects of their own heads and bodies! Hearne relates that they will eat with a relish whole handfuls of maggots that have been produced in meat by the eggs of the bluebottle fly! On the other hand, they held cannibalism in horror, whereas for two-two's their Amerindian neighbours on the west and south would eat human flesh without repugnance.

The Eskimo, though occasicnally tall, are as a rule stumpy and thickset, with very small hands and feet, broad faces, and projecting cheekbones, a narrow nose without the aquiline bridge of the Amerindian, slanting narrow eyes, and long heads containing large well-developed brains. In disposition the Eskimo are nearly always merry, affectionate to one another, honest, and modest. Modern travellers in the Arctic regions give them invariably a high character; but Frobisher, Davis, and the explorers of the sixteenth and seventeenth centuries accused them of treachery and an inclination to steal. Iron in any shape or form they could hardly resist taking. Moreover, if they are the same people as the Skraellings of the Norse traditions they must have been of a fiercer disposition a thousand years ago.

The Amerindians who inhabited (more or less) the rest of the Canadian Dominion, and the whole remainder of the New World, differed in physical appearance from the Eskimo mainly in being taller and better proportioned, with shorter and rounder heads, larger, fuller eyes, a bigger nose, and a handsomer personal appearance. The skin colour, as a rule, was darker and browner than the greyish- or pinkish-yellow of the Eskimo.

The various human types that went to form the Amerindian race (beside the Eskimo element in them) seem to have entered north-west America from Asia, and first to have peopled the Pacific slopes of the Rocky Mountains, after which they wandered farther and farther south till they got into a warmer climate. Then they crossed the Rocky Mountains and peopled the centre and east of what is now the United States. As they pushed their way north up the valleys of the great rivers, they no doubt killed, mingled with, or pushed back the Eskimo. At last their northernmost extensions reached to the Mackenzie River, the vicinity of Hudson's Bay, Labrador, and Newfoundland. But in all the middle, west, and even east of Canada they seem to have been *relatively recent arrivals*,[1] not to have inhabited the country for a great many centuries before the white man came, and all their recorded and legendary movements in North America have been from the south-west towards the north-east (after they had got across the Rocky Mountains). The few cultivated plants they had, such as maize (Indian corn), tobacco, and pumpkins, they brought with them or received from the south.

The only domestic animal possessed by either Eskimo or Amerindian was the dog. We are most of us by now familiar with the type of the Eskimo dog—a large, wolf-like animal with prick ears and a bushy tail curled over its back. In this carriage of the tail the Eskimo and most other true dogs differ from wolves, with whom the tail droops between the hind quarters. But there is a small wild American wolf—the coyote—which carries its tail more upright, like that of the true dog; and the coyote seems indeed an intermediate form between the wolf and the original wild dog. Most of the domestic dogs of the Amerindians[2] (as distinguished from those of the Eskimo)

[1] There may have been an earlier race inhabiting north-east America which was killed out or driven away by the last Glacial period.

[2] "The dogs of the Northern Indians are of various sizes and colours, but all of them have a foxy or wolf-like appearance, sharp noses, bushy tails, and sharp ears standing erect" (Samuel Hearne).

Hearne also remarks that the northern Indians had a superstitious reverence and liking for the wolf. They would frequently go to the mouth of the burrows where the female wolves lived with their young, take out the puppies and play with them, and even paint the faces of the young wolves with vermilion or red ochre.

When first observed by Europeans the unhappy Beothiks (of Newfoundland) had apparently no domestic dogs, only "tame wolves", whom they distinguished from the wild wolves by marking their ears. They were made more angry by the European seamen attacking and killing the wolves than by anything else they did. Apparently some kind of alliance had been struck up between the Beothiks—a nation of hunters—and the wolf packs which followed in their tracks; and the Newfoundland wolves were on the way to becoming domesticated "dogs". Later on it was realized that the island *did* produce a special breed—the celebrated Newfoundland dog—the original type of which was much smaller than the modern type, nearly or entirely black in colour, with a sharper muzzle and less pendulous ears. But its feet were as strongly seem to have been derived from the coyote or small wolf of central North America.

On the Pacific coast there were other types of domestic dog, resembling greatly breeds that are found in eastern Asia and the Pacific islands. Some of these were naked, and others grew silky hair, which was woven by the natives into cloth (see p. 323). The Eskimo dog almost certainly has been derived from northern Asia, and is closely related to the well-known Chinese breed—the chow dog—and the domestic breeds of ancient Europe. Even the commonest type of house dog in the Roman Empire was very much like an Eskimo or a chow in appearance. There is a true wild dog, however, in the Yukon province of the Canadian Dominion and in Alaska—*Canis pambasileus*—a dark, blackish-brown in colour. This may have been a parent of the Eskimo dog, but it is also doubtless closely allied to the original (extinct) wild dog of northern Asia, from which the chow and many other breeds are directly descended. The Eskimo never under ordinary circumstances ate their dogs; on the other hand, the Amerindians were fond of dog's flesh, and in some tribes simply bred dogs for the table.

When Europeans first reached America all these Amerindian tribes, and also the Eskimo, were still, for all practical purposes, in the Stone Age. Those who lived in the north had discovered the use of copper and had shaped for themselves knives and spear blades out of copper, but not even this metal was in use to any great extent, and for the most part they relied, down to the end of the eighteenth century, for their implements and weapons, on polished and sharpened stones, on deer's antlers, buffalo

webbed and its habits as aquatic as those of the "Newfoundland" of the modern breed. Some people have noticed the resemblance between the farmers' dogs in Norway and the Newfoundland type, and have thought that the latter may not be altogether of wolf extraction, but be descended from the dogs brought from Norway and Iceland by the Norse adventurers who visited Newfoundland in the tenth and eleventh centuries.

horns, sticks, sharp shells, beavers' incisor teeth,[1] the claws or spines of crustaceans, flints, and suchlike substances —in short, they were leading the same life and using almost exactly the same tools as the long-since-vanished hunter races of Europe of five thousand to one hundred thousand years ago—the people who pursued the mammoth, the bison, the Irish "elk", and the other great beasts of prehistoric Europe. Indeed, North America represented to some extent, as late as a hundred years ago, what Europe must have looked like in the days of palæolithic Man.

The AMERINDIANS of the Canadian Dominion (when the country first became known to Europeans) belonged to the following groups and tribes. The order of enumeration begins in the east and proceeds westwards. I have already mentioned the peculiar *Beothiks* of Newfoundland.[2] In Nova Scotia, Prince Edward Island, New Brunswick, and the Gaspé Peninsula there were the *Mikmak* Indians belonging to the widespread ALGONKIN family or stock. West and south of the Mikmaks, in New Brunswick and along the borders of New England, were other tribes of the Algonkin group: the Etchemins, Abenakis, Tarratines, Penobscots, *Mohikans*, and Adirondacks. North of these, in the eastern part of the Quebec province, on either side of the Gulf of St. Lawrence, were the *Montagnais*. This name, though it looks like a French word meaning "mountaineers", was also spent Montagnet, and in various other ways, showing that it was originally a native name, pronounced Montanyé. The Montagnais in various clans extended northwards across Labrador until they touched the Eskimo, with whom they constantly fought. The interior of Labrador was inhabited by another Algonkin tribe, the *Naskwapi*, living in a state of rude

[1] Of which they made very serviceable chisels.

[2] See also pp. 156, 164, 186, and 199. In this list I have put in italics the names of the tribes more important in history, and in capitals the principal group names.

savagery. The *Algonkins* proper, whose tribe gave their name to the whole stock because the French first became acquainted with them as a type, dwelt in the vicinity of Montreal, Lake Ontario, and the valley of the St. Lawrence. In upper Canada, about the great lakes and the St. Lawrence valley, were the Chippeways, or *Ojibwés*, and the Ottawas. West and north of Lake Michigan were the Miamis, the Potawátomis, and the Fox Indians (the Saks or Sawkis). Between Lake Winnipeg and Lake Superior were the *Cheyennes* (Shians); between North and South Saskatchewan, the *Blackfeet* or Siksika Indians (sections of which were also called Bloods, Paigans, Piegans, &c.). North of Lake Winnipeg, as far as Lake Athabaska, and almost from the Rocky Mountains to the shores of Hudson's Bay, were the widespread tribe of the *Kris*, or *Knistino*.[1] The Gros Ventres or Big Bellies —properly called *Atsina*—inhabited the southern part of the middle west, between the Saskatchewan and the Missouri basins; and the Monsoni or Maskegon were found in eastern Rupert Land.

All the above-enumerated tribes, except the Beothik indigenes of Newfoundland, belong to the great and widespread ALGONKIN group. (Algonkin is a word derived from the "Algommequin" of Champlain.) In the valley of the St. Lawrence the French first encountered those Indians whom they called *Huron*. This was a French word meaning "crested", because these people wore their hair in a great crest over the top and back of the head, which reminded the French of the appearance of a wild boar (*Hure*). The real name of the Hurons, who dwelt at a later date between Lakes Huron, Erie, Ontario, and the neighbourhood of Montreal, was *Waiandot* (Wyandot); but they went under a variety of other names, according to the clans, such as the Eries and the Atiwándoran or Neutral Nation. They were also called the "Good" Iro-

[1] Kinistino, Kiristineaux, Kilistino; called "Crees" or "Kris" for short.

quois, to distinguish them from the six other nations, the IROQUOIS proper of the French Canadians, who signalized themselves by fiendish and frightful warfare against the French and the various tribes of Algonkin Indians. The Hurons and the rest of the six tribes grouped under the name of IROQUOIS[1] were of the same stock originally, forming a separate group like that of the Algonkins, though they are supposed to be related distantly to the Dakota or Siou. Amongst the "Six Nations" or tribes banded together in warfare and policy were the celebrated "Mohawks" who dwelt on the southern borders of the St. Lawrence basin and near Lake Champlain. As the others of the six nations (including the Senekas and Onondagas) inhabited the eastern United States, well outside the limits of Canada, they need not be referred to here.

Between the South Saskatchewan, the Rocky Mountains, and Lake Superior, nearly outside the limits of the Canadian Dominion, was the great DAKOTA, or SIOU group,[2] divided into the distinct tribe of *Assiniboin* or "Stone" Indians (because they used hot stones in cooking), the "Crows" or Absaroka, the Hidatsa or Minitari (also called Big Bellies, like the quite distinct Atsina of the Algonkin family), the Menómini (the most north-eastern amongst the Siouan tribes, and the first met with by the British and French Canadians south-west of Lake Superior), the Winnebagos on the southern borders of Manitoba, the Yanktons or Yanktonnais, the "*Santi Siou*" proper—generally calling themselves *Dakota* or Mdewakanton—and the "Tétons" along the northern Dakota frontier and into the Rocky Mountains—also

[1] "Iroquois" was a name invented by Champlain (see p. 69). Apparently this confederation called themselves *Hodenosauni*. The termination "ois" in all French-American names is pronounced "-wa"—Irokwá.

[2] The far-famed term *Siou* is said to have been an abbreviation of one of the original French names for this type of Amerindian, *Nadouessiou*. In early books they are often called the Nadouessies.

known as *Blackfeet*, Sans Arcs ("without bows"), "Two-kettles", "Brulés" or "Burnt" Indians, &c.

Next must be mentioned the very important and wide-spread ATHAPASKAN or Déné (Tinné) group, named after Lake Athapaska (or Athabaska), because that sheet of water became a great rallying place for these northern tribes. The Athapaskan group of Indians indeed represents the "Northern Indians" of the Hudson's Bay Company's reports and explorers. They drew a great distinction between the Northern Indians (the Athapaskan tribes) and the Southern Indians, which included all the other Amerindian groups dwelling to the south of the Athapaskan domain. But although nowadays so much associated with the far north and north-west of America, the Athabaskan group evidently came from a region much farther south, and has been cut in half by other tribal movements, wars, and migrations; for the Athapaskan family also includes the Apaches and the Navaho of the south-western portions of the United States and the adjoining territories of Mexico. The northern and southern divisions of the Athapaskan group are separated by something like twelve hundred miles. The following are the principal tribes into which the Northern ATHAPASKAN group was divided at the time of the first explorations of the north-west. There were the *Chippewayan* Indians[1] round about Lake Athapaska, and the Caribou Eaters or Ethen-eldeli between Lake Athapaska and Reindeer Lake. The "*Slaves*", or Slave Indians of the Great Slave Lake and the upper Mackenzie River; the Beaver and Sarsi Indians (known also as the Tsékehn), about the Peace River and the northern part of Alberta province; and the *Yellow Knives*, or Totsan-ottine (so called from their being

[1] These northern Indians are described by Hearne as having very low foreheads, small eyes, high cheekbones, Roman noses, broad cheeks, and long, broad chins. Their skins were soft, smooth and polished, somewhat copper-coloured, and inclining towards a dingy brown. The hair of the head was black, strong, and straight. They were not in general above middle size, though well proportioned.

found with light-coloured copper knives when first discovered by Europeans), north-east of the Great Slave Lake and along the Coppermine River: the *Dogribs* between the Great Slave Lake and Great Bear Lake, perhaps (except in Alaska) the most northern extension of the Amerindian type towards the Arctic regions. West of the Dogribs dwelt—and still dwell—the interesting tribe of *Hare* Indians, or Kawcho-Tinné. They extend northwards to the Anderson River, on the verge of the Arctic Ocean. West of the lower Mackenzie River, and stretching thence to the Porcupine or Yukon Rivers, are the Squinting Indians ("Loucheux", or Kuchin), who in former times were met with much farther to the south-east than at the present day. Finally, there are the Nahani Indians, who have penetrated through the Rocky Mountains to the Stikine River, reaching thus quite close to the Pacific Ocean. This penetration northwards of groups of Athapaskan Indians into districts inhabited for the most part by Amerindian tribes differing widely in language and customs from all those *east* of the Rocky Mountains, explains the way in which stories of the great western sea—the Pacific—reached, by means of trading intercourse, those Amerindian tribes of the middle-west and upper Canada, and so stirred up the French and English explorers of the seventeenth and eighteenth centuries to make the marvellous journeys which are recounted in this book.

*West* of the Rocky Mountains, in British Columbia and Vancouver Island (besides southern Alaska), the Amerindian tribes form the Nūtka-Columbian group, which is markedly distinct from the Amerindians *east* of the Rocky Mountains, from whom they differ *widely* in language, type, and culture. They are divided into quite a large number of small separate groups—the Wakashan or *Nūtkas* of Vancouver Island and south-western British Columbia, the Shahaptian or "Nez percés" Indians of the

c 312 Photo Thompson

AN AMERINDIAN TYPE OF BRITISH COLUMBIA

Columbia basin, and the Chinūks of the lower Columbia River, the *Salishan* or "Flathead" group (including the Atnās) of the Fraser and Thompson Rivers and central British Columbia; and the *Haida* Indians of Queen Charlotte's Islands and the north-west coast of British Columbia. It must be remembered that these different groups are only based on the relationships of their component tribes in language or dialect, and do not always imply that the tribes belonging to them had the same customs and dispositions; but they were generally able to communicate with one another in speech, whereas if they met the Indians of another group the language might be so totally different that they could only communicate by means of signs.

Sign and gesture language[1] was extraordinarily developed amongst all the Amerindian races from the Arctic Ocean to the Antarctic. Not only that, but they were quick to understand the purpose of pictures. They could draw maps in the sand to explain the geography of their country, and Europeans could often make them understand what they required by rough drawings. They themselves related many events by means of a picture language—the beginning of hieroglyphics; and in the south-eastern parts of Canada, as in the United States, these signs or pictographs were recorded in bead-shell work—the celebrated "wampum".

All these tribes, of course, varied very much in personal appearance, though not in disposition. The van-

[1] "It is surprising how dexterous all these natives of the plains are in communicating their ideas by signs. They hold conferences for several hours, upon different subjects, during the whole of which time not a single word is pronounced upon either side, and still they appear to comprehend each other perfectly well. This mode of communication is natural to them; their gestures are made with the greatest ease, and they never seem to be at a loss for a sign to express their meaning" (Alex. Henry the Younger, 1800). But it should also be noted that during the last hundred years the peoples belonging to the Nūtka-Columbian group have developed a trade language which they use in common. This is a mixture of Chinūk, English, French, Chinese, and Hawaaian.

ished Beothiks of Newfoundland are described as having been a good-looking tall people, with large black eyes and a skin so light, when washed free from dirt or paint, that the Portuguese compared them to gipsies; and the writer of Fabian's *Chronicle*, who saw two of them (brought back by Cabot) at Henry VII's Court, in 1499, took them for Englishmen when they were dressed in English clothes. It was these people—subsequently killed out by the British settlers on Newfoundland—who originated the term "Red Indians", or, in French, *Peaux Rouges*, because their skins, like those of so many other Amerindians, were painted with red ochre.

Many of the British Columbian peoples made themselves artificially ugly by flattening the sides of the head. To press the skull whilst it was soft, they squeezed the heads of their children between boards; others, such as the warlike tribes of the upper Missouri, had a passion for submitting themselves to mutilation by the medicine man of the clan, in order to please the sun god. Such would submit to large strips being cut from the flesh of their shoulders, arms, or legs, or having their cheeks slashed. The result, of course, was to leave their limbs and features horribly scarred when they healed up. In some tribes, however, a young man could not obtain—or retain—a wife unless he had shown his bravery by submitting to this mutilation. Women often cut off one or more joints of their fingers to show their grief for the death of children.

In some tribes, especially of the far north-west and of the Rocky Mountains, the personal habits of men and women, or of the women only, were so filthy, and their dislike to bathing so pronounced, that they became objects of loathing to white men; in other tribes personal cleanliness was highly esteemed, especially on the sea-coast of British Columbia or along the banks of the great rivers. Usually the men were better looking and better developed than the women—for one reason, because they were better fed.

Here is a description by PETER GRANT—a pioneer of the North-West Company—of the Ojibwé Indians dwelling near the east end of Lake Superior at the beginning of the nineteenth century:—

"Their complexion is a whitish cast of copper colour, their hair black, long, straight, and of a very strong texture. The young men allow several locks of the hair to fall down over the face, ornamented with ribbons, silver brooches, &c. They gather up another lock from behind the head into a small clump, and wrap it up with very thin plates of silver, in which they fix the tail feathers of the eagle or any other favourite bird with the wearing of which they have distinguished themselves in war. They are very careful with their hair, anointing it with bears' oil, which gives it a smooth and glossy appearance. The teeth are of a beautiful ivory white, the cheeks rather high and prominent, the eyes black and lively. Their countenances are generally pleasant, and they might often be called handsome. The ears are pierced in infancy, and the lobe is extended to an unnatural size by suspending lead or any other heavy metal from the outer rim, which in time brings them down near the shoulder. The nose ornaments hang down half an inch, and nearly touch the upper lip.

"The men are bold, manly, and graceful in their gait, always carrying their bodies erect and easy. On the other hand, the women, by walking with the toes of their feet turned inwards, have a disagreeable and lame appearance. The men are specially fond of painting their faces and bodies with vermilion, white and blue clay, charcoal or soot mixed with a little grease or water. With this colour they daub the body, legs, and thighs in bars and patches, and take the greatest pains about painting the face, usually with red and black. Their skins are generally tattooed with figures representing the sun, stars, eagles, serpents, &c., especially objects which have appeared to them in their dreams. The women's faces are much less painted, usually a spot of red on each cheek and a circle of red round the roots of the hair or eyes."

Here is a summary of what Alexander Henry, sen., wrote of the *Kri* or *Knistino* Indians of Lake Athabaska about 1770:—

"The men in general tattoo their bodies and arms very much. The women confine this ornamentation to the chin, having three perpendicular lines from the middle of the chin to the lip, and one or more running on each side, nearly parallel with the corner of the mouth. Their dress consists of leather; that of the men is a pair of leggings, reaching up to the hip and fastened to the girdle. Between the legs is passed a strip of woollen stuff, but when this cannot be procured they use a piece of dressed leather about nine inches broad and four feet long, whose ends are drawn through the girdle and hang down before and behind about a foot. . . . The shirt is of soft dressed leather, either from the prong-buck or young red deer, close about the neck and hanging to the middle of the thigh; the sleeves are of the same, loose and open under the arms to the elbows, but thence to the wrist sewed tight. The cap is commonly a piece of leather, or skin with the hair on, shaped to fit the head, and tied under the chin; the top is usually decorated with feathers or other ornament. Shoes are made of buffalo (bison) hide, dressed in the hair, and mittens of the same. Over the whole a buffalo robe is thrown, which serves as covering day and night.

"Such is their common dress, but on particular occasions they appear to greater advantage, having their cap, shirt, leggings, and shoes perfectly clean and white, trimmed with porcupine quills and other ingenious work of their women, who are supposed to be the most skilful hands in the country at decorations of this kind. The women's dress consists of the same materials as the men's. Their leggings do not reach above the knee, and are gathered below that joint; their shoes always lack decoration. The shift or body garment reaches down to the calf, where it is generally fringed and trimmed with quillwork; the upper part is fastened over the shoulders by strips of leather; a flap or cape hangs down about a foot before and behind, and is ornamented with quillwork and fringe. This covering is quite loose, but tied around the waist with a belt of stiff parchment fastened on the side, where also some ornaments are suspended. The sleeves are detached from the body garment; from the wrist to the elbow they are sewed, but thence to the shoulder they are open underneath and drawn up to the neck, where they are fastened across the breast and back.

"Their ornaments are two or three coils of brass wire twisted around the rim of each ear, in which incisions are made for that purpose; blue beads, brass rings, quillwork, and fringe occasionally answer. Vermilion (a red clay) is much used by the women to paint the face.

"Their hair is generally parted on the crown and fastened behind each ear in large knots, from which are suspended bunches of blue beads or other ingenious work of their own. The men adjust their hair in various forms; some have it parted on top and tied in a tail on each side, while others make one long *queue* which hangs down behind, and around which is twisted a strip of otter skin or dressed buffalo entrails. This tail is frequently increased in thickness and length by adding false hair, but others allow it to flow loose naturally. Combs are seldom used by the men, and they never smear the hair with grease, but red earth is sometimes put upon it. White earth daubed over the hair generally denotes mourning. The young men sometimes have a bunch of hair on the crown, about the size of a small teacup, and nearly in the shape of that vessel upside down, to which they fasten various ornaments of feathers, quillwork, ermine tails, &c. Red and white earth and charcoal are much used in their toilets; with the former they usually daub their robes and other garments, some red and others white. The women comb their hair and use grease on it."

The Slave Indians (a tribe of the Athapaskan family) tattooed their cheeks with charcoal inserted under the skin, also daubed their bodies, robes, and garments profusely with red earth (generally called, in the text of travellers, vermilion), but they had another favourite pigment, procured from the regions on the west of the Rocky Mountains, some kind of graphite, like the lead of lead pencils. With this they marked their faces in black lead after red earth has been applied, and thus gave themselves a ghastly and savage appearance. Their dress consists of a leather shirt trimmed with human hair and porcupine-quill work, and leggings of leather. Their shoes and caps were made of bison leather, with the hair outside. Their necklaces were strings of grizzly-bear claws, and a "buffalo" robe was thrown over all occasionally. Some of them occasionally had quite light skins—when free of dirt or paint—and grey eyes, and their hair, instead of being black, was greyish-brown. These last features (grey eyes and brown hair) characterized many individuals among the northern British-Columbian tribes.

The Naskwapis of inland Labrador—allied in speech to the Kris and the Montagnais, but in blood to the Eskimo—are described as above the middle size in height, slender, and long-legged, their cheeks being very prominent, eyes black, nose rather flat, mouth large, lips thick, teeth white, hair rough and black, and the complexion a yellowish "frog" colour. They were dressed in elaborate and warm garments made of reindeer skin. The ordinary covering for the head of the men was the skin of a bear's head. "Thus accoutred, with the addition of a bow and quiver, a stone axe, and a bone knife, a Naskwapi man possessed no small degree of pride and self-importance" (James M'Kenzie).

The handsomest tribes of Amerindians encountered by the Canadian pioneers seem to have been the Ojibwés of Lake Superior, the Iroquois south of the St. Lawrence, and the Mandans of the upper Missouri.

Until well on in the nineteenth century none of the Canadian Amerindians were particular about wearing clothes if the weather was hot. The men, especially, were either quite oblivious of what was seemly in clothing (except perhaps the Iroquois) or thought it necessary to go naked into battle, or to remove all clothing before taking part in religious ceremonies.

It is commonly supposed that the Red Man was a rather glum person, seldom seen to smile and averse to showing any emotion. That is not the impression one derives from the many pen portraits of Amerindians in the journals of the great pioneers. Here, on the contrary, you see the natives laughing, smiling, kissing eagerly their wives and children after an absence, displaying exuberant and cordial friendship towards the white man who treated them well, having love quarrels and fits of raging jealousy, moods of deep remorse after a fight, touching devotion to their comrades or chiefs, and above all to their children. They are most emotional, indeed, and, apart from this chapter you will find frequent descriptions of how they wept at times over the remembrance of their dead relations and friends.

Hearne remarked, in 1772, that when two parties of Athapaska Indians met, the ceremonies which passed between them were very formal. They would advance within twenty or thirty yards of each other, make a full halt, and then sit or lie down on the ground, not speaking for some minutes. At length one of them, generally an elderly man, broke silence by acquainting the other party with every misfortune that had befallen him and his companions from the last time they had seen or heard of each other, including all deaths and other calamities which had happened to any other Indians during the same period. When he finished, another orator, belonging to the other party, related in like manner all the bad news that had come to *his* knowledge. If these orations contained any news that in the least affected either party, it would not be long before some of them began to sigh and sob, and soon after to break out into a loud cry, which was generally accompanied by most of the grown persons of both sexes; and sometimes it was common to hear them all—men, women, and children—joining in one universal howl. When the first transports of grief had subsided, they advanced by degrees, and both parties mixed with each other, the men with the men, the women with the women. They then passed round tobacco pipes very freely, and the conversation became general. They had now nothing but good news left to tell, and in less than half an hour probably nothing but smiles and cheerfulness would be seen on every face.

One direction in which the Amerindians did not shine was in their treatment of women. This perhaps was worse than in other uncivilized races. Woman was very badly used, except perhaps for the first year of courtship and marriage. Courtship began by the young man throwing sticks at the girl[1] who pleased his fancy, and if she responded he asked her in marriage. But not long after she had become a mother she sank into the position of a household drudge and beast of burden. For example, amongst the Beaver Indians, an Athapaskan tribe of the

[1] The manner of courtship among the Ojibwés seemed to Peter Grant not only singular, but rude. "The lover begins his first addresses by gently pelting his mistress with bits of clay, snowballs, small sticks, or anything he may happen to have in his hand. If she returns the compliment, he is encouraged to continue the farce, and repeat it for a considerable time, after which more direct proposals of marriage are made by word of mouth."

far north-west, it is related by Alexander Mackenzie that the women are permanently crippled and injured in physique by the hardships they have to undergo. "Having few dogs for transport in that country, the women alone perform that labour which is allotted to beasts of burden in other countries. It is not uncommon whilst the men carry nothing but a gun, that their wives and daughters follow with such weighty burdens that if they lay them down they cannot replace them; nor will the men deign to perform the service of hoisting them on to their backs. So that during their journeys they are frequently obliged to lean against a tree for a small degree of temporary relief. When they arrive at the place which their tyrants have chosen for their encampment, they arrange the tent in a few minutes by forming a curve of poles meeting at the top and expanding into a circle of twelve or fifteen feet in diameter at the bottom, covered with dressed skins of the moose sewn together. During these preparations the men sit down quietly to the enjoyment of their pipes, if they happen to have any tobacco."

Among the Ojibwé and Huron Indians of the Great Lakes the men sometimes obliged their wives to bring up and nourish young bears instead of their own children, so that the bears might eventually be fattened for eating. If food was scarce, the women went without before even the male slaves of the tribe were unprovided with food. Women might never eat in the society of males, not even if these males were slaves or prisoners of war. If food was very scarce, the husband as likely as not killed and ate a wife; perhaps did this before slaying and eating a valuable dog. (On the other hand, Mackenzie instances the case of a woman among the Slave Indians who, in a winter of great scarcity, managed to kill and devour her husband and several relations.) So terrible was the ill-treatment of the women in some tribes that these wretched beings sometimes committed suicide to end their tortures. Even in this, however, they were not let off lightly, for the Siou men invented as a tenet of their religion the saying that "Women who hang themselves are the most miserable of all wretches in the other world".

On the other hand, the kind treatment of children by fathers as well as mothers is an "Indian" trait commented on by writer after writer. Here is a typical description by Alexander Henry the Elder, concerning the children of the Ojibwé tribe:

"As soon as the boys begin to run about, they are provided with bows and arrows, and acquire, as it were 'by instinct', an astonishing dexterity in shooting birds, squirrels, butterflies, &c. Hunting in miniature may be justly said to comprise the whole of their education and childish diversion. Such as excel in this kind of exercise are sure of being particularly distinguished by their parents, and seldom punished for any misbehaviour, but, on the contrary, indulged in every degree of excess and caprice. I have often seen grown-up boys of this description, when punished for some serious fault, strike their father and spit in his face, calling him 'bad dog', or 'old woman', and, sometimes, carrying their insolence so far as to threaten to stab or shoot him, and, what is rather singular, these too-indulgent parents seem to encourage such unnatural liberties, and even glory in such conduct from their favourite children. I heard them boast of having sons who promised at an early age to inherit such bold and independent sentiments. . . . Children of nine or ten years of age not only enjoy the confidence of the men, but are generally considered as companions and very deliberately join in their conversations."

When death overtook anybody the grief of the female relations was carried to great excess. They not only cut their hair, cried and howled, but they would some-

c 312

CARIBOU SWIMMING A RIVER

times, with the utmost deliberation, employ some sharp instrument to separate the nail from the finger and then force back the flesh beyond the first joint, which they immediately amputated. "Many of the old women have so often repeated this ceremony that they have not a complete finger remaining on either hand" (Mackenzie).

The Amerindians of North America were religious and superstitious, and had a firm faith in a world of spiritual agencies within or outside the material world around us. Most of them believed in the existence of "fairies",—woodland, earth, mountain, or water spirits—whom they declared they could see from time t. time in human semblance. Or such spirit or demi-god might assume for a time or permanently the form of an animal. To all such spirits of earth, air, and water, or to the sacred animals they inhabited, sacrifices would be offered and prayers made. Great importance was attributed to dreams and visions. They accustomed themselves to make long fasts, so that they might become light-headed and see visions, or hear spirit voices in a trance. To prepare their minds for this state they would go four or five days without food, and even abstain from drinking.

Undoubtedly their "medicine men" developed great mesmeric powers, and this force, combined with rather clumsy juggling and ventriloquism, enabled them to perform a semblance of "miracles". The Iroquois offered much opposition to Christianity, thinking it would tame their warriors too quickly and affect their national independence; but by the greater part of the Amerindians the message of the Gospel brought by the French priests was eagerly received, and the converts became many and most sincere. Their reverence for the missionaries and belief in them was increased when they saw how effectually they were able to protect them from too-rapacious white adventurers, fierce soldiers, and unscrupulous traders.

The Miamis of Lake Michigan held the symbol of the cross in great respect. A young Frenchman who was trading with them got into a passion and drew his sword to avenge himself for a theft committed on his goods. The Miama chieftain, to appease him, showed him the cross, which was planted in the ground at the end of his lodge, and said to him: "Behold the tree of the Black Gown; he teaches us to pray and not to lose our temper,"—of course, referring to the missionary in the black gown who had been amongst them. Before the cross was planted here these Miamis kept in their houses one or more bogies, to which they appealed in times of distress or sickness. One of these was the skull of the bison with its horns. Another was the skin of the bear raised on a pole in the middle of the hut and retaining the head, which was usually painted green. The women sometimes died of terror from the stories told them by the men about these idols, and the Jesuits did a great deal of good by getting them abolished in many places.

The Supreme Being of the Eskimos was a goddess rather than a god: a mother of all things who lived under the sea. On the other hand, most of the Amerindian tribes believed in one great God of the Sky—Manito, as He was called by the peoples of Algonkin stock, Nainubushan by the Siou and their kindred. This Being was usually kindly disposed towards man; but they also (in most cases) believed in a *bad* Manito, who was responsible for most of the harm in the world. But sometimes the Great Manito was capricious, or apparently made many mistakes which he had afterwards to rectify. Thus the Siou tribes of Assiniboia believed that the Supreme Being (whom they called Eth-tom-é) first created mankind and all living things, and then, through some oversight or mistake, caused a great flood to cover the earth's surface. So in a hurry he was obliged to make a very large canoe of twigs and branches, and into this he put a pair of every kind of bird and beast, besides a family of human beings, who were thus saved from drowning, and began the world afresh when the waters subsided. This legend was something like the story of Noah's ark, but seems in some form or another to have existed in the mind of all the North-American peoples before the arrival of Christian missionaries. Much the same story was told by the Ojibwés about the Great Hare-God, Nainiboju.

The Siou and the Ojibwé (and other tribes also) believed that after death the soul lay for a time in a trance, and then found itself floating towards a River which must be crossed. Beyond the River lay the Happy Hunting Grounds, the Elysian fields; but to oppose the weary soul anxious to reach this paradise there ramped on the other side a huge, flaming-red bison bull. If it had been ordained by the Great Spirit that the soul's time was not yet come, this red bison pushed it back, and the soul was obliged to re-enter the body, which then awoke from its trance or swoon and resumed its worldly activities.

Suicide was regarded as the most heinous of crimes. Any man killing himself deliberately, fell into the river of the ghost world and was never heard of again, while women who hanged themselves "were regarded as the most miserable of all wretches in the other world".

Their belief in spirits—even ancestral spirits—taking up an abode in the bodies of beasts, birds, or reptiles, or even in plants or stones, caused them to view with respect of a superstitious kind many natural objects. Some one thing—a beast, bird, reptile, fish, plant, or strange stone had been fixed on as the abode of his tutelary spirit by some father of a family. The family grew into a clan, and the clan to a tribe, and the object sacred in the eyes of its father and founder became its "totem", crest, or symbol. As a rule, whatever thing was the *totem* of the individual or the clan was held sacred in their eyes, and, if it was an animal, was not killed, or, if killed, not eaten. Many of the northern Indians would refrain from killing the wolf or the glutton, or if they did so, or did it by accident, they would refuse to skin the animal. The elder people amongst the Athapaskan Indians, in Hearne's day, would reprove the young folk for "speaking disrespectfully" of different beasts and birds.

Their ideas of medicine and surgery were much mixed up with a belief in magic and in the mysterious powers of their "medicine men". This person, who might be of either sex, certainly knew a few simple medicines to be made from herbs or decoctions of bark, but for the most part he attempted to cure the sick or injured by blowing lustily on the part affected or, more wisely, by massage. A universal cure, however, for all fevers and mild ailments was sweating. Sweating huts were built in nearly every settlement. They were covered over in a way to exclude air as much as possible. The inside was heated with red-hot stones and glowing embers, on to which from time to time water was poured to fill the place with steam. The Amerindians not only went through these Turkish baths to cure small ailments but also with the idea of clearing the intelligence and as a fitting preliminary to negotiations —for peace, or alliance, or even for courtship. In many tribes if a young "brave" arrived with proposals of marriage for a man's daughter he was invited to enter the sweating house with her father, and discuss the bargain calmly over perspiration and the tobacco pipe.

Tobacco smoking indeed was almost a religious ceremony, as well as a remedy for certain maladies or states of mind. The "pipe of peace" has become proverbial. Nevertheless tobacco was still unknown in the eighteenth century to many of the Pacific-coast and far-north-west tribes, as to the primitive Eskimo. It was not a very old practice in the Canadian Dominion when Europeans first arrived there, though it appeared to be one of the most characteristic actions of these red-skinned savages in the astonished eyes of the first pioneers. They used pipes for smoking, however, long before tobacco came among them, certain berries taking the place of tobacco.

The Amerindians of the southern parts of Canada and British Columbia were more or less settled peoples of towns or villages, of fixed homes to which they returned at all seasons of the year, however far afield they might range for warfare, trade, or hunting. But the more northern tribes were nomads: people shifting their abode from place to place in pursuit of game or trade. Unlike the people of the south and west (though these only grew potatoes) they were not agriculturists: the only vegetable element in their food was the wild rice of the marshes, the sweet-tasting layer between the bark and the wood of certain trees, and the fruits or fungi of the forest or the lichen growing on the rocks. Though these people might in summertime build some hasty wigwam of boughs and moss, their ordinary dwelling place was a tent.

The Wood Indians, or Opimitish Ininiwak, of the Athapaskan group (writes Alexander Henry, sen.) had no fixed villages; and their lodges or huts were so rudely fashioned as to afford them very inadequate protection against the weather. The greater part of their year was spent in travelling from place to place in search of food. The animal on which they chiefly depended was the *hare*—a most prominent animal in Amerindian economy and tradition. This they took in springes. From its skin they made coverings with much ingenuity, cutting it into narrow strips and weaving this into the shape of a blanket, which was of a very warm and agreeable quality.

The Naskwapi Algonkins of inland Labrador were savages that led a wandering life through the bare, flat parts of that country, subsisting chiefly upon flesh, and clothing themselves with the skin of the caribou, which they caught in pitfalls or shot with the bow and arrow. "Very few sights, I believe, can be more distressing to the feelings of humanity than a Labrador savage, surrounded by his wife and five or six small children, half-famished with cold and hunger in a hole dug out of the snow and screened from the inclemency of the weather by the branches of the trees. Their whole furniture is a kettle hung over the fire, not for the purpose of cooking victuals, but for melting snow" (James M'Kenzie).

A description of the tents of the Kris or Knistino (Algonkins of the Athabaska region), written by Alexander Henry, sen., applies with very little difference to all the other tribes dwelling to the east of the Rocky Mountains.[1]

These tents were of dressed leather, erected with poles, generally seventeen in number, of which two were tied together about three feet from the top. The first two poles being erected and set apart at the base, the others were placed against them in a slanting position, meeting at the top, so that they all formed nearly a circle, which was then covered with the leather. This consisted of ten to fifteen dressed skins of the bison, moose, or red deer, well sewed together and nicely cut to fit the conical figure of the poles, with an opening above, to let out smoke and admit the light. From this opening down to the door the two edges of the tent were brought close together and well secured with wooden pegs about six inches long, leaving for the door an oval aperture about two feet wide and three feet high, below which the edges were secured with similar pegs. This small entrance did well enough for the natives, who would be brought up to it from infancy, but a European might be puzzled to get through, as a piece of hide stretched upon a frame of the same shape as the door, but somewhat larger, hung outside, and must be first raised by the hand of the incomer.

Such tents were usually spacious, measuring twenty

[1] See also p. 249.

feet in diameter. The fire was always made in the centre, around which the occupants generally placed a range of stones to prevent the ashes from scattering and to keep the fire compact. New tents were perfectly white; some of them were painted with red and black figures. These devices were generally derived from the dreams of the Amerindians, being some mythical monster or other hideous animal, whose description had been handed down from their ancestors. A large camp of such tents, pitched regularly on a level plain, had a fine effect at a distance, especially when numerous bands of horses were seen feeding in all directions.

The "lodges" or long houses made of poles, fir branches, moss, &c., wherein, among the Iroquois, Algonkin, and Siou peoples, several families made a common habitation, are described here and there in the course of the narrative. The houses of the coast tribes of British Columbia were bigger, more elaborate, and permanent, and in this region the natives had acquired some idea of carpentry, and had learnt to make planks of wood by splitting with wedges or hewing with adzes.

One of these British Columbian houses was measured, and found to be seventy feet long by twenty-five feet wide; the entrance in the gable end was cut through a plank five and a half feet wide, and nearly oval. A board suspended on the outside answered for a door; on the other side of the broad plank was rudely carved a large painted figure of a man, between whose legs was the passage. But other houses on the Pacific coast, visited by Cook or Vancouver, are said to have been large enough to accommodate seven hundred people. These houses of the Pacific coast region were exceedingly filthy, sturgeon and salmon being strewn about in every direction. The men inhabiting them were often disgusting in their behaviour, while the women are declared to have been "devoid of shame or decency".

According to Mackenzie, such habitations swarmed

with fleas, and even the ground round about them "was alive with this vermin". The Alexander Henrys, both uncle and nephew, complain of the flea plague (partly due to the multitude of dogs) in every Indian village or encampment.

The domestic implements of the Amerindians were few. Pottery seems to have been unknown amongst the northern tribes to the east and north of the Mississippi valley, but earthen jars and vessels were made by the Dakota-Siou group in the valley of the Mississippi. Amongst these agricultural Indians the hoe was made of a buffalo's blade bone fastened to a crooked wooden handle. The Ojibwés manufactured chisels out of beavers' teeth. The Eskimo and some of the neighbouring Amerindian tribes used oblong "kettles" of stone—simply great blocks of stone chipped, rubbed, and hollowed out into receptacles, with handles at both ends. (It is suggested that they borrowed the idea of these stone vessels for cooking from the early Norse settlers of Greenland; see p. 18.)

The Amerindians of the regions west of the Rocky Mountains made kettles or cooking vessels out of blocks of "cedar" (*Juniper*) wood; east of the Rocky Mountains the birch-bark kettle was universal. Of course these vessels of wood or bark could not be placed on the fire or embers to heat or boil the contents, as was possible with the "kettles" of stone or the cooking pots of clay. So the people using them heated the water in which the food or the soup was boiled by making stones red-hot in the fire and then dropping them into the birch-bark or cedar-wood tubs. Many of the northern Indians got into the way of eating their food raw because of the difficulty of making a fire away from home.

In regard to food, neither Amerindian nor Eskimo was squeamish. They were almost omnivorous, and specially delighted in putrid or noisome substances from which a

European would turn in loathing, and from the eating of which he might conceivably die.

It was only in the extreme south of Canada or in British Columbia (potatoes only) that any agriculture was carried on and that the natives had maize, pumpkins, and pease to add to their dietary; but (as compared to the temperate regions of Europe and Asia) Nature was generous in providing wild fruits and grain without trouble of husbandry. The fruits and nuts have been enumerated elsewhere, but a description might be given here of the "wild oats" (*Avena fatua*) and the "wild rice" of the regions of central Canada and the middle west. The wild oats made a rough kind of porridge, but were not so important and so nourishing as the wild rice which is so often mentioned in the stories of the pioneers, who liked this wild grain as much as the Indians did.

This wild rice (*Zizania aquatica*) grew naturally in small rivers and swampy places. The stems were hollow, jointed at intervals, and the grain appeared at the extremity of the stalk. By the month of June they had grown two feet above the surface of the shallow water, and were ripe for harvesting in September. At this period the Amerindians passed in canoes through the water-fields of wild rice, shaking the ears into the canoes as they swept by. The grain fell out easily when ripe, but in order to clean it from the husk it was dried over a slow fire on a wooden grating. After being winnowed it was pounded to flour in a mortar, or else boiled like rice, and seasoned with fat. "It had a most delicate taste", wrote Alexander Henry the Elder.

Fish was perhaps the staple of Amerindian diet, because in scarcely any part of the Canadian Dominion is a lake, river, or brook far away. In the region of the Great Lakes fish were caught in large quantities in October, and exposed to the weather to be frozen at nighttime. They were then stored away in this congealed state, and lasted good — more or less — till the following April.

Pemmican—that early form of potted meat so familiar to the readers of Red-Indian romances—was made of the lean meat of the bison. The strips of meat were dried in the sun, and afterwards pounded in a mortar and mixed with an equal quantity of bison fat. Fish "pemmican" was sun-dried fish ground to powder.

A favourite dish among the northern Indians was blood mixed with the half-digested food found in the stomach of a deer, boiled up with a sufficient quantity of water to make it of the consistency of pease porridge. Some scraps of fat or tender flesh were shredded small and boiled with it. To render this dish more palatable they had a method of mixing the blood with the contents of the stomach in the paunch itself, and hanging it up in the heat and smoke of the fire for several days—in other words, the Scotch haggis. The kidneys of both moose and buffalo were usually eaten *raw* by the southern Indians, for no sooner was one of those beasts killed than the hunter ripped up its belly, snatched out the kidneys, and ate them warm, before the animal was quite dead. They also at times put their mouths to the wound the ball or the arrow had made, and sucked the blood; this, they said, quenched thirst, and was very nourishing.

The favourite drink of the Ojibwé Indians in the winter-time was hot broth poured over a dishful of pure snow.

The Amerindians of the Nipigon country (north of Lake Superior) and the Ojibwés and Kris often relapsed into cannibalism when hard up for food. Indeed some of them became so addicted to this practice that they simply went about stalking their fellow Indians with as much industry as if they were hunting animals. "These prowling ogres caused such terror that to sight the track of one of them was sufficient to make twenty families decamp in all the speed of their terror" (Alexander Henry). It was deemed useless to attempt any resistance when these monsters were coming to kill and eat. The people would even make them presents of clothes and provisions to allow them and their children to live. There were women cannibals as well as men (see p. 171).

As the greater part of their food came from the chase, and their only articles of commerce likewise, they devoted themselves more entirely to hunting and fishing than to any other pursuit. The women did most of the fishing (and all the skin-curing for the fur market and for their own dress), while the men pursued with weapons the beasts of the chase, trapped them in pitfalls or snares, or drove them into "pounds" (excavated enclosures).

Illustrating the wonderful sagacity of the Amerindians as game trackers, Alexander Henry the Elder tells the following story in the autumn of 1799:—

"We had not gone far from the house before we fell upon the fresh tracks of some red deer (wapiti), and soon after discovered the herd in a thicket of willows and poplars; we both fired, and the deer disappeared in different directions. We pursued them, but to no purpose, as the country was unfavourable. We then returned to the spot where we had fired, as the Indian suspected that we had wounded some of them. We searched to see if we could find any blood; on my part, I could find tracks, but no blood. The Indian soon called out, and I went to him, but could see no blood, nor any sign that an animal had been wounded. However, he pointed out the track of a large buck among the many others, and told me that from the manner in which this buck had started off he was certain the animal had been wounded. As the ground was beaten in every direction by animals, it was only after a tedious search that we found where the buck had struck off. But no blood was seen until, passing through a thicket of willows, he observed a drop upon a leaf, and next a little more. He then began to examine more strictly, to find out in what part of the body the animal had been wounded; and, judging by the height and other signs, he told me the wound must have been somewhere between the shoulder and neck. We advanced about a mile, but saw nothing of the deer, and no more blood. I was for giving up the chase; but he assured me the wound was mortal, and that if the animal should lie down he could not rise again. We proceeded two miles farther, when, coming out upon a small open space, he told me the animal was at no great distance, and very probably in this meadow. We accordingly advanced a few yards, and there we found the deer lying at the last gasp. The wound was exactly as I had been told. The sagacity of the Saulteurs [Ojibwés] in tracing big wood animals is astonishing. I have frequently witnessed occurrences of this nature; the bend of a leaf or blade of grass is enough to show the hunter the direction the game has taken. Their ability is of equally great service to war parties, when they discover the footsteps of their enemies."

The Assiniboin Indians (a branch of the Sious) down to about fifty years ago captured the bison of the plains in hundreds at a time by driving them into large excavated areas below the level of the ground.

Alexander Henry, jun., gives the following description of this procedure in 1810:—

"The pounds are of different dimensions, according to the number of tents in one camp. The common size is from sixty to one hundred paces or yards in circumference, and about five feet in height. Trees are cut down, laid upon one another, and interwoven with branches and green twigs; small openings are left to admit the dogs to feed upon the carcasses of the (old) bulls, which are generally left as useless. This enclosure is commonly made between two hummocks, on the declivity or at the foot of rising ground. The entrance is about ten paces wide, and always fronts the plains. On each side of this entrance commences a thick range of fascines, the two ranges spreading asunder as they extend to the distance of one hundred yards, beyond which openings are left at intervals; but the fascines soon become more thinly planted, and continue to spread apart to the right and left until each range has been extended about three hundred yards from the pound. The labour is then diminished by only placing at intervals three or four cross sticks, in imitation of a dog or other animal (sometimes called 'dead men'); these extend on the plain for about two miles, and double rows of them are planted in several other directions to a still greater distance. Young men are usually sent out to collect and bring in the buffalo—a tedious task, which requires great patience, for the herd must be started by slow degrees. This is done by setting fire to dung or grass. Three young men will bring in a herd of several hundred from a great distance. When the wind is aft it is most favourable, as they can then direct the buffalo with great ease. Having come in sight of the ranges, they generally drive the herd faster, until it begins to enter the ranges, where a swift-footed person has been stationed with a buffalo robe over his head, to imitate that animal; but sometimes a horse performs this business. When he sees buffaloes approaching he moves slowly toward the pound until they appear to follow him; then he sets off at full speed, imitating a buffalo as well as he can, with the herd after him. The young men in the rear now discover themselves, and drive the herd on with all possible speed. There is always a sentinel on some elevated spot to notify the camp when the buffalo appear; and this intelligence is no sooner given than every man, woman, and child runs to the ranges that lead to the pound to prevent the buffalo from taking a wrong direction. Then they lie down between the fascines and cross sticks, and, if the buffalo attempt to break through, the people wave their robes, which causes the herd to keep on, or turn to the opposite side, where other persons do the same. When the buffalo have been thus directed to the entrance of the pound, the Indian who leads them rushes into it and out at the other side, either by jumping over the enclosure or creeping through an opening left for that purpose. The buffalo tumble in pell-mell at his heels, almost exhausted, but keep moving around the enclosure from east to west, and never in a direction against the sun. What appeared extraordinary to me on those occasions was that, when word was given to the camp of the near approach of the buffalo, the dogs would skulk away from the pound and not approach until the herd entered. Many buffaloes break their legs and some their necks in jumping into the pound, as the descent is generally six or eight feet, and stumps are left standing there. The buffalo being caught, the men assembled at the enclosure, armed with bows and arrows; every arrow has a particular mark of the owner, and they are let fly until the whole herd is killed. Then the men enter the pound, and each claims his own; but commonly there is what they term the master of the pound, who divides the animals and gives each tent an equal share, reserving nothing for himself. But in the end he is always the best provided for; everyone is obliged to send him a certain portion, as it is in his tent that the numerous ceremonies relating to the pound are observed. There the young men are always welcome to feast and smoke, and no women are allowed to enter, as that tent is set apart for the affairs of the pound. Horses are sometimes used to collect and bring in buffalo, but this method is less effectual than the other; besides, it frightens the herds and soon causes them to withdraw to a great distance. When horses are used the buffalo are absolutely driven into the pound, but when the other method is pursued they are in a manner enticed to their destruction."

A somewhat similar method was adopted by the

northern Kris and Athapascans for the capture of reindeer.

As regards means of transport, the use of dogs as draught animals was by no means confined to the Eskimo: they were used in wintertime to draw sledges over the snow or ice by nearly all the northern Indian tribes, and by the people of the Rocky Mountains and Pacific coast. After the Amerindians of the prairies and plains received horses (indirectly through the Spaniards of Mexico)[1] they sometimes employed the smaller and poorer kind of ponies as pack animals; but for the most part throughout the summer season of the Canadian Dominion—from May to October—transport and travel by canoe was the favourite method.

There were four very well marked types of canoe or boat in British North America. There was the already-described Eskimo *kayak*, made of leather stretched over a framework of wood or bone; the Amerindians of the Dominion, south of the Eskimo and east of the Rocky Mountains, used the familiar "birch-bark" canoe;[2] the peoples of the Pacific coast belt possessed something more like a boat, made out of a hollowed tree trunk and built up with planks; and the tribes of the Upper Mississippi used round coracles. Here are descriptions of all three kinds of Amerindian canoe from the pens of eighteenth-century pioneers: The birch-bark canoe used on the Great Lakes was about thirty-three feet long by four and a half feet broad, and formed of the smooth rind or bark of the birch tree fastened outside a wooden framework. It was lined with small splints of juniper cedar, and the vessel was further strengthened with ribs of the same wood, of which the two ends were fastened to the gunwales. Several bars rather than seats were laid across

[1] See p. 150.

[2] In the far north-west, on the rivers of the Pacific slope, the natives used spruce-fir bark instead of birch.

the canoe from gunwale to gunwale, the small roots of the spruce fir afforded the fibre with which the bark was sewn or stitched, and the gum of the pine tree supplied the place of tar and oakum. Bark, some spare fibre, and gum were always carried in each canoe for repairs, which were constantly necessary (one continually reads in the diaries of the pioneers of "stopping to gum the canoe"). The canoes were propelled with paddles, and occasionally a sail.

The aborigines of Newfoundland—the Beothiks—are said to have known the birch-bark canoe, framework canoe, but to have employed "dug-outs"—hollowed tree trunks. The canoes of the Mandans of the upper Missouri basin were like coracles, of circular form, made of a framework of bent willow branches over which was stretched a raw bison-hide with the hair inside. This was sewn tightly round the willow rim. In lieu of a paddle they use a pole about five feet long, split at one end to admit a piece of board about two feet long and half a foot broad, which was lashed to the pole and so formed a kind of cross. There was but one for each canoe. The paddler of this coracle made directly for the opposite shore; every stroke he gave turned his "dish" almost entirely round; to recover his position and go on his intended route, he must give a stroke on the other side, which brought him up again; and so on till he got over, not without drifting down sometimes nearly a mile.

Alexander Henry, jun., thus describes a canoe of the Clatsop people on the Lower Columbia (Pacific coast, opposite Vancouver Island): "This was a war canoe—the first of the kind I had seen. She was about thirty-six feet long and wide in proportion, the stem rising upright about six feet, on top of which was a figure of some imaginary monster of uncouth sculpture, having the head of a carnivorous animal with large erect ears but no body, clinging by arms and legs to the upper end of the canoe, and grinning horribly. The ears were painted green, the other parts red and black. The stern also rose about five feet in height, but had no figure carved on it. On each side of both stem and stern broad strips of wood rose about four feet, having holes cut in them to shoot arrows through. She had a high sprit-sail made of handkerchiefs and pieces of gunny-cloth or jute, forming irregular stripes, I am told these Indians commonly have pieces of squared timber, not unlike a three-inch plank, high and broad, perforated to shoot arrows through; this is fixed on the bow of the war canoe to serve as bulwarks in battle."

Canoe voyages were mainly embarked on for trading; but in all probability before the coming of the European there was little trading done between one tribe and another, except in the region *west* of the Rocky Mountains, in which—especially to the north—the Amerindians were so different in their habits and customs from those dwelling east of the mountains as to suggest that they must very occasionally have been in touch with some world outside America, such as Hawaii, Kamschatka, or Japan. In these Pacific coastlands they used a white seashell as a currency and a medium of exchange. So also did the Iroquois people and the southern Algonkin tribes, in the form of "wampum". The principal articles of barter were skins of fur animals, porcupine quills, dogs, slaves, and women.

First Hunting (to supply food), then Trading in the products of the chase, and lastly War were the main subjects which occupied the Amerindian's thoughts before the middle of the nineteenth century. They usually went to war to turn other tribes out of profitable hunting grounds or productive fisheries; or because they wanted slaves or more wives; or because a chief or a medicine man had a dream; or because some other notability felt he had given way too much to tears over some personal or public sorrow, and must show his manliness by killing the people of another tribe. In their wars they knew no mercy when their blood was up, and frequently perpetrated frightful cruelties for the sheer pleasure of seeing human suffering. Yet these devilish moods would alternate with fits of sentimentality. A man or a woman would suddenly take a war prisoner, or a person who was wounded or half-tortured to death, under their protection, and a short time afterwards the whole war party would be greeting this rescued wretch (usually a man—they were far more pitiless towards women) as brother, son, or friend, and even become quite maudlin over a scratch or a bruise; whereas an hour or so before they were on the point of disembowelling, or of driving splinters up the nails and setting them on fire. In warfare they often gave way to cannibalism.

Though extremely fond of singing—they sang when they were merry; when they thought they were going to die; when they were victorious in hunting, love, or war; when they were defeated; when they were paddling a canoe or sewing a moccasin—they had but a poor range of musical instruments. Most of the tribes used flutes made out of the wing bones of cranes or out of reeds, and some had small trumpets of wood, bark, or buffalo horn. The Pacific coast Indians made gongs or "xylophones" out of blocks or slabs of resonant wood.

Here is a specimen of Amerindian singing. It is the song which accompanied the famous Calumet dance in celebration of the peacemaking qualities of tobacco-smoking. It was taken down by the Jesuit missionaries in the seventeenth century from the Ilinwa (Illinois) Algonkin Indians of the middle west, and its notation reminds one of Japanese music.

## THE CALUMET OR TOBACCO-PIPE DANCE

Ninahani, &c., ongo; ninahani, &c., hoho; ninahani, &c.
Kawa bannoge atchicha Koge ake awā;
Banoge atchicha shagobe hé hé hé! Mintingo mitade
Pini pini hé! Atchicha lé machi mi nam ba miktande,
Miktande pini pini hé!

Dancing was little else than posturing and jumping in masks—usually made to look like the head of a wild beast. But the men were usually very athletic. Wrestling competitions were almost universal, especially as a means of winning a wife. The conqueror in a wrestling match took the wife or wives of the defeated man. Their running powers for endurance and speed became justly celebrated.

"Their principal and most inveterate game is that of the hoop," writes Alexander Henry, sen., "which proves as ruinous to them as the platter does to the Saulteurs (Ojibwé)." This game was played in the following manner. A hoop was made about two feet in diameter, nearly covered with dressed leather, and trimmed with quillwork, feathers, bits of metal, and other trinkets, on which were certain particular marks. Two persons played at the same time, by rolling the hoop and accompanying it, one on each side; when it was about to fall, each gently threw one arrow in such a manner that the hoop might fall upon it, and according to that mark on the hoop which rested on the arrows they reckoned the game. They also played another game by holding some article in one hand, or putting it into one of two shoes, the other hand or shoe being empty. They had another game which required forty to fifty small sticks, as thick as a goose quill and about a foot long; these were all shuffled together and then divided into two bunches, and according to the even or odd numbers of sticks in the bunch chosen, the players lost or won.

A favourite game amongst the Ojibwé is described as "the hurdle", which is another name for the Canadian national game of La Crosse. When about to play, the men, of all ages, would strip themselves almost naked, but dress their hair in great style, put ornaments on their arms, and belts round their waists, and paint their faces and bodies in the most elaborate style. Each man was provided with "a hurdle", an instrument made of a small stick of wood about three feet long, bent at the end to a small circle, in which a loose piece of network is fixed, forming a cavity big enough to receive a leather ball about the size of a man's fist. Everything being prepared, a level plain about half a mile long was chosen, with proper barriers or goals at each end. Having previously formed into two equal parts, they assembled in the very middle of the field, and the game began by throwing up the ball perpendicularly in the air, when instantly both parties (writes an eyewitness) "formed a singular group of naked men, painted in different colours and in the most comical attitudes imaginable, holding their rackets elevated in the air to catch the ball". Whoever was so fortunate as to catch it in his net ran with it to the barrier with all his might, supported by his party; whilst the opponents were pursuing and endeavouring to knock the ball out of the net. He who succeeded in doing so ran in the same manner towards the opposite barrier, and was, of course, pursued in his turn. If in danger of being overtaken, he might throw it with his hurdle towards any of his associates who happened to be nearer the barrier than himself. They had a particular knack of throwing it a great distance in this manner, so that the best runners had not always the advantage; and, by a peculiar way of working their hands and arms while running, the ball never dropped out of their "hurdle".

"The best of three heats wins the game, and, besides the honour acquired on such occasions, a considerable prize is adjudged to the victors. The vanquished, however, generally challenge their adversaries to renew the game the next day, which is seldom refused. The game then becomes more important, as the honour of the whole village is at stake, and it is carried on with redoubled impetuosity, every object which might impede them in their career is knocked down and trodden under foot without mercy, and before the game is decided, it is a common thing to see numbers sprawling on the ground with wounded legs and broken heads, yet this never creates any disputes or ill-will after the play is decided" (Alexander Henry, sen.).

It has been computed that in the middle of the eighteenth century the Amerindian population of the vast territories now known as the Dominion of Canada numbered about 300,000. It now stands at an approximate 110,000. The chief diminution has taken place in Newfoundland, Lower and Upper Canada, New Brunswick, Assiniboia, and British Columbia. There may even have been an increase in the north and north-west. The first great blow to the Amerindians of these regions was the smallpox epidemic of 1780. The next was the effect of the strong drink[1] introduced by the agents of the Hudson's Bay and, still more, the two North-west Companies. Phthisis or pulmonary consumption also seems to have been introduced from Europe (though Hearne thought that the Northern Indians had it before the white man came). In fact, before the European invaded America neither Eskimo nor Amerindian seem to have had many diseases. They suffered from ulcers, scurvy, digestive troubles, rheumatism, headache, bronchitis, and heart complaints, but from few, if any, "germ" diseases.

Some of the agents of the North-west Company apologize in their writings for the amount of rum that was circulated among the Amerindians at the orders of that

[1] Before the white man came to *North* America the natives had no form of intoxicating drink.

company to stimulate trade, by saying that it was seven parts water. Nevertheless it excited them to madness, as the following extracts show. These are mostly taken from the journals of Alexander Henry the Younger, but they are typical of what was recorded by many other writers who describe the far interior of British North America between 1775 and 1835.

"To see a house full of drunken Indians, consisting of men, women, and children, is a most unpleasant sight; for, in that condition, they often wrangle, pull each other by the hair, and fight. At times, ten or twelve of both sexes may be seen fighting each other promiscuously, until at last they all fall on the floor, one upon another, some spilling rum out of a small kettle or dish which they hold in their hands, while others are throwing up what they have just drunk. To add to this uproar, a number of children, some on their mothers' shoulders, and others running about and taking hold of their clothes, are constantly bawling, the elder ones, through fear that their parents may be stabbed, or that some other misfortune may befal them in the fray. These shrieks of the children form a very unpleasant chorus to the brutal noise kept up by their drunken parents."

"In a drinking match at the Hills yesterday, Gros Bras (Thick Arms) in a fit of jealousy stabbed Aupusoi to death with a hand-dague (dagger); the first stroke opened his left side, the second his belly, and the third his breast; he never stirred, although he had a knife in his belt, and died instantly. Soon after this Aupusoi's brother, a boy about ten years of age, took the deceased's gun, loaded it with two balls, and approached Gros Bras's tent. Putting the muzzle of the gun through the door the boy fired the two balls into his breast and killed him dead, just as he was reproaching his wife for her affection for Aupusoi, and boasting of the revenge he had taken. The little fellow ran into the woods and hid. Little Shell (Petite Coquille) found the old woman, Aupusoi's mother, in her tent; he instantly stabbed her. Ondainoiache then came in, took the knife, and gave her a second stab. Little Shell, in his turn taking the knife, gave a third blow. In this manner did these two rascals continue to murder the old woman, as long as there was any life in her. The boy escaped into Langlois' house, and was kept hid until they were all sober. Next morning a hole was dug in the ground, and all three were buried together. This affair kept the Indians from hunting, as Gros Bras was nearly related to the principal hunters."

"Grand' Gueule stabbed Perdrix Blanche with a knife in six places. Perdrix Blanche fighting with his wife, fell in the fire and almost roasted, but had strength enough left notwithstanding his wounds to bite her nose off."

"In the first drinking match a murder was committed in an Assiniboine tent, but fortunately it was done by an Ojibwé. L'Hiver stabbed Mishewashence to the heart three times, and killed him instantly. The wife and children cried out, and some of my people ran to the tent just as L'Hiver came out with the bloody knife in his hand, expecting we would lay hold of him. The first person he met was William Henry, whom he attempted to stab in the breast; but Henry avoided the stroke, and returned the compliment with a blow of his cudgel on the fellow's head. This staggered him; but instantly recovering he made another attempt to stab Henry. Foiled in this design, and observing several coming out of the fort, he took to his heels and ran into the woods like a deer. I chased him with some of my people, but he was too fleet for us. We buried the murdered man, who left a widow and five helpless orphans, having no relations on this river. The behaviour of two of the youngest was really piteous while we were burying the body; they called upon their deceased father not to leave them, but to return to the tent, and tried to prevent the men from covering the corpse with earth, screaming in a terrible manner; the mother was obliged to take them away."

"Men and women have been drinking a match for three days and nights, during which it has been drink, fight—drink, fight—drink, and fight again—guns, axes, and knives being their weapons—very disagreeable."

"Mithanasconce was so troublesome (in drink) that we were obliged to tie him with ropes to prevent his doing mischief. He was stabbed in the back in three different places about a month ago. His wounds were still open, and had an ugly appearance; in his struggling to get loose they burst out afresh and bled a great deal. We had much trouble to stop the blood, as the fellow was insensible to pain or danger; his only aim was to bite us. We had some narrow escapes, until we secured his mouth, and then he fell asleep."

"Some Red Lake Indians having traded here for liquor which they took to their camp, quarrelled amongst themselves. One jumped on another and bit his nose off. It was some time before the piece could be found; but, at last, by tumbling and tossing the straw about, it was recovered, stuck on, and bandaged, as best the drunken people could, in hopes it would grow again" (Alexander Henry, jun.).

As regards drunkenness, several authors among the early explorers declared that the French Canadian voyageurs were more disagreeable when drunk even than the Amerindians, for their quarrels were noisier and more deadly. "Indeed I had rather have fifty drunken Indians in the fort than sixty-five drunken Canadians", writes Alexander Henry in 1810. And yet the extracts I have given from his journal show that it would be hard to beat the Amerindians for disagreeable ferocity when intoxicated.

Henry, summing up his experiences before leaving for the Pacific coast in 1811, writes these remarks in his diary:—

"What a different set of people they would be, were there not a drop of liquor in the country! If a murder is committed among the Saulteurs (Ojibwés), it is always in a drinking match. We may truly say that liquor is the root of all evil in the north-west. Great bawling and lamentation went on, and I was troubled most of the night for liquor to wash away grief."

As a rule, the treatment of the Amerindians by the British and French settlers was good, except the thrusting of alcohol on them. But in Newfoundland a great crime was perpetrated. Between the middle of the seventeenth and the beginning of the nineteenth centuries the British fishermen and settlers on the coasts of Newfoundland had *destroyed* the native population of Beothik Indians.

Before the English arrived on the coasts of Newfoundland the Beothiks lived an ideal life for savages. They were well clothed with beasts' skins, and in the winter these were supplemented by heavy fur robes. Countless herds of reindeer roamed through the interior, passing from north to south in the autumn and returning in the spring. Vast flocks of willow grouse (like ptarmigan) were everywhere to be met with; the many lakes were covered with geese, swans, and ducks. The woods were full of pigeons; the salmon swarmed up the rivers to

c 312

GREAT AUKS, GANNETS, PUFFINS, AND GUILLEMOTS

breed; the sea round the coasts was — except in the wintertime — the richest fishery in the world. They caught lobsters in the rock pools, and speared or clubbed seals and great walruses for their flesh and oil. An occasional whale provided them with oil, blubber, and meat. The Great Auk—which could not fly—swarmed in millions on the cliffs and islets. So abundant was this bird, and so fat, that its body was sometimes used as fuel, or as a lamp. In the summertime their fish and flesh diet could be varied by the innumerable berries growing wild—strawberries, raspberries, currants, cranberries, and whortleberries. The *capillaire* plant yielded a lusciously sweet, sugary substance.[1]

The Beothiks were a tall, good-looking people, with large black eyes and a light-coloured skin. The early French and Biscayan seamen, who resorted to the coasts of Newfoundland for the whale fisheries, reported these "Red Indians" to be "an ingenious and tractable people, if well used, who were ready to help the white men with great labour and patience in the killing, cutting-up, and boiling of whales, and the making of train oil, without other expectation of reward than a little bread or some such small hire".

Yet from the beginning of the seventeenth century the Beothiks—then about four thousand in number—were ill-treated by the European fishermen who frequented the Newfoundland coasts. They soon greatly decreased in numbers, and became very shy of white men. The French, when they occupied the south coast of Newfoundland, brought over Mikmak Indians to chase and kill the Beothiks or "Red" Indians. The Eskimo attacked them from Labrador. Finally, when Newfoundland became British in the eighteenth century, the English fishermen settlers and fur hunters attacked and slew the harmless Beothiks with a wanton ferocity (described by

[1] This was the Moxie plum or creeping snowberry (*Chiogenes hispidula*

horror-struck officers of the British navy) which is as bad as anything attributed to the Spaniards in Cuba and Hispaniola. By about 1830 they were all extinct. As late as 1823 the following anecdote is recorded of two English settlers whose names are hidden behind the initials C and A. "When near Badger Bay they fell in with an Indian man and woman, who approached, apparently soliciting food. The man was first killed, and the woman, who was afterwards found to be his daughter, in despair remained calmly to be fired at, when she was also shot through the chest and immediately expired. This was told Mr. Cormack by the man who did the deed." Even English women in the late eighteenth century were celebrated for their skill "in shooting Red Indians and seals".

"For a period of nearly two hundred years this barbarity had continued, and it was considered meritorious to shoot a Red Indian. 'To go to look for Indians' came to be as much a phrase as to look for partridges (ptarmigan). They were harassed from post to post, from island to island; their hunting and fishing stations were unscrupulously seized by the invading English. They were shot down without the least provocation, or captured to be exposed as curiosities to the rabble at the fairs of the western towns of Christian England at twopence a piece."[1]

Too late—when the worry and anxiety of the Napoleonic wars were over—the British Government sent a commission of naval officers to enquire into the treatment of the Beothiks by the settlers. One woman alone remained, as a frightened semi-captive, to be consoled and soothed. There are Indians in the south of Newfoundland at the present day, but they are Mikmaks who come over from the adjoining regions of Cape Breton and Nova Scotia. So tender, indeed, is the modern government of the island

[1] These are the remarks of an English chaplain in the island, quoted by the Rev. George Patterson, who contributed a most interesting article on the vanished Beothiks of Newfoundland to the Royal Society of Canada in 1891.

towards these (out of compunction for the past) that they are allowed to kill the reindeer and other wild animals without the licence which is exacted from white people, and so are actually injuring Newfoundland's resources!

Since the great Dominion of Canada was brought into existence in 1871 as a unified, responsible government, the treatment of the remaining Amerindian natives of British North America has been admirable; and splendid work has been done in reclaiming them to a wholesome civilization by the Moravian, Roman Catholic, and Church of England missionaries.

## CHAPTER VIII

# The Hudson Bay Explorers and the British Conquest of all Canada

In a general way the discovery of the main features of the vast Canadian Dominion may be thus apportioned amongst the different European nations. First came the British, led by an Italian pilot. They discovered Cape Breton Island, Nova Scotia, and Newfoundland. Then came the Portuguese, who discovered the north-east of Newfoundland and the coast of Labrador, while a French expedition under an Italian captain reached to Nova Scotia and southern Newfoundland. A Spanish expedition under a Portuguese leader shortly afterwards reached the coast of New Brunswick. After that the French from Brittany, Normandy, and the west coast of France laid bare the *west* coast of Newfoundland, the Gulf of St. Lawrence, the River St. Lawrence, and the Great Lakes.

Sir Francis Drake led the way in the exploration of the north-west coast of North America. He reached, in 1579, as far north on that side as the country of Oregon, which he christened New Albion. This action stirred up the Spaniards, who explored the coast of California, and in 1591–2 sent an Ionian Island pilot, Apostolos Valeriano (commonly called Juan de Fuca), in charge of an expedition to discover the imagined Straits of Anian. He gave strength to this idea of a continuous water route across temperate North America by entering (in 1592) the straits, since called Juan de Fuca, between Vancouver Island and the modern State of Washington, and passing thence into the Straits of Georgia, which bear a striking resemblance in their features to the Straits of Magellan.

French explorers and adventurers, as we have seen, penetrated from the basin of the St. Lawrence to the north and west until they touched the southern extension of Hudson Bay (James's Bay), discovered Lake Winnipeg and the Saskatchewan Rivers, the upper Missouri and the whole course of the Mississippi, and finally recorded the existence of the Rocky Mountains.

Parallel with these movements the British discovered the broad belt of sea between Greenland and North America and the whole area of Hudson Bay. After the French had ceased to reign in North America, the British were to reveal the great rivers flowing into the Arctic Ocean, the coasts and islands of the Arctic Ocean, the Yukon River, and the coasts and islands of British Columbia and Alaska.

The first Europeans, however, to reach Alaska were Russians led by Vitus Bering, a great Danish sea captain in the Russian service. Bering was born in 1680 at Horsens, in the province of Aarhuus, E. Denmark, and entered the service of Peter the Great, who was desirous of knowing where Asia terminated and America began. Bering discovered the straits which bear his name in 1728, and in 1741 was wrecked and died on Bering's Island. Captain James Cook, the British discoverer of Australia and of so many Pacific islands, completed the work of Bering in 1788 in charting the north-west American coast right into the Arctic Ocean.

It has already been related in Chapter III how the Hudson's Bay Chartered Company came to be founded. Soon after their first pioneers were established, in 1670, at Fort Nelson, on the west coast of Hudson Bay, near where York Factory now stands, there was born — or brought out from England as an infant — a little boy named Henry Kellsey, who as a child took a great fancy to the Amerindians who came to trade at Fort Nelson. As he played with them, and they returned his affection, he learnt their language, and—for some inconceivable reason—this gave great offence to the stupid governor of the fort (indeed, when Kellsey as a grown man, some years afterwards, compiled a vocabulary of the Kri language for the use of traders, the Hudson's Bay Company ordered it to be suppressed). Stupid Governor Geyer not only objected to Kellsey picking up the Kri language, but punished him most severely for that and for his boyish tricks and jokes; so much so, that Kellsey, when he was about ten years old, ran away with the returning Indians, some of whom had grown very fond of him whilst they stayed at Fort Nelson.

Six years afterwards an Indian brought to the governor of the fort a letter written by Kellsey in charcoal on a piece of white birch bark. In this he asked the governor's pardon for running away, and his permission to return to the fort. As a kind reply was sent, Kellsey appeared not long afterwards grown into a young man, accompanied by an Indian wife and attended by a party of Indians. He was dressed exactly like them, but differed from them in the respect which he showed to his native wife. She attempted to accompany her husband into the factory or place of business, and the governor stopped her; but Kellsey at once told him in English that he would not enter himself if his wife was not suffered to go with him, and so the governor relented. After this Kellsey (who must then have been about seventeen) seems to have regularly enrolled himself in 1688 in the service of the Company, and he was employed as a kind of commercial traveller who made long journeys to the north-west to beat up a fur trade for the Company and induce tribes of Indians to make long journeys every summer to the Company's factory with the skins they had secured between the autumn and the spring. In this way Kellsey penetrated into the country of the Assiniboines, and he finally reached a more distant tribe or nation called by the long name of Néwátamipoet.[1] Kellsey first of all made for Split Lake, up the Nelson River, and thence paddled westwards in his canoe for a distance of 71 miles. Here he abandoned the canoe, and, for what he estimated as 316 miles, he tramped through a wooded country, first covered with fir and pine trees, and farther on with poplar and birch. Apparently he then reached a river flowing into Reindeer Lake. In a general way his steps must have taken him in the direction of Lake Athapaska.

On the way he had much trouble with the Assiniboin Indians and Kris, with whom he had caught up, and with whom he was to travel in the direction of these mysterious Néwátamipoets. The last-named tribe, who were probably of the Athapaskan group, had killed, a few months previously, three of the Kri women, and the Kri Indians who belonged to Kellsey's party were bent, above all things, on attacking the Néwátamipoets and punishing them for this outrage. Kellsey only wished to open up peaceful relations with them and create a great trade in furs with the Hudson's Bay Company, so he kept pleading with the Indians not to go to war with the Néwátamipoets. On this journey, however, one of the Kri Indians fell ill and died. The next day the body was burnt with much ceremony—first the flesh, and then the bones—and after this funeral the companions of the dead man began to reason as to the cause of his death, and suddenly blamed Kellsey. Kellsey had obstructed them from their purpose of avenging their slain women, therefore the gods of the tribe were angry and claimed this victim in the man who had died. Kellsey was very near being sent to the other world to complete the sacrifice; but he arranged for "a feast of tobacco"—in other words, a calm deliberation and the smoking of the pipe of peace. He explained to the angry

[1] Spelt in the documents of the Hudson's Bay Company, Naywatame-poet.

Indians that his Company had not supplied him with guns and ammunition with which to go to war, but to induce them to embark on the fur trade and to kill wild animals for their skins. If, instead of this, they went to war, or injured him, they need never again go down to Fort Nelson for any further trade or supplies. Four days afterwards, however, the attention of the whole party was concentrated on bison.

Bison could now be seen in abundance. Kellsey was already acquainted with the musk ox, which he had seen in the colder regions near to Hudson Bay; but the bison seemed to him quite different, with horns growing like those of an English ox, black and short. In the middle of September he reached the country of the Néwâtamipoets, and presented to their chief, on behalf of the Hudson's Bay Company, a present of clothes, knives, awls, tobacco, and a gun, gunpowder, and shot. On this journey Kellsey encountered the grizzly bear, a more common denizen of the western regions of North America. According to his own account, he and one of the Indians with him were attacked by two grizzly bears and obliged to climb into the branches of trees. The bears followed them; but Kellsey fired and killed one, and later on the other also. For this feat he was greatly reverenced by the Indians, and received the name of Mistopashish, or "little giant". Kellsey afterwards rose to be governor of York Fort, on the west coast of Hudson Bay.

The next great explorer ranging westward from Hudson Bay was Anthony Hendry.[1] Anthony Hendry left York factory in 1754, with a company of Kri Indians, to

[1] The young or old reader of this and other books dealing with the exploration of the Canadian Dominion will be indeed puzzled between the various Hendrys and Henrys. The last-named was a prolific stock, from which several notable explorers and servants of the fur-trading companies were drawn. In this book a careful distinction must be made between the *Anthony* Hendrey or Hendey, who commenced his exploration of the west in 1754; the unrelated *Alexander* Henry the Elder, who journeyed between 1761 and 1776; and the nephew of the last-named, Alexander Henry the Younger, whose pioneering explorations occurred between 1799 and 1814.

EASTERN CANADA and NEWFOUNDLAND
Scale, 1:20,000,000
English Miles
0 50 100 200 300 400
Hudson's Bay
James Bay
York Factory
Nelson R.
L. St. Joseph
Albany R.
English R.
L. of the Woods
Rainy L.
Rainy R.
Nipigon
Duluth
MINNESOTA
Upper Mississippi R.
L. Superior
Sault Ste. Marie
Str. of Michilli-Makinak
Green Bay
Fox R.
L. Michigan
MICHIGAN
L. Huron
Georgian Bay
L. Simcoe
Toronto
L. St. Clair
Detroit
L. Erie
Niagara R. and Falls
Rochester
Oneida L.
L. Ontario
Kingston
Ottawa
Ottawa R.
French R.
L. Nipissing
Montreal
Three Rivers
Quebec
L. St. John
Saguenay R.
Tadoussac
Orleans
Adirondack Mts.
L. Champlain
Richelieu R.
White Mts.
Albany
Hudson R.
Catskill Mts.
Boston
MASSACHUSETTS
Massachusetts Bay
C. Cod
Buzzard's Bay
Martha's Vineyard
Nantucket I.
Portland
Gulf of Maine
MAINE
NEW ENGLAND
NEW BRUNSWICK
B. of Fundy
Annapolis
NOVA SCOTIA
Halifax
C. Sable
Sable I.
Gut of Canso
C. Breton I.
Louisbourg
PRINCE EDWARD I.
Chaleur B.
Gaspé Peninsula
Gaspé B.
Gulf of St. Lawrence
Magdalen Is.
Anticosti I.
St. Lawrence
Cabot Straits
C. Ray
Miquelon
St. Pierre
C. Race
Avalon Pen.
St. Johns
Funk I.
NEWFOUNDLAND
Str. of Belle Isle
Blanc Sablon
Melville Lake
LABRADOR
Ungava
Labrador or Ungava Peninsula
ONTARIO
QUEBEC
UNITED STATES
ATLANTIC OCEAN

make a great journey of exploration to the west, and with the deliberate intention of wintering with the natives and not returning for that purpose to Hudson Bay. By means of canoe travel and portages he reached Oxford Lake. From here he gained Moose Lake, and soon afterwards "the broad waters of the Saskatchewan—the first Englishman to see this great river of the western plains".[1] Twenty-two miles upstream from the point where it reached the Saskatchewan he came to a French fort which had only been standing for a year, and which represented probably the farthest advance northwards of the French Canadians.

The situation was a rather delicate one, for the Hudson's Bay Company was a thorn in the side of French Canada. However, in this year—1754—the two nations were not actually at war, and the two Frenchmen in charge of the fort received him "in a very genteel manner", and invited him into their home, where he readily accepted their hospitality. At first they spoke of detaining him till the commandant of the fort returned, but abandoned this idea after reflection, and Hendry continued his journey up the Saskatchewan. He then left the river and marched on foot over the plains which separate the North and the South Saskatchewan Rivers. The South Saskatchewan was found to be a high stream covered with birch, poplar, elder, and fir. He and his Indian guides were searching for the horse-riding Blackfeet Indians.[2] All the Amerindians known to the Hudson's Bay Company hitherto travelled on foot, using snowshoes in the winter; but vague rumours had reached the Company that in the far south-west there were great nations of Indians which did all their hunting on horseback.

Hendry had now found them, and he also met a small tribe of Assiniboins—the Mekesue or Eagle Indians—who differed from the surrounding tribes by going about,

[1] *The Search for the Western Sea*, by Lawrence J. Burpee.
[2] See p. 159.

at any rate in the summertime, absolutely naked. Here, too, between the two Saskatchewans, they saw herds of bison on the plains grazing like English cattle. But they also found elk (moose), wapiti or red deer, hares, grouse, geese, and ducks. He records in his journal: "I went with the young men a-buffalo-hunting, all armed with bows and arrows; killed several; fine sport. We beat them about, lodging twenty arrows in one beast. So expert were the natives that they will take the arrows out of the buffalo when they are foaming and raging with pain and tearing up the ground with their feet and horns until they fall down." The Amerindians killed far more of these splendid beasts than they could eat, and from these carcasses they merely took the tongues and a few choice pieces, leaving the remainder to the wolves and the grizzly bears.

At last they arrived at the temporary village of the Blackfeet. Two hundred tents or *tipis* were pitched in two parallel rows, and down this avenue marched Anthony Hendry, gazed at silently by many Blackfeet Indians until he reached the large house or lodge of their great chief, at the end of the avenue of tents. This lodge was large enough to contain fifty persons. The chief received him seated on the sacred skin of a white buffalo. The pipe of peace was then produced and passed round in silence, each person taking a ceremonial puff. Boiled bison beef was then brought to the guests in baskets made of willow branches. Hendry told the great chief of the Blackfeet that he had been sent by the great leader of the white men at Hudson Bay to invite the Blackfeet Indians to come to these eastern waters in the summertime, and bring with them beaver and wolf skins, for which they would get, in return, guns, ammunition, cloth, beads, and other trade goods. But this chief, though he listened patiently, pointed out that this fort on Hudson Bay was situated at a very great distance, that his men only knew how to ride horses, and not how to paddle canoes. Moreover, they could not live without bison beef, and disliked fish.

After leaving the headquarters of the Blackfeet, Hendry rambled over the beautiful country of fir woods and pine woods until he must have got within sight of the Rocky Mountains, though these are not mentioned in his journal. Then, after passing the winter (which did not begin as regards cold weather till the 2nd of December, and was over at the end of March) he returned to the French fort on the Saskatchewan, where he was received by the Commandant, de La Corne, with great kindness and hospitality. These Frenchmen, he found, were able to speak in great perfection several Indian languages; they were well dressed, and courtly in manners, and led a civilized life in these distant wilds. They had excellent trade goods and were sincerely liked by the Indians, but for some reason or other they lacked Brazilian tobacco, which seems to have been a commodity much in favour amongst the Indians. With this the Hudson's Bay Company were kept well supplied, and that alone enabled them in any degree to compete with the French. But in ten years more this French fort would be abandoned owing to the cession of Canada to Britain.

The British, in fact, all through the first half of the eighteenth century, by their superiority in sea power, were steadily strangling the French empire in North America. Acadia, or Nova Scotia, and New Brunswick had been, as we have seen, recognized as British in 1713, and Newfoundland, also, subject to certain conditions, giving France the exclusive right to fish on the *western* and *northern* coasts of Newfoundland. The result was that when "New France", or Canada and Louisiana combined, was at its greatest extent of conquered and administered territory, France held but a very limited seacoast from which to approach it—just the mouth of the Mississippi, and a little bit of Alabama on the south and Cape Breton Island on the east. Cape Breton Island was commanded by the immensely strong fortress of Louisburg, and the possession of this place gave the French some security in entering the Gulf of St. Lawrence through Cabot Straits. But Louisburg was captured by the British colonists of New England (United States) in 1745; and although it was given back to France again, it was reoccupied in 1758, and served as a basis for the armaments which were directed against Quebec in 1759, and which resulted at the close of that year in the surrender of that important city. In 1763 all Canada was ceded to the British, and Louisiana (which had become tne western barrier of the about-to-be-born United States) was ceded to Spain· the French flag flew no more on the Continent of North America, save in the two little islands of St. Pierre and Miquelon adjoining Newfoundland, wherein it still remains as a reminder of the splendid achievements of Frenchmen in America.

## CHAPTER IX

# The Pioneers from Montreal: Alexander Henry the Elder

After 1763, when the two provinces of Canada were definitely ceded to Great Britain, the exploring energies of the Hudson's Bay Fur-trading Company revived. But before this rather sluggish organization could take full advantage of the cessation of French opposition, independent British pioneeers were on their way to explore the vast north-west and west, soon carrying their marvellous journeys beyond the utmost limits reached by La Verendrye and his sons. Eventually these pioneers, who had Montreal for their base and who wisely associated themselves in business and exploration with French Canadians, founded in 1784 a great trading association known as the North-west Trading Company. A few years later certain Scottish pioneers brought a rival exploration and trading corporation into existence and called it the "X. Y. Company". In 1804 these rival Montreal fur-trading associations were fused into a new North-west Trading Company. Between this and the old Hudson's Bay Company an intensely bitter rivalry and enmity—almost at times a state of war—arose, and continued until 1821, when the North-west Company and that of Hudson's Bay amalgamated. It is necessary that these dry details should be understood in order that the reader may comprehend the motives and reasons which prompted the journeys which are about to be described.

Jonathan Carver, of Boston, U.S.A., was perhaps the pioneer of all the British traders into the far west of Canada, beyond Lake Superior, after Canada had been handed over to the British.[1] In 1766–7 he reached the Mississippi at its junction with the St. Peter or Minnesota River, and journeyed up it to the land of the Dakota. Thomas Currie, of Montreal, in 1770 travelled as far as Cedar Lake,[2] where there had been established the French post of Fort Bourbon. He was succeeded the next year by James Finlay, who extended his explorations to the Saskatchewan, whither he was followed by Alexander Henry the Elder in 1775.

Alexander Henry (styled The Elder to distinguish him from his famous nephew of the same name) was a native of New Jersey (U.S.A.), where he was born in 1739. His parents were well-to-do people of the middle class who are believed to have emigrated at the beginning of the eighteenth century from the West of England, and to have been related to Matthew Henry, the Bible commentator. Their son, Alexander, received a good education, and after some commercial apprenticeship at Albany (New York) came to Quebec when Canada was occupied by the British in 1760; at which period he was about twenty-one years old. He was in such a hurry to try a trading adventure in the country of the great lakes that he ventured into central Canada before it was sufficiently calmed down and reconciled to British rule. The hostility, curiously enough, manifested itself much more among the Amerindians than the settlers of French blood. These white men had not been so well treated by the arrogant French officers and officials as much to mind the change to the greater freedom of British government. But the Indian chiefs and

[1] Carver was not so remarkable for his actual journeys as for his confident predictions of a feasible transcontinental route being found to the Pacific coast.

[2] The white-barked conifer, which gives its name to this lake, is *Thuja occidentalis*. There are no real "cedars" in America.

people loved the French, largely owing to the goodness and solicitude of the missionaries.

"The hostility of the Indians", wrote Henry in his journal, travelling along the coast of Lake Huron, "was exclusively against the English. Between them and my Canadian attendants, there appeared the most cordial goodwill. This circumstance suggested one means of escape, of which, by the advice of my friend, Campion, I resolved to attempt availing myself; namely, that of putting on the dress usually worn by such of the Canadians as pursue the trade into which I had entered, and assimilating myself, as much as I was able, to their appearance and manners. To this end I laid aside my English clothes and covered myself only with a cloth passed about the middle; a shirt, hanging loose; a 'molton', or blanket coat, and a large, red worsted cap. The next thing was to smear my face and hands with dirt and grease; and, this done, I took the place of one of my men, and, when the Indians approached, used the paddle with as much skill as I possessed. I had the satisfaction to find, that my disguise enabled me to pass several canoes without attracting the smallest notice."

When he reached Fort Michili-makinak[1] he wrote: "At two o'clock in the afternoon, the Chipeways came to my house, about sixty in number, and headed by Minavávâná, their chief. They walked in single file, each with his tomahawk in one hand and scalping knife in the other. Their bodies were naked from the waist upward, except in a few examples, where blankets were thrown loosely over the shoulders. Their faces were painted with charcoal, worked up with grease; their bodies, with white clay, in patterns of various fancies. Some had feathers thrust through their noses, and their

[1] The famous place of call (the name means "Turtle Island") in the narrow strait between Lakes Huron and Michigan, and near Lake Superior. (See p. 230.) But some authorities declare that Michili-makinak means "Island of the great wounded person".

heads decorated with the same. . . . It is unnecessary to dwell on the sensations with which I beheld the approach of this uncouth, if not frightful assemblage.

"The chief entered first, and the rest followed without noise. On receiving a sign from the former, the latter seated themselves on the floor.

"Minavávâná appeared to be about fifty years of age. He was six feet in height, and had, in his countenance, an indescribable mixture of good and evil. . . . Looking steadfastly at me, where I sat in ceremony, with an interpreter on either hand and several Canadians behind me, he entered at the same time into conversation with Campion, enquiring how long it was since I left Montreal, and observing that the English, as it would seem, were brave men, and not afraid of death, since they dared to come, as I had done, fearlessly among their enemies."

The Indians now gravely smoked their pipes, whilst Henry inwardly endured tortures of suspense. At length, the pipes being finished, a long pause of silence followed. Then Minavávâná, taking a few strings of wampum in his hand, began a long speech, of which it is only necessary to give a few extracts:—

"Englishman, it is to you that I speak, and I demand your attention!

"Englishman, although you have conquered the French, you have not yet conquered us! We are not your slaves. These lakes, these woods and mountains, were left to us by our ancestors. They are our inheritance, and we will part with them to none. Your nation supposes that we, like the white people, cannot live without bread—and pork—and beef! But, you ought to know, that He, the Great Spirit and Master of Life, has provided food for us in these spacious lakes, and on these woody mountains.

"Englishman, our father, the King of France, employed our young men to make war upon your nation.

In this warfare many of them have been killed, and it is our custom to retaliate, until such time as the spirits of the slain are satisfied. But the spirits of the slain are to be satisfied in either of two ways. The first is by the spilling of the blood of the nation by which they fell; the other by covering the bodies of the dead, and thus allaying the resentment of their relations. This is done by making presents.

"Englishman, your king has never sent us any presents, nor entered into any treaty with us, wherefore he and we are still at war; anɑ, until he does these things, we must consider that we have no other father, nor friend, among the white men, than the King of France; but, for you, we have taken into consideration, that you have ventured your life among us in the expectation that we should not molest you. You do not come armed with an intention to make war; you come in peace, to trade with us, and supply us with necessaries, of which we are in want. We shall regard you, therefore, as a brother, and you may sleep tranquilly, without fear of the Chipeways. . . . As a token of our friendship, we present you with this pipe to smoke."

When Minavávâná had finished his harangue, an Indian presented Henry with a pipe, the which, after he had drawn smoke through it three times, was carried back to the chief, and after him to every person in the room. This ceremony ended, the chief arose, and gave the Englishman his hand, in which he was followed by all the rest.

At the Sault Ste Marie, on the river connecting Lake Superior and Huron, Henry spent part of the spring of 1763-4, and engaged with a few French Canadians and Indians in making maple sugar, the season for which —April—was now at hand.

A temporary house for eight persons was built in a convenient part of the maple woods, distant about three miles from the fort. The men then gathered the bark of white birch trees, and made out of it vessels to hold the sap which was to flow from the incisions they cut in the bark of the maple trees. Into these cuts they introduced wooden spouts or ducts, and under them were placed the birch-bark vessels. When these were filled, the sweet liquid was poured into larger buckets, and the buckets were emptied into bags of elkskin containing perhaps a hundred gallons. Boilers (probably of metal, introduced by the French) were next set up in the camp over fires kept burning day and night, and the maple sap thus boiled became, by concentration, maple sugar.

The women attended to all the business of sugar manufacture, while the men cut wood and went out hunting and fishing to secure food for the community; though, as a matter of fact, sugar and syrup were their main sustenance during all this absence from home. "I have known Indians", wrote Henry, "to live for a time wholly on maple sugar and syrup and become fat." The sap of the maple had certain medicinal qualities which were exceedingly good for persons who had previously been eating little else than meat and fish, so that the three weeks of sugar-boiling in Canada was, no doubt, a splendid assistance to the health of the natives. On this particular occasion described by Henry, the party returned, after three weeks' absence, to the Sault Ste Marie with 1600 lb. of maple sugar, and 36 gallons of syrup.[1]

Henry returned in the summer of 1763 to Fort Michilimakinak. The place was then held by a British garrison under Major Etherington. Shortly after Henry's arrival, an Ojibwe chief named Wáwatam came often to his lodgings, and, taking a great fancy to the Englishman, asked leave to become his blood brother. He was about forty-

[1] There are at least two species of maple in Canada yielding sugar from their sap; but the best is *Acer saccharinum*. The maple leaf is the national emblem of Canada.

five years of age, and of an excellent character amongst his nation. He warned Henry that he, Wáwátam, had had bad dreams during the winter, in which he had been disturbed "by the noises of evil birds", and gave him other roundabout warnings that the Indians of different tribes were going to attack the British garrison at Michili-Makinak, and endeavour to destroy all the English in Upper Canada. Henry did not pay over much attention to this warning, because "the Indian manner of speech is so extravagantly figurative".

The King's birthday was celebrated with, no doubt, somewhat tipsy rejoicings in the summer of 1763. The Ojibwé Indians outside the fort pretended they were going to have a great game of La Crosse with the Sāki or "Fox" Indians. This game was got up to find a pretext for entering the fort and taking the British officers and garrison at a disadvantage. Some of the officers and soldiers, suspecting nothing in the way of danger, were outside the fort by the waterside. However, the sport commenced, and suddenly the ball was struck over the pickets of the fort. At once the Ojibwés, pretending great ardour in their game, came leaping, struggling and shouting over the defences into the fort as though "in the unrestrained pursuit of a rude, athletic exercise". Once inside the fortifications, they attacked the unsuspicious and unarmed soldiers and officers, of whom they killed seventy out of ninety.

Henry had not gone with the others, but had stayed in his room writing letters. Suddenly he heard the Indian warcry and a noise of general confusion. Looking out of his window he saw a crowd of Indians inside the fort furiously cutting down and scalping every Englishman they could reach. Meantime, the French Canadian inhabitants of the fort looked on calmly, neither intervening to stop the Indians, nor suffering any injury from them. Realizing that all his fellow countrymen were practically destroyed, Henry endeavoured to hide himself. He entered the house of his next-door neighbour, a Frenchman, and found the whole family at the windows gazing at the scene of blood before them. He implored this Frenchman to put him into some place of safety until the massacre was over. The latter merely shrugged his shoulders and intimated that he could do nothing for him; but a Pani Indian woman, a slave of this Frenchman, beckoned to Henry to follow her, and hid him in a garret. Then the Indians burst into the house and asked the Frenchman if he had got any Englishmen concealed, the latter returned an evasive answer, telling them to search for themselves. Henry hid himself under a heap of birch-bark vessels, which were used in maple-sugar manufacture. The door was unlocked, the four Indians dashed in, their bodies covered with blood, and armed with tomahawks. The hidden man thought that the throbbing of his heart must make a noise loud enough to betray him. The Indians searched the garret, and one of them approached Henry so closely as almost to touch him; yet he remained undiscovered, possibly owing to the dark colour of his clothes and the dim light in the room. Then the Indians, after describing to the Frenchman how many they had killed and scalped, returned downstairs, and the door was locked behind them.

But the next day the Indians insisted on a further search, and, regarding every attempt at concealment as vain, Henry, by a desperate resolve, rose from his bed and presented himself in full view to the Indians as they entered the room. They were all in a state of intoxication and entirely naked. One of them, upwards of six feet in height, had all his face and body covered with charcoal and grease, but with a large white ring encircling each of his eyes. This man, walking up to Henry, seized him with one hand by the collar of his coat, and in the other held up a large carving knife, making a feint as if to plunge it into his breast, his eyes meanwhile fixed steadfastly on those of the Englishman. At length, after some seconds of the most anxious suspense, he dropped Henry's arm, saying: "I won't kill you," adding that he had often fought in war with the English and brought away many scalps, but that on a certain occasion he had lost a brother whose name was Musinigon, and that he would adopt Henry in his place.

One would like the story to have stopped here at this happy turn of events, but Wenniway (as this saviour of Henry was called) entertained a very fickle regard for his adopted brother, and, though he once or twice intervened, subsequently took no great pains to see that his life was spared. However, for the time being he was reprieved, and regarded Wenniway as his "master". Nevertheless, he was soon haled out of the house by another Indian, apparently coming with Wenniway's authority. This man ordered him to undress, and then took away all his clothes, giving him such dirty rags or strips of leather as he possessed himself. He frankly owned that his motive for stripping him was that, as he wished afterwards to kill him, Henry's clothes might not be stained with blood! With the intention of assassinating him, in fact, he dragged Henry along to a region of bushes and sandhills, and then produced a knife and attempted to execute his purpose. But with the rage and strength of absolute despair Henry wrenched himself free, pushed his would-be murderer on one side, and ran for his life towards the fort.

Here Wenniway rather indifferently helped him to take refuge in the house of the Frenchman in which he had formerly hidden, but the same night he was roused from sleep and ordered to come below, where to his surprise he found himself in the presence of three of the British officers who had formerly commanded in this fort, and who were now prisoners of the Ojibwés. The Indian chiefs for the time being had handed these men over to the surveillance of the French Canadians, together with the seventeen surviving English soldiers and traders. Henry, like the others, was almost without clothes. The French Canadian in whose house he had taken refuge refused to give him as much as a blanket, but another Canadian, less indifferent to the sufferings of a fellow white man, did give him a blanket, but for which he would certainly have perished from cold.

The next day he and the other English prisoners were embarked in canoes and taken away to Lake Michigan. On reaching the mouth of that lake, at the Beaver Islands, the Ojibwé canoes, on account of the fog, were obliged to approach the lands of the Ottawa Indians. These last suddenly seized the canoes as they entered shallow water, and professed great indignation at the capture of Fort Michili-Makinak and the slaughter of the Englishmen. They declared their intention of saving the survivors, and charged the Ojibwés with being about to kill and eat them. By the Ottawa Indians, therefore, the twenty Englishmen were carried back again and deposited in Fort Michili-Makinak, which was now taken possession of by the Ottawas. The English were still held as prisoners. After hearing all the Ojibwés had to say, and receiving from them large presents, the Ottawas finally decided to restore their English prisoners to the Ojibwés, who consequently took them away with ropes tied round their necks, and put them into an Indian habitation. Here, as they were starving, they were offered loaves of bread, but with the horrible accompaniment of seeing the slices cut with knives still covered with the blood of the murdered English. The Ojibwes moistened this blood on the knife blades with their spittle, and rubbed it on the slices of bread, offering this food then to their prisoners, so that they might force them to eat the blood of their countrymen.

The next morning, however, there appeared before Ménéhewéhná, the great war chief of the Ojibwes, Henry's friend and adopted brother, Wáwátam. This man made an earnest speech to the council of Ojibwé chiefs and braves, in which he pleaded hard for the Englishman's life, at the same time tendering from out of his own goods a considerable ransom. After much pipe-smoking and an embarrassing silence, the war chief rose to his feet and accepted the ransom, giving Wáwátam permission to take away into safety his adopted brother. "Wáwátam led me to his lodge, which was at the distance of a few yards only from the prison lodge. My entrance appeared to give joy to the whole family; food was immediately prepared for me; and I now ate the first hearty meal which I had made since my capture. I found myself one of the family; and, but that I had still my fears as to the other Indians, I felt as happy as the situation could allow."

The next day seven of the English prisoners were killed by the Ojibwés, and Henry actually saw their dead bodies being dragged out into the open. They had been killed in cold blood by an Indian chief who had just arrived from a hunting expedition, and who, not having been present at the attack on the fort, now desired to satisfy his warlike instincts and his agreement with the policy of the Ojibwés by going into the lodge where the English officers and men were tied up, and slaughtering seven of them in cold blood.

Shortly afterwards two of the Ojibwés took the fattest amongst the dead men, cut off his head, and divided his body into five parts, one of which was put into each of five kettles hung over as many fires, which were kindled for this purpose at the door of the house in which the other prisoners were tied up. They then sent to insist on the attendance at their cannibal feast of Wáwátam, the adopted brother and protector of Henry. The invitation was delivered after the Amerindian fashion. A small cutting of cedar wood about four inches in length supplies the place of the written or printed invitation to dinner of European civilization, and the man who bore the slip of cedar wood gave particulars as to place and time by word of mouth. Guests on these occasions were expected to bring their own dish and spoon.

In spite of repugnance, Wáwátam, to save his life and that of Henry, was obliged to go. He returned after an absence of half an hour, bringing back in his dish the portion given to him—a human hand and a large piece of flesh. His objection to eat this gruesome food was apparently not very deep or persistent. He excused the custom by saying that amongst all Amerindian nations there existed this practice of making a war feast from out of the bodies of the slain after a successful battle.

Soon after this episode of horror the Ojibwés abandoned Fort Michili-Makinak, for fear the English should come to attack it. Henry was hidden by his adopted brother, Wàwatam, in a cave, where he found himself by the light of the next morning sleeping on a bed of human bones, which the night before he had taken to be twigs and boughs. The whole of the cave was, in fact, filled with these human remains. No one knew or remembered the reason. Henry thought that the cave had been an ancient receptacle for the bones of persons who had been sacrificed and devoured at war feasts; for, however contemptuous they may be of the flesh, the Amerindians paid particular attention to the bones of human beings—whether friends, relations, or enemies—preserving them unbroken, and depositing them in some place kept exclusively for that purpose.

The great chief of the Ojibwés, however, advised that Henry, who had rejoined Wáwátam, should be dressed in disguise as an Indian to save him from any further harm, for the natives all round about were preparing for what they believed to be an inevitable war with the English.

"I could not but consent to the proposal, and the chief was so kind as to assist my friend and his family in effecting that very day the desired metamorphosis. My hair was cut off, and my head shaved, with the exception of a spot on the crown, of about twice the diameter of a crown piece. My face was painted with three or four different colours; some parts of it red, and others black. A shirt was provided for me, painted with vermilion, mixed with grease. A large collar of wampum[1] was put round my neck, and another suspended on my breast. Both my arms were decorated with large bands of silver above the elbow, besides several smaller ones on the wrists; and my legs were covered with *mitasses*, a kind of hose, made, as is the favourite fashion, of scarlet cloth. Over all I was to wear a scarlet blanket or mantle, and on my head a large bunch of feathers. I parted, not without some regret, with the long hair which was natural to it, and which I fancied to be ornamental; but the ladies of the family, and of the village in general, appeared to think my person improved, and now condescended to call me handsome, even among Indians."

He then went away to live with his protectors, and with them passed a by no means unhappy autumn, winter, and spring, hunting and fishing.

Here are some of his adventures at this period.

"To kill beaver, we used to go several miles up the rivers, before the approach of night, and after the dusk came on, suffer the canoe to drift gently down the current, without noise. The beavers, in this part of the evening, come abroad to procure food, or materials for repairing their habitations, and as they are not alarmed by the canoe, they often pass it within gunshot.

[1] Shell beads.

"On entering the River Aux Sables, Wáwátam took a dog, tied its feet together, and threw it into the stream, uttering, at the same time, a long prayer, which he addressed to the Great Spirit, supplicating his blessing on the chase, and his aid in the support of the family, through the dangers of a long winter. Our 'lodge' was fifteen miles above the mouth of the stream. The principal animals, which the country afforded, were red deer (wapiti), the common American deer, the bear, racoon, beaver, and marten.

"The beaver feeds in preference on young wood of the birch, aspen, and poplar tree[1]; but, in defect of these, on any other tree, those of the pine and fir kinds excepted. These latter it employs only for building its dams and houses. In wide meadows, where no wood is to be found, it resorts, for all its purposes, to the roots of the rush and water lily. It consumes great quantities of food, whether of roots or wood; and hence often reduces itself to the necessity of removing into a new quarter. Its house has an arched dome-like roof, of an elliptical figure, and rises from three to four feet above the surface of the water. It is always entirely surrounded by water; but, in the banks adjacent, the animal provides holes or *washes*, of which the entrance is below the surface, and to which it retreats on the first alarm.

"The female beaver usually produces two young at a time, but not unfrequently more. During the first year, the young remain with their parents. In the second, they occupy an adjoining apartment, and assist in building, and in procuring food. At two years old, they part, and build houses of their own; but often rove about for a considerable time before they fix upon a spot. There are beavers, called, by the Indians, *old bachelors*, who live by themselves, build no houses, and work at no dams, but shelter themselves in holes. The usual method of taking these

[1] *Populus nigra*, called by the French Canadians *liard*.

is by traps, formed of iron, or logs, and baited with branches of poplar.

"According to the Indians, the beaver is much given to jealousy. If a strange male approaches the cabin, a battle immediately ensues. Of this the female remains an unconcerned spectator, careless as to which party the law of conquest may assign her. The Indians add that the male is as constant as he is jealous, never attaching himself to more than one female.

"The most common way of taking the beaver is that of breaking up its house, which is done with trenching tools, during the winter, when the ice is strong enough to allow of approaching them; and when, also, the fur is in its most valuable state.

"Breaking up the house, however, is only a preparatory step. During this operation, the family make their escape to one or more of their *washes*. These are to be discovered by striking the ice along the bank, and where the holes are, a hollow sound is returned. After discovering and searching many of these in vain, we often heard the whole family together in the same wash. I was taught occasionally to distinguish a full wash from an empty one, by the motion of the water above its entrance, occasioned by the breathing of the animals concealed in it. From the washes, they must be taken out with the hands; and in doing this, the hunter sometimes receives severe wounds from their teeth. Whilst I was a hunter with the Indians, I thought beaver flesh was very good; but after that of the ox was again within my reach, I could not relish it. The tail is accounted a luxurious morsel.

"One evening, on my return from hunting, I found the fire put out, and the opening in the top of the lodge covered over with skins—by this means excluding, as much as possible, external light. I further observed that the ashes were removed from the fireplace, and that dry sand was spread where they had been. Soon after, a fire was made withoutside the cabin, in the open air, and a kettle hung over it to boil.

"I now supposed that a feast was in preparation. I supposed so only, for it would have been indecorous to enquire into the meaning of what I saw. No person, among the Indians themselves, would use this freedom. Good breeding requires that the spectator should patiently wait the result.

"As soon as the darkness of night had arrived, the family, including myself, were invited into the lodge. I was now requested not to speak, as a feast was about to be given to the dead, whose spirits delight in uninterrupted silence.

"As we entered, each was presented with his wooden dish and spoon, after receiving which we seated ourselves. The door was next shut, and we remained in perfect darkness.

"The master of the family was the master of the feast. Still in the dark, he asked everyone, by turn, for his dish, and put into each two boiled ears of maize. The whole being served, he began to speak. In his discourse, which lasted half an hour, he called upon the manes of his deceased relations and friends, beseeching them to be present, to assist him in the chase, and to partake of the food which he had prepared for them. When he had ended, we proceeded to eat our maize, which we did without other noise than what was occasioned by our teeth. The maize was not half boiled, and it took me an hour to consume my share. I was requested not to break the spikes,[1] as this would be displeasing to the departed spirits of their friends.

"When all was eaten, Wáwátam made another speech, with which the ceremony ended. A new fire was kindled, with fresh sparks, from flint and steel; and the pipes being smoked, the spikes were carefully buried, in a hole

[1] The grains of maize (Indian corn) grow in compact cells, round a pithy core.

made in the ground for that purpose, within the lodge. This done, the whole family began a dance, Wáwátam singing, and beating a drum. The dance continued the greater part of the night, to the great pleasure of the lodge. The night of the feast was that of the first day of November."

In the month of January, Henry happened to observe that the trunk of a very large pine tree was much torn by the claws of a bear, made both in going up and down. On further examination he saw there was a large opening, in the upper part, near which the smaller branches were broken. From these marks, and from the additional circumstances that there were no tracks on the snow, there was reason to believe that a bear lay concealed in the tree.

He communicated his discovery to his Indian friends, and it was agreed that all the family should go together in the morning to cut down the tree, the girth of which was not less than eighteen feet! This task occupied them for one and a half days with their poor little axes, till about two o'clock in the second afternoon the tree fell to the ground. For a few minutes everything remained quiet, and Henry feared that all his expectations would be disappointed; but, as he advanced to the opening, there came out a female bear of extraordinary size, which he had shot and killed before she had proceeded many yards.

"The bear being dead, all my assistants approached, and all, but more particularly my old mother, (as I was won't to call her), took the bear's head in their hands, stroking and kissing it several times; begging a thousand pardons for taking away her life; calling her their relation and grandmother; and requesting her not to lay the fault upon them, since it was truly an Englishman that had put her to death.

"This ceremony was not of long duration; and if it was I that killed their grandmother, they were not themselves behindhand in what remained to be performed. The skin being taken off, we found the fat in several places six inches deep. This, being divided into two parts, loaded two persons; and the flesh parts were as much as four persons could carry. In all, the carcass must have exceeded five hundredweight.

"As soon as we reached the lodge, the bear's head was adorned with all the trinkets in the possession of the family, such as silver armbands and wristbands, and belts of wampum; and then laid upon a scaffold, set up for its reception, within the lodge. Near the nose was placed a large quantity of tobacco.

"The next morning no sooner appeared, than preparations were made for a feast to the manes. The lodge was cleaned and swept; and the head of the bear lifted up, and a new Stroud blanket, which had never been used before, spread under it. The pipes were now lit; and Wáwatam blew tobacco smoke into the nostrils of the bear, telling me to do the same, and thus appease the anger of the bear, on account of my having killed her.

"At length, the feast being ready, Wáwátam commenced a speech, resembling, in many things, his address to the manes of his relations and departed companions; but, having this peculiarity, that he here deplored the necessity under which men laboured, thus to destroy their *friends*. He represented, however, that the misfortune was unavoidable, since without doing so, they could by no means subsist. The speech ended, we all ate heartily of the bear's flesh; and even the head itself, after remaining three days on the scaffold, was put into the kettle. The fat of our bear was melted down, and the oil filled six porcupine-skin bags. A part of the meat was cut into strips, and fire-dried, after which it was put into the vessels containing the oil, where it remained in perfect preservation, until the middle of summer."

In the spring of 1762 Henry once more returned to Fort Michili-Makinak, and went sugar-making with his Indian companions. Whilst engaged in this agreeable task, a child belonging to one of the party fell into a kettle of boiling syrup. It was instantly snatched out, but with little hope of its recovery. So long, however, as it lived, a continual feast was observed; and this was made "to the Great Spirit and Master of Life", that he might be pleased to save and heal the child. At this feast Henry was a constant guest; and often found some difficulty in eating the large quantity of food which, on such occasions as these, was put upon his dish.

Several sacrifices were also offered; among which were dogs, killed and hung upon the tops of poles, with the addition of blankets and other articles. These, also, were yielded to the Great Spirit, in the humble hope that he would give efficacy to the medicines employed. But the child died. To preserve the body from the wolves it was placed upon a scaffold, and then later carried to the borders of a lake, on the border of which was the burial ground of the family.

"On our arrival there, which happened in the beginning of April, I did not fail to attend the funeral. The grave was made of a large size, and the whole of the inside lined with birch bark. On the bark was laid the body of the child, accompanied with an axe, a pair of snowshoes, a small kettle, several pairs of common shoes, its own strings of beads, and—because it was a girl—a carrying belt and a paddle. The kettle was filled with meat. All this was again covered with bark; and at about two feet nearer the surface logs were laid across, and these again covered with bark, so that the earth might by no means fall upon the corpse.

"The last act before the burial, performed by the mother, crying over the dead body of her child, was that of taking from it a lock of hair for a memorial. While she did this, I endeavoured to console her by offering the usual arguments: that the child was happy in being released from the miseries of this present life, and that she should forbear to grieve, because it would be restored to her in another world, happy and everlasting. She answered that she knew it, and that by the lock of hair she should discover her daughter; for she would take it with her. In this she alluded to the day when some pious hand would place in her own grave, along with the carrying belt and paddle, this little relic, hallowed by maternal tears."

After many ups and downs of hope and despair, and many narrow escapes of being killed and made into broth for warlike Ojibwés, Henry at length obtained permission to travel with a party of Ojibwé Indians who were invited to visited Sir William Johnson at Niagara. This British Governor of Canada was attempting to enter into friendly relations with the Amerindian tribes, and induce them to accept quietly the transference of Canada from French to English control.

Before starting, however, to interview this great White Governor, the Ojibwés decided to consult their oracle, the Great Turtle, after which Fort Michili-Makinak was named.[1] Behind Fort Michili-Makinak is an extraordinary mound or hill of stone supposed to resemble this reptile exactly, and in fact to be in some way the residence of a supernatural giant turtle.

For invoking and consulting the Great Turtle, the first thing to be done was to build a large house, within which was placed a kind of tent, for the use of the priest and reception of the spirit. The tent was formed of moose skins, hung over a framework of wood made out of five pillars of five different species of timber, about ten feet in

[1] Michili, pronounced "Mishili", means "great", and Makinak, "turtle", in the translation of some Canadian writers. The turtle in question is, of course, not the turtle of sea waters, but the Snapping Turtle (*Chelydra serpentina*) found in most Canadian lakes and the big rivers of North America, east of the Rocky Mountains.

c 312

SCENE ON CANADIAN RIVER: WILD SWANS FLYING UP DISTURBED BY BEAR

height and eight inches in diameter, set up in a circle of four feet in diameter, with their bases two feet deep in the soil. At the top the pillars were bound together by a circular hoop of withies. Over the whole of this edifice were spread the moose skins, covering it at top and round the sides, and made fast with thongs of the same, except that on one side a part was left unfastened, to admit of the entrance of the priest.

The ceremonies did not commence till the approach of night. To give light inside the house several fires were kindled round the tent. Nearly the whole village assembled in the house, Alexander Henry among the rest. It was not long before the priest appeared, almost in a state of nakedness. As he approached the tent the skins were lifted up, as much as was necessary to allow of his creeping under them on his hands and knees. His head was scarcely within side when the edifice, massive as it has been described, began to shake; and the skins were no sooner let fall than the sounds of numerous voices were heard beneath them — some yelling, some barking as dogs, some howling like wolves; and in this horrible concert were mingled screams and sobs of despair, anguish, and the sharpest pain. Articulate speech was also uttered, as if from human lips, but in a tongue unknown to any of the audience.

After some time these confused and frightful noises were succeeded by a perfect silence; and now a voice, not heard before, seemed to manifest the arrival of a new character in the tent. This was low and feeble, resembling the cry of a young puppy. The sound was no sooner distingushed than all the Indians clapped their hands for joy, exclaiming that this was the Chief Spirit, the Turtle, the Spirit that never lied! Other voices, which they had distinguished from time to time, they had previously hissed, as recognizing them to belong to evil and lying spirits, the deceivers of mankind.

Then came from the tent a succession of songs, in which a diversity of voices met the ear. From his first entrance, till these songs were finished, we heard nothing in the proper voice of the priest. But now he addressed the multitude, declaring the presence of the Great Turtle, and the spirit's readiness to answer such questions as should be proposed. The questions were to come from the chief of the village, who was silent, however, till after he had put a large quantity of tobacco into the tent, introducing it at the aperture. This was a sacrifice offered to the spirit; for the spirits were supposed by the Indians to be as fond of tobacco as themselves. This done, the chief desired the priest to enquire: Whether or not the English were preparing to make war upon the Indians? and whether or not there were at Fort Niagara a large number of English troops?

The priest was heard to put the questions, and then the tent shook and rocked so violently that Henry expected to see it levelled with the ground. But apparently answers were given, after which a terrific cry announced, with sufficient intelligibility, the departure of the Turtle. Subsequently the priest interpreted the Great Turtle's answers, which gave a great deal of information regarding the disposition and numbers of the English soldiers, and the presents which Sir William Johnson was preparing for the Ojibwes; and which finally approved the wisdom of the embassy proceeding on its way.

Journeying along the shores of Lake Huron, they stopped to avoid a gale of wind and to rest. Henry, gathering firewood, disturbed a rattlesnake which manifested hostile intentions. He went back to the canoe to fetch his gun; but upon telling the Ojibwés that he was about to kill a rattlesnake they begged him to desist. They then seized their pipes and tobacco pouches and returned with him to the place where he had left the rattlesnake, which was still coiled up and angry.

"The Indians, on their part, surrounded it, all addressing it by turns, and calling it their *grandfather*; but yet keeping at some distance. During this part of the ceremony they filled their pipes; and now each blew the smoke towards the snake, who, as it appeared to me, really received it with pleasure. In a word, after remaining coiled, and receiving incense for the space of half an hour, it stretched itself along the ground, in visible good humour. Its length was between four and five feet. Having remained outstretched for some time, at last it moved slowly away, the Indians following it, and still addressing it by the title of grandfather, beseeching it to take care of their families during their absence, and to be pleased to open the heart of Sir William Johnson, so that he might *show them charity*, and fill their canoe with rum.

"One of the chiefs added a petition, that the snake would take no notice of the insult which had been offered him by the Englishman, who would even have put him to death, but for the interference of the Indians, to whom it was hoped he would impute no part of the offence."

Early the next morning they proceeded on their way, with a serene sky and very little wind, so that to shorten the journey they determined to steer across the lake to an island which just appeared on the horizon. But after hoisting a sail the wind increased, and the Indians, beginning to be alarmed, frequently called on the rattlesnake to come to their assistance. By degrees the waves grew high, and at last it blew a hurricane, Henry and his companions expecting every moment to be swallowed up. From prayers the Indians now proceeded to sacrifices, both alike offered to the god-rattlesnake, or *manito-kinibik*. One of the chiefs took a dog, and, after tying its fore legs together, threw it overboard, at the same time calling on the snake to preserve the party from being drowned, and desiring him to satisfy his hunger with the carcass of the dog. The snake was unpropitious, and the wind increased.

Another chief sacrificed another dog, with the addition of some tobacco. In the prayer which accompanied these gifts he besought the snake, as before, not to avenge upon the Indians the insult which he had received from the Englishman. "He assured the snake that I was *absolutely* an Englishman, and of kin neither to him nor to them."

"At the conclusion of this speech, an Indian, who sat near me, observed, that if we were drowned it would be for my fault alone, and that I ought myself to be sacrificed, to appease the angry manito; nor was I without apprehensions, that in case of extremity this would be my fate; but, happily for me, the storm at length abated, and we reached the island safely."

The next day they arrived at the shore of Lake Ontario. Here they remained two days to make canoes out of the bark of the elm tree, in which they might travel to Niagara. For this purpose the Indians first cut down a tree, then stripped off the bark in one entire sheet of about eighteen feet in length, the incision being lengthwise. The canoe was now complete as to its bottom and sides. Its ends were next closed, by sewing the bark together; and a few ribs and bars being introduced, the architecture was finished. In this manner they made two canoes; of which one carried eight men, and the other nine.

A few days later Henry was handed over safe and sound to Sir William Johnson at Niagara. He was then given the command of a corps of Indian allies which was to accompany the expedition under General Bradstreet to raise the siege of Detroit, which important place had been long invested by a great Indian chief, Pontiac, who still carried on the war on behalf of King Louis XV. This enterprise was successful, and British control was extended to many places in central Canada. Henry returned to Fort Michili-Makinak and regained much of the property which he had lost in the Indian attacks. As some compensation for his former sufferings he received from the

British commandant of Michili-Makinak the exclusive fur trade of Lake Superior.

The currency at that period, and long before, in Canadian history, was in beaver skins, which were approximately valued at the price of two shillings and sixpence a pound. Otter skins were valued at six shillings each, and marten skins at one shilling and sixpence, and others in proportion; but all these things were classed at being worth so many beaver skins or proportion of beaver skins. Thus, for example, the native canoemen and porters engaged by Henry for his winter hunts were paid each at the rate of a hundred pounds weight of beaver skins.[1]

At various places on the River Ontonagan, which flows into Lake Superior, Henry was shown the extraordinary deposits of copper, which presented itself to the eye in masses of various weight. The natives smelted the copper and beat it into spoons and bracelets. It was so absolutely pure of any alloy that it required nothing but to be beaten into shape. In one place Henry saw a mass of copper weighing not less than five tons, pure and malleable, so that with an axe he was able to cut off a portion weighing a hundred pounds. He conjectured that this huge mass of copper had at some time been dislodged from the side of a lofty hill and thence rolled into the position where he found it. Farther to the north of Lake Superior he found pieces of virgin copper remarkable for their form, some resembling leaves of vegetables, and others the shapes of animals.

In these journeys he collected some of the native traditions, amongst others that of the Great Hare, Naniboju, who was represented to him as the founder or creator of the Amerindian peoples. An island in Lake Superior was called Naniboju's burial place. Henry landed there,

[1] The smallest change, so to speak, was the skin of a marten, worth one shilling and sixpence. If you went to a canteen for a drink you paid your score with a marten skin, unless the value of your refreshment exceeded the sum of eighteen pence.

and "found on the projecting rocks a quantity of tobacco, rotting in the rain; together with kettles, broken guns, and a variety of other articles. His spirit is supposed to make this its constant residence; and here to preside over the lake, and over the Indians, in their navigation and fishing."

In the spring of the following year (1768), whilst the snow still lay many feet thick on the ground, he and his men made sugar from the maple trees on a mountain, and for nearly three weeks none of them ate anything but maple sugar, consuming a pound a day, desiring no other food, and waxing fat and strong on this diet. Then they returned to the banks of the Ontonagan River, where the wild fowl appeared in such abundance that one man, with a muzzle-loading gun, could kill in a day sufficient birds for the sustenance of fifty men. As soon as the ice and snow had melted, parties of Indians came in from their winter's hunt, bringing to Henry furs to pay him for all the goods he had advanced. In this way the whole of his outstanding credit was satisfied, with the exception of thirty skins, which represented the contribution due from one Indian who had died. In this case even, the man's family had sent all the skins they could gather together, and gradually acquitted themselves of the amount due, in order that the spirit of the dead man might rest in peace, which it could not do if his debts were not acquitted.

In the following autumn he had an experience which showed him how near famine was to great abundance, and how ready the Amerindians were in cases of even slight privation to turn cannibal, kill and eat the weaker members of the party. He was making an excursion to the Sault de Sainte Marie, and took with him three half-breed Canadians and a young Indian woman who was journeying in that direction to see her relations. As the distance was short, and they expected to obtain much fish by the way, they only took with them as provisions a quart of maize for each person. On the first night of their journey they encamped on the island of Naniboju and set their net to catch fish. But there arose a violent storm, which continued for three days, during which it was impossible for them to take up the net or to leave the island. In consequence of this they ate up all their maize. On the evening of the third day the storm abated, and they rushed to examine the net. It was gone! It was impossible to return to the point of their departure, where there would have been plenty of food, on account of the strong wind against them. They therefore steered for the Sault de Sainte Marie. But the wind veered round, and for nine days blew a strong gale against their progress in this direction, making the waves of the lake so high that they were obliged to take refuge on the shore.

Henry went out perpetually to hunt, but all he got during those nine days were two small snow-buntings. The Canadian half-breeds with him then calmly proposed to kill and feed upon the young woman. One of these men, indeed, admitted that he had had recourse to this expedient for sustaining life when wintering in the north-west and running out of food. But Henry indignantly repudiated the suggestion. Though very weak, he searched everywhere desperately for food, and at last found on a very high rock a thick lichen, called by the French Canadians *tripe de roche*,[1] looking, in fact, very much like slices of tripe. Henry fetched the men and the Indian woman, and they set to work gathering quantities of this lichen. The woman was well acquainted with the mode of preparing it, which was done by boiling it into a thick mucilage, looking rather like the white of an egg. On this they made hearty meals, though it had a bitter and disagreeable taste. After the ninth day of their sufferings the wind fell, they continued their journey, and met with

[1] See p. 128.

kindly Indians, who supplied them with as many fish as they wanted. Nevertheless, they all were so ill afterwards that they nearly died, from the effects of the lichen diet.

Some time after this Henry resolved to search for the marvellous island of Yellow Sands,[1] an island of Lake Superior which, it is true, the French had discovered, but about which they kept up a good deal of mystery. The Indian legend was that the sands of this small island consisted of gold dust, and the Ojibwé Indians, having discovered this, and attempting to bring some away, they were disturbed by a supernatural being of amazing size, sixty feet in height, which strode into the water and commanded them to deliver back what they had taken away. Terrified at his gigantic stature, they complied with his request, since which time no Indian has ever dared to approach the haunted coast. Henry, however, with his men, finally discovered this Island of Yellow Sands in 1771, in the north-east part of Lake Superior. It was much smaller than he had been led to expect, and very low and studded with small lakes, probably made by the action of beavers damming up the little streams. He found no supernatural monster to dispute the island with him, but a number of large reindeer, so unused to the sight of man that they scarcely got out of his way, so that he was able to shoot as many as he wanted. The ancestors of these reindeer may have reached the island either by floating ice or by swimming. They seem, with the birds, to have been the island's only inhabitants, and to have increased and multiplied to a remarkable extent, small portions of the island's surface being actually formed of immense accumulations of reindeer bones.

Amongst the birds of the island, besides geese and pigeons, were hawks. No serpents whatever were seen

[1] The Isle of Yellow Sands, famed in legend for its terrible serpents and ogre sixty feet high, was subsequently identified with the Ile de Pont Chartrain, which is distant sixty miles from the north shore of Lake Superior.

by the party, but Henry remarks that the hawks nearly made up for them in abundance and ferocity. They appeared very angry at the intrusion of these strangers on the sacred island, and hovered round perpetually, swooping at their faces and even carrying off their caps.

In 1775 Henry, having been greatly disappointed over an attempt to work the copper of Lake Superior, entered with vigour into a fur trade with the north-west. He penetrated from Lake Superior to the Lake of the Woods and reached the great Lake Winnipeg. Here he encountered the Kristino,[1] Knistino, or Kri Indians. He found these people very different in appearance from the other Amerindian tribes farther south. The men were almost entirely naked in spite of the much colder climate. Their bodies were painted with an ochre or clay so red that it was locally known by the French Canadians as vermilion. Every man and boy had his bow strung and in his hand, with the arrow, ready to attack in case of need. Their heads were shaved all over except for a large spot on the crown. Here the hair grew very long, and was rolled and gathered into a tuft; and this tuft, which was the object of the greatest care, was covered with a piece of skin. The lobes of their ears were pierced, and through the opening was inserted the bones of fish or small beasts. The women wore their hair in great length all over the head. It was divided by a parting, and on each side was collected into a roll fastened above the ear and covered with a piece of painted skin or ornamented with beads. The clothing of the women was of leather, the dressed skins of buffalo or deer. This cloak was fastened round the waist by a girdle, and the legs were covered with leather gaiters. The Kristino men were eager that their women should marry Europeans, because the half-breed children proved to be bolder warriors and better hunters than themselves, Henry found that although the Kris

[1] See p. 166.

were much addicted to drunkenness they were peaceable when inebriated, and, moreover, detached two of their number, who refused ever to touch the liquor under such circumstances, in order that they might guard the white men, and not allow any drunken Indian to approach their camp.

Henry and his party, after crossing Lake Winnipeg, ascended the Saskatchewan (in the autumn of 1775). On their way up this river they came to a village of Paskwaya Indians, which consisted of thirty families, who were lodged in tents of a circular form, composed of dressed bison skins stretched upon poles twelve feet in length. On their arrival the chief of this village, named Chatik, which name meant Pelican,[1] called the party rather imperiously into his lodge or meeting house, and then told them very plainly that his armed men exceeded theirs in number, and that he would put the whole of the party to death unless they were very liberal in their presents. To avoid misunderstanding, he added that he would inform them exactly what it was that he required: Three casks of gunpowder, four bags of shot and ball, two bales of tobacco, three kegs of rum, and three guns, together with knives, flints, and other articles. He went on to say that he had already seen white men, and knew that they promised more than they performed. He, personally, was a peaceful man, who contented himself with moderate views in order to avoid quarrels; nevertheless, he desired that an immediate answer should be given before the strangers quitted his lodge. A hurried consultation took place, and Henry could do nothing but comply with the chief's demands, for he was powerless to resist. Having, therefore, intimated his acceptance of these demands, he was invited to smoke the pipe of peace, and then obtained permission to depart. After this the goods demanded were handed

[1] Elsewhere Henry observes the great numbers of pelicans to be seen on Lake Winnipeg.

over, but Chatik managed to snatch more rum from them before they got safely away.

In the winter of 1776 Henry, who, together with his party, had received welcome hospitality from the Hudson's Bay Company's station at Cumberland House, resolved to reach the western region known as the Great Plains, or Prairies—that immense tract of country through which flow the Athabaska, the Saskatchewan, the Red River, and the Missouri. He and his party, of course, travelled on snowshoes, and their goods were packed on sledges made of thin boards, and drawn after them by the men. The cold was intense, so that, besides wearing very warm woollen clothes, they were obliged to wrap themselves in blankets of beaver skin and huge bison robes. On these plains there were occasional knolls covered with trees, which were usually called "islands". These provided the precious fuel which alone enabled the travellers to support the intense cold of the nights.

After fifteen days of very difficult travel, during which it had been impossible to kill any game, as the beasts were mostly hidden in the dense woods on these rare hillocks, the situation of his party became alarming. They were now on the borders of the plains, and the trees were getting small and scanty. On the twentieth day of their journey they had finished the last remains of their provisions. But Henry had taken the precaution of concealing a large cake of chocolate[1] as a reserve in case of great need. His men had walked till they were exhausted, and had lost both strength and hope, when Henry informed them of the treasure which was still in store. They filled the big kettle with snow. It held two gallons of water, and into this was put one square of the

[1] Chocolate from St. Domingue (Haiti) was a favourite form of portable nutriment among the French Canadians, who also provided a means of subsistence for long journeys called *praline*. This was made of roasted Indian corn on which sugar had been sprinkled. It was a most nourishing food, as well as being an agreeable sweetmeat.

chocolate. The quantity was scarcely sufficient to give colour to the water, but each man drank off a gallon of this hot liquor and felt much refreshed. The next day they marched vigorously for six hours on another two gallons of chocolate and water. For five days the chocolate kept them going, though more by faith than by any actual nourishment that it imparted. They now began to be surrounded by large herds of wolves, who seemed to be conscious of their dire extremity and the probability that they would soon fall an easy prey, yet were cunning enough to keep out of gunshot. At last, however, at sunset on the fifth day, they discovered on the ice the remains of an elk's carcass on which the wolves had left a little flesh. From these elk bones a meal of strong and excellent soup was soon prepared, and the men's bodies thrilled with new life.

"Want had lost his dominion over us. At noon we saw the horns of a red deer, standing in the snow, on the river. On examination we found that the whole carcass was with them, the animal having broken through the ice in the beginning of the winter, in attempting to cross the river, too early in the season; while his horns, fastening themselves in the ice, had prevented him from sinking. By cutting away the ice we were enabled to lay bare a part of the back and shoulders, and thus procure a stock of food amply sufficient for the rest of our journey. We accordingly encamped, and employed our kettle to good purpose, forgot all our misfortunes, and prepared to walk with cheerfulness the twenty leagues which, as we reckoned, still lay between ourselves and Fort des Prairies. Though the deer must have been in this situation ever since the month of November, yet its flesh was perfectly good. Its horns alone were five feet high or more, and it will therefore not appear extraordinary that they should be seen above the snow."

The next day they reached the Fort des Prairies,

established by the Hudson's Bay people, on the verge of the Assiniboin country. The journey was resumed in company with Messrs. Patterson and Holmes, and accompanied by a band of natives. They had entered the bison country, and were regaled by the Indians with bison tongue and beef.

"Soon after sunrise we descried a herd of oxen (bison) extending a mile and a half in length, and too numerous to be counted. They travelled, not one after another, as, in the snow, other animals usually do, but, in a broad phalanx, slowly, and sometimes stopping to feed. . . . Their numbers were so great that we dreaded lest they should fairly trample down the camp; nor could it have happened otherwise, but for the dogs, almost as numerous as they, who were able to keep them in check. The Indians killed several when close upon their tents, but neither the fire of the Indians nor the noise of the dogs could soon drive them away." The poor animals were more frightened of the frightful snowstorm which was raging than of what man or dog might do to them in the shelter of the woods.

At last the party reached the residence of the great chief of the Assiniboins, whose name was "Great Road". These Amerindians received Henry and his people with the greatest respect, giving them a bodyguard, armed with bows and spears, who escorted them to the lodge or tent prepared for their reception. This was of circular form, covered with leather, and not less than twenty feet in diameter. On the ground within, bison skins were spread for beds and seats.

"One-half of the tent was appropriated to our use. Several women waited upon us, to make a fire and bring water, which latter they fetched from a neighbouring tent. Shortly after our arrival these women brought us water, unasked for, saying that it was for washing. The refreshment was exceedingly acceptable, for on our march we had become so dirty that our complexions were not very distinguishable from those of the Indians themselves."

Invited to feast with the great chief, they proceeded to the tent of "Great Road", which they found neither more ornamented nor better furnished than the rest. At their entrance the chief arose from his seat, saluted them in the Indian manner by shaking hands, and addressed them in a few words, in which he offered his thanks for the confidence which they had reposed in him in trusting themselves so far from their own country. After all were seated, on bearskins spread on the ground, the pipe, as usual, was introduced, and presented in succession to each person present. Each took his whiff, and then let it pass to his neighbour. The stem, which was four feet in length, was held by an officer attendant on the chief. The bowl was of red marble or pipe stone.

When the pipe had gone its round, the chief, without rising from his seat, delivered a speech of some length, after which several of the Indians began to weep, and they were soon joined by the whole party. "Had I not previously been witness" (writes Henry) "to a weeping scene of this description, I should certainly have been apprehensive of some disastrous catastrophe; but, as it was, I listened to it with tranquillity. It lasted for about ten minutes, after which all tears were dried away, and the honours of the feast were performed by the attending chiefs." This consisted in giving to every guest a dish containing a boiled bison's tongue. Henry having enquired why these people always wept at their feasts, and sometimes at their councils, he was answered that their tears flowed to the memory of their deceased relations, who were formerly present on these occasions, and whom they remembered as soon as they saw the feast or the conference being got ready.[1]

[1] The Assiniboins (whom Henry calls the Osinipoilles) are the Issati of older travellers, and have sometimes been called the Weeper Indians, from their tendency to tears.

The chief to whose kindly reception they were so much indebted was about five feet ten inches high, and of a complexion rather darker than that of the Indians in general. His appearance was greatly injured by the condition of his head of hair, and this was the result of an extraordinary superstition.

"The Indians universally fix upon a particular object, as sacred to themselves; as the giver of their prosperity, and as their preserver from evil. The choice is determined either by a dream, or by some strong predilection of fancy; and usually falls upon an animal, or part of an animal, or something else which is to be met with, by land, or by water; but 'Great Road' had made choice of his *hair*—placing, like Samson, all his safety in this portion of his proper substance! His hair was the fountain of all his happiness; it was his strength and his weapon, his spear and his shield. It preserved him in battle, directed him in the chase, watched over him on the march, and gave length of days to his wife and children. Hair, of a quality like this, was not to be profaned by the touch of human hands. I was assured that it had never been cut nor combed from his childhood upward, and, that when any part of it fell from his head, he treasured up that part with care: meanwhile, it did not escape all care, even while growing on the head; but was in the special charge of a spirit, who dressed it while the owner slept. All this might be; but the spirit's style of hairdressing was at least peculiar; the hair being suffered to remain very much as if it received no dressing at all, and matted into ropes, which spread themselves in all directions."

From this Assiniboin village Henry saw, for the first time, one of those herds of horses which the Assiniboins possessed in numbers. The herd was feeding on the skirts of the plain. The horses were provided with no fodder, but were left to find food for themselves, which they did in winter by removing the snow with their feet till they reach the grass. This was everywhere on the ground in plenty.

Amongst these people they saw the paunch or stomach of a bison employed as a kettle. This was hung in the smoke of a fire and filled with snow. As the snow melted, more was added, till the paunch was full of water. The lower orifice of the organ was used for drawing off the water, and stopped with a plug and string.

Henry also noticed amongst the Assiniboins the celebrated lariat. This is formed of a stone of about two pounds weight, which is sewed up in leather and made fast to a wooden handle two feet long. In using it the stone is whirled round the handle by a warrior sitting on horseback and riding at full speed. Every stroke which takes effect brings down a man, a horse, or a bison. To prevent the weapon from slipping out of the hand, a string, which is tied to the handle, is also passed round the wrist of the wearer.

Alexander Henry extended his travels in the northwest within four hundred and fifty miles of Lake Athabaska. He met at this point some Chipewayan slaves in the possession of the Assiniboins, and heard from them (1) of the Peace River in the far west which led one through the Rocky Mountains (he uses that name) to a region descending towards a great sea (the Pacific Ocean); and (2) of the Slave River which, after passing through several lakes, also reached a great sea on the north. This, of course, was an allusion to the Mackenzie River. Here were given and recorded the chief hints at possible lines of exploration which afterwards sent Alexander Mackenzie and other explorers on the journeys that carried British-Canadian enterprise and administration to the shores of the Pacific and Arctic Oceans.

After 1776 Alexander Henry ceased his notable explorations of the far west. In that year he paid a visit to England and France, returning to Canada in 1777. Whilst in France he was received at the French Court and had the privilege of relating to Queen Marie Antoinette some of his wonderful adventures and experiences. After two more visits to England he settled down at Montreal as a merchant (autumn of 1780), and in 1784 he joined with other great pioneers in founding, at Montreal, The North-west Trading Company. Eventually he handed over his share in this enterprise to his nephew, Alexander Henry the Younger, and established himself completely in a life of ease and quiet. He died at Montreal in 1824, aged eighty-five years.

## CHAPTER X

## Samuel Hearne

The first noteworthy explorer of the far north was SAMUEL HEARNE,[1] who had been mate of a vessel in the employ of the whale fishery of Hudson Bay. He entered the service of the Hudson's Bay Company about 1765, and was selected four years afterwards by the Governor of Prince of Wales's Fort (a certain Moses Norton, a half-breed) to lead an expedition of discovery in search of a mighty river flowing northwards, which was rumoured to exist by the Eskimo. This "Coppermine" River was said to flow through a region rich in deposits of copper. From this district the northern tribes of Indians derived their copper ornaments and axeheads.

Samuel Hearne started on the 6th of November, 1769, from Prince of Wales's Fort at the mouth of the Churchill River, on the north-west coast of Hudson Bay. Presumably he and the two "common white men" who were with him travelled on snowshoes and hauled small sledges after them. Travelling westward they passed over bleak hills with very little vegetation—"the barren grounds, where, in general, we thought ourselves well off if we could scrape together as many shrubs as would make a fire; but it was scarcely ever in our power to make any

[1] Hearne was born in London in 1745. He entered the Royal Navy as a midshipman at the tender age of eleven, and remained in the Navy till about 1765, when he went out to Hudson Bay with the rank of quartermaster. He must have acquired a considerable education, even in botany and zoology. He not only wrote well, and was a good surveyor for rough map making, but he had a considerable talent as a draughtsman.

other defence against the weather than by digging a hole in the snow down to the moss, wrapping ourselves up in our clothing, and lying down in it, with our sledges set up edgeways to windward". But the principal Indian guide that he engaged was so obviously determined to make the expedition a failure that Hearne returned to his base, Prince of Wales's Fort, and made a second start on the 23rd of February, 1770, this time taking care not to be accompanied by any other white men, and insisting that the Indians who accompanied him should be more carefully chosen.

It must be remembered that in all these early expeditions, French and English, the explorers relied for their food almost entirely on what could be obtained as they went along, in the way of venison, grouse, geese, fish, and wild fruits. In the springtime they would probably get goose eggs and some form of maple sugar through the Indians. From the summer to the autumn there would be an abundance of wild fruits and nuts, but for the rest of the year it would be a diet almost entirely of flesh or fish. As a stand-by there was probably *pemmican*, made in times of plenty from fish, from bison meat and fat, or from the dried flesh of deer or musk oxen; but tea, coffee, bread, biscuits, and such like accessories were absolutely unknown to them, in fact they lived exactly as the Amerindians did. Their habitations, of course, were the tents or houses of the natives, or what they made for themselves.

In order to pitch an Indian tent in winter it was first necessary to search for a level piece of dry ground, and this could only be ascertained by thrusting a stick through the snow, down to the ground, all over the proposed plot. When a suitable site had been found the snow was then cleared away down to the very moss, in the shape of a circle. When a prolonged stay was contemplated, even the moss was cut up and removed, as it was very liable when dry to catch fire. A quantity of poles were then procured, proportionate in number and length to the size of the tent cloth and the number of persons the tent was intended to contain. Two of the longest poles were tied together at the top and raised to an angle of about 45 degrees from the ground, so that the lower ends extended on either side as widely as the proposed diameter of the tent. The other poles were then arranged on either side of the first two, so that they formed a complete circle round the bottom, and their points were tied together at the top. The tent cloth was usually of thin moose leather, and in shape resembled the vane of a fan, so that the large outer curve enclosed the bottom of the poles, and the smaller one fitted round the apex of the poles at the top, leaving an open space which let out the smoke and let in air and light. The fire was made on the ground in the centre of the floor, which floor was covered all over with small branches of firs and pines serving as seats and beds. Pine foliage and branches were laid round the bottom of the poles on the outside, and a quantity of snow was packed all round the exterior of the tent, thus excluding a great part of the external air, and contributing much to the warmth within.

For a month or more Hearne camped in this fashion by the side of a lake, waiting till the season was sufficiently open for him to continue his journey by water. He and his party of Indians lived mainly on fish, but when these became scarce they attempted to snare grouse or kill deer. In the intervals of rare meals all the party smoked or slept, unless they were obliged to go out to hunt and fish. They would delight, after killing deer, in securing as much as possible of the blood and turning it into broth by boiling it in a kettle with fat and scraps of meat. This was reckoned a dainty dish. Their spoons, dishes, and other necessary household furniture were cut out of birch bark.

c 312

Photo. Thompson

LAKE LOUISE, THE ROCKY MOUNTAINS

By the 19th of May, geese, swans, ducks, gulls, and other birds of passage were so plentiful, flying from south to north, and halting to rest at the lake, that Hearne felt the time had come to resume his journey, provisions being now very plentiful and the worst of the thaw over. The weather was remarkably fine and pleasant as the party travelled northwards.

There must have been good patent medicines even in those days. Of these Hearne possessed "Turlington's Drops" and "Yellow Basilicon", and with these he not only healed the terrible wounds of a valuable Indian who had cut his leg most severely (when making birch-bark dishes, spoons, &c.), but also the hand of another Indian, which was shattered with the bursting of a gun. These medicines soon restored the use of his hand, so that in a short time he was out of danger, while the carver of birch-bark spoons was able to walk. Nevertheless, although they were to the south of the 60th degree of latitude, the snow was not completely melted until the end of June.

All at once the weather became exceedingly hot, the sledges had to be thrown away, and each man had to carry on his back a heavy load. For instance, Hearne was obliged to carry his quadrant for taking astronomical observations, and its stand; a trunk containing books and papers, &c.; a large compass; and a bag containing all his wearing apparel; also a hatchet, a number of knives, files, &c., and several small articles intended for presents to the natives—in short, a weight of *sixty pounds*. Moreover, the barren ground was quite unsuited to the pitching of the southern type of tent, the poles of which obviously could not be driven into the bare rock, so that Hearne was obliged to sleep in the open air in all weathers. Very often he was unable to make a fire, and was constantly reduced to eating his meat quite raw. "Notwith standing these accumulated and complicated hardships, we continued in perfect health and good spirits." The average day's walk was twenty miles, sometimes without any other subsistence than a pipe of tobacco and a drink of water.

At last they saw three musk oxen grazing by the side of a small lake. This seemed a splendid piece of fortune, but, to their mortification, before they could get one of them skinned, a tremendous downpour of rain ensued, so as to make it out of their power to have a fire, for their only form of fuel was moss. And the flesh of the musk ox eaten raw was disgusting; it was coarse and tough, and tasted so strongly of musk that Hearne could hardly swallow it. "None of our natural wants," he writes, "except thirst, are so distressing or hard to endure as hunger. . . . For want of action, the stomach so far loses its digestive powers that, after long fasting, it resumes its office with pain and reluctance." After these prolonged fasts, his stomach was scarcely able to contain two or three ounces of food without producing the most agonizing pain. "We fasted many times two whole days and nights, and twice for three days; once for nearly seven days, during which we tasted not a mouthful of anything, except a few cranberries, water, scraps of old leather, and burnt bones."

At a place 63° north latitude he bought a canoe for a single knife "the full value of which did not exceed one penny", having been told that they would soon reach rivers through which they could not wade. And, moreover, they found an Indian who was willing to carry it. In July his guide persuaded him to join an encampment of natives—about six hundred persons living in seventy tents—asserting that, as it was no use proceeding much farther north in their search for the Coppermine River that season, it would be well to winter to the west, and resume their northern journey in the spring. The country, though quite devoid of trees, and mostly barren rock, was covered with a herb or shrub called by the Indian name of Wishakapakka,[1] from which the European servants of the Hudson's Bay Company had long been used to prepare a kind of tea by steeping it in boiling water. Here there were multitudes of reindeer feeding on the *Cladina* lichen and the Indians with Hearne killed large numbers for the food of the party, and also for their skins and the marrow in their bones.

The Indian who had volunteered to carry the canoe proved unequal to his task. But Hearne found another of his carriers who was willing to take the burden. In order, therefore, to be readier with his gun to shoot deer, he transferred a portion of his own load to the ex-canoe carrier. This portion consisted of the invaluable quadrant and its stand, and a bag of gunpowder. The gunpowder was of such importance to Hearne and his party that one wonders he made this exchange; for if he lost this powder he had no means of killing game, and was entirely dependent for food on the troop of Indians with whom he was travelling, and whom he knew to be most niggardly and inhospitable. Judge, therefore, of his horror when, at the end of a day's march, this weakly Indian porter was missing with his load. All night Hearne was unable to sleep with anxiety, and the whole of the next day he spent searching the rocky ground for miles to discover some sign of the missing man. At that season of the year it was like looking for a needle in a pottle of hay, for there was no snow, and equally no herbage, on which a man's foot could leave traces. However, at last, by some miracle, they discovered the load by the banks of a little river where a party of Indians had crossed.

Shortly afterwards, leaving his quadrant on its stand for a few minutes, whilst he went to eat his dinner, a violent wind arose and blew the whole thing on to the

[1] This word is said to be a corruption or altered form of *Wishakagamiū*, a liquid or broth (Kri language). The drink made from this shrub or herb (*Ledum palustre*) is now known as Labrador tea. It is a bitter aromatic infusion.

rocks, so that the quadrant was smashed and rendered useless. On this account he determined once more to return to Fort Prince of Wales. The Northern Indians[1] with whom Hearne travelled backwards towards the fort were most inhospitable, not to say dangerous. They robbed him of most of his goods, and refused to allow their women to assist his people to dress the reindeer skins out of which it would be necessary shortly to make coverings to protect them from the severe cold of the autumn. In fact Hearne was in rather a desperate condition by September, 1770, when he was joined by a party of Indians under a famous leader, whom he calls Matonabi.

Matonabi, though of Athapaskan stock, had, when a boy, resided several years at Prince of Wales's Fort, and learnt a little English, and, above all, was a master of several Algonkin dialects or languages, so that he could discourse with the Southern Indians. As soon as he heard of Hearne's distress he furnished him with a good, warm suit of skins, and had the reindeer skins dressed for the Indian carriers who accompanied Hearne. In journeying together, Matonabi invited him to return once more, with himself as guide, to discover the copper mines.

"He attributed all our misfortunes to the misconduct of my guides, and the very plan we pursued, by the desire of the Governor, in not taking any women with us on this journey, was, he said, the principal thing that occasioned all our wants. 'For,' said he, 'when all the men are heavy laden, they can neither hunt nor travel to any considerable distance; and in case they meet with success in hunting, who is to carry the produce of their labour?' 'Women,' added he, 'were made for labour; one of them

[1] The Indians of the Athapaskan or Déné group were usually called the *Northern Indians* by the Hudson Bay people, in comparison to all the other tribes of the more temperate regions farther south, who were known as the *Southern Indians* (Algonkins, &c.).

can carry, or haul, as much as two men can do. They also pitch our tents, make and mend our clothing, keep us warm at night; and, in fact, there is no such thing as travelling any considerable distance, or for any length of time, in this country, without their assistance.' 'Women,' said he again, 'though they do everything, are maintained at a trifling expense; for as they always stand cook, the very licking of their fingers in scarce times is sufficient for their subsistence.'

"This," added Hearne, "however odd it may appear, is but too true a description of the situation of women in this country: it is at least so in appearance; for the women always carry the provisions, though it is more than probable they help themselves when the men are not present."

On the 7th of December, 1770, Samuel Hearne started again from Prince of Wales's Fort, Hudsons Bay, but under very much happier circumstances, Matonabi being practically in charge of the expedition.

Unfortunately, on reaching the Egg River, where Matonabi's people had made a *cache* or hiding place in which they had stored a quantity of provisions and implements, they found that other Indians had discovered this hiding place and robbed it of nearly every article. This was a great disappointment to Matonabi's people; but Hearne remarks the fortitude with which they bore this, nor did one of them ever speak of revenge. But the expedition's scarcity of food obliged them to push on from morning till night, day after day; yet the road being very bad, and their sledges heavy, they were seldom able to do more than eighteen miles a day. Hearne himself writes that he never spent so dull a Christmas. For the last three days he had not tasted a morsel of anything, except a pipe of tobacco and a drink of snow water, yet he had to walk daily from morning till night heavily laden. However, at the end of December they reached Island Lake, where they entered a camp of Matonabi's people, and here they found a little food in the way of fish and dried venison. From Island Lake they made their way in a zigzag fashion, stopping often to drive reindeer into pounds to secure large supplies of venison and of skins, till, in the month of April, 1771, they reached a small lake with an almost unpronounceable name, which meant "Little Fish Hill", from a high hill which stood at the west end of this sheet of water.

On an island in this lake they pitched their tents, as deer were very numerous. During this time also they were busily employed in preparing staves of birch wood, about seven or eight feet long, to serve as tent poles in the summer, and in the winter to be converted into snow-shoe frames. Here also Chief Matonabi purchased another wife. He had now with him no less than seven, most of whom would for size have made good grenadiers. He prided himself much on the height and strength of his wives, and would frequently say few women could carry off heavier loads. In fact in this country wives were very seldom selected for their beauty, but rather for their strength.

"Ask a Northern Indian," wrote Hearne, "What is beauty?' He will answer: 'A broad, flat face, small eyes, high cheekbones, three or four broad black lines across each cheek, a low forehead, a broad chin, a clumsy hook nose, and a tawny hide.'"

But the model woman amongst these Indians was one who was capable of dressing all kinds of skins and making them into clothing, and who was strong enough to carry a load of about a hundred pounds in weight in summer, and to haul perhaps double that weight on a sledge in winter. "As to their temper, it is of little consequence; for the men have a wonderful facility in making the most stubborn comply with as much alacrity as could possibly be expected." When the men kill any large beast the women are always sent to bring it to the tent. When it

SAMUEL HEARNE

c 212

ALEXANDER MACKENZIE

is brought there, every operation it undergoes, such as splitting, drying, pounding, is performed by the women. When anything is prepared for eating it is the women who cook it; and when it is done, not even the wives and daughters of the greatest chiefs in the country are served until all the males—even the male slaves—have eaten what they think proper. In times of scarcity it was frequently the lot of the women to be left without a single mouthful; though, no doubt, they took good care to help themselves in secret.

Hearne mentions that in this country among the Northern Indians the names of the boys were various and generally derived from some place, or season of the year, or animal; whilst the names of the girls were chiefly taken from some part or property of a marten,[1] such as the white marten, the black marten, the summer marten, the marten's head, foot, heart, or tail.

From the Lake of Little Fish Hill the party moved on to Lake Clowey, and here the Northern Indians set to work to build their canoes in the warm and dry weather, which was about to come in at the end of May. These canoes were very slight and simple in construction and wonderfully light, which was necessary, for some of the northern portages might be a hundred to one hundred and fifty miles in length, over which the canoes would have to be carried by the Indians. All the tools employed in those days, in building such canoes and making snowshoes and all the other furniture and utensils of Indian life, consisted of a *hatchet*, a *knife*, a *file*, and an *awl* obtained from the stores of the Hudson's Bay Company. In the use of these tools they were so dexterous that everything they manufactured was done with a neatness which could not be excelled by the most expert mechanic. These northern canoes were flat-bottomed, with straight, upright sides, and sharp prow and peak. The stern part of the

[1] A fur-bearing animal (*Mustèla americana*), very like the British pine marten.

canoe was wider than the rest in order to receive the baggage. The average length of the canoe would be from twelve to thirteen feet, and the breadth in the widest part about two feet. Generally but a single paddle was used, and that rather attenuated. When transporting the canoes from one river to another, a strong band of bark or fibre would be fastened round the thwarts of the canoe, and then slung over the breast and shoulders of the Indian that was carrying it.

From Lake Clowey the northern progress was made on foot, steady and fatiguing walking over the barren grounds. The wooded region had been left behind to the south; but for a distance of about twenty miles outside the living woods there was a belt of dry stumps more or less ancient. According to Hearne, these vestiges of trees to the north of the present forest limit were an indication that the climate had grown colder during the seventeenth and eighteenth centuries, because, according to the traditions of the Indians and the remembrances of their old people, the forest had formerly extended much farther to the north.

Whilst they were staying for the canoe building at Lake Clowey, Hearne was a great deal bothered by the domestic troubles of his Indian friend Matonabi. This man had been constantly trying to add to his stock of wives as he passed up country, and at Clowey he had met the former husband of one of these women whom he had carried off by force. The man ventured to reproach him, whereupon Matonabi went into his tent, opened one of his wives' bundles, and with the greatest composure took out a new, long, box-handled knife; then proceeded to the tent of the man who had complained, and without any parley whatever took him by the collar and attempted to stab him to death. The man had already received three bad knife wounds in the back before other people, rushing in to his assistance, prevented Matonabi from finishing him. After this, Matonabi returned to his tent as though nothing had happened, called for water, washed the blood off his hands and knife, and smoked his pipe as usual, asking Hearne if he did not think he had done quite right!

"It has ever been the custom among those people for the men to wrestle for any woman to whom they are attached; and of course the strongest party always carries off the prize. A weak man, unless he be a good hunter and well beloved, is seldom permitted to keep a wife that a stronger man thinks worth his notice; for at any time when the wives of those strong wrestlers are heavy laden either with furs or provisions, they make no scruple of tearing any other man's wife from his bosom and making her bear a part of his luggage. This custom prevails throughout all their tribes, and causes a great spirit of emulation among their youth, who are upon all occasions, from their childhood, trying their strength and skill in wrestling. This enables them to protect their property, and particularly their wives, from the hands of those powerful ravishers, some of whom make almost a livelihood by taking what they please from the weaker parties without making them any return. Indeed it is represented as an act of great generosity if they condescend to make an unequal exchange, as, in general, abuse and insult are the only return for the loss which is sustained.

"The way in which they tear the women and other property from one another, though it has the appearance of the greatest brutality, can scarcely be called fighting. I never knew any of them receive the least hurt in these *rencontres*; the whole business consists in hauling each other about by the hair of the head; they are seldom known either to strike or kick one another. It is not uncommon for one of them to cut off his hair and to grease his ears immediately before the contest begins. This, however, is done privately; and it is sometimes truly laughable to see one of the parties stiutting about with an air of great importance, and calling out: 'Where is he? Why does he not come out?' when the other will bolt out with a clean-shorn head and greased ears, rush on his antagonist, seize him by the hair, and, though perhaps a much weaker man, soon drag him to the ground, while the stronger is not able to lay hold of him. It is very frequent on those occasions for each party to have spies, to watch the other's motions, which puts them more on a footing of equality. For want of hair to pull, they seize each other about the waist, with legs wide extended, and try their strength by endeavouring to vie who can first throw the other down."

"Early in the morning of the twenty-ninth 'Captain' Keelshies (an Indian) joined us. He delivered to me a packet of letters and a two-quart keg of French brandy, but assured me that the powder, shot, tobacco, knives, &c., which he received at the fort for me, were all expended. He endeavoured to make some apology for this by saying that some of his relations died in the winter, and that he had, according to native custom, thrown all his own things away; after which he was obliged to have recourse to my ammunition and other goods to support himself and a numerous family. The very affecting manner in which he related this story, often crying like a child, was a great proof of his extreme sorrow, which he wished to persuade me arose from the recollection of his having embezzled so much of my property; but I was of a different opinion, and attributed his grief to arise from the remembrance of his deceased relations. However, as a small recompense for my loss, he presented me with four ready-dressed moose skins, which was, he said, the only retribution he could then make. The moose skins, though not the twentieth part of the value of the goods which he had embezzled, were in reality more acceptable to me than the ammunition and the other articles would have been, on account of their great use as shoe leather, which at that time was a very scarce article with us, whereas we had plenty of powder and shot."

During Hearne's stay at Lake Clowey a great number of Indians entered into a combination with those of his party to travel together to the Coppermine River, with no other intent than to murder the Eskimo who frequented that river in considerable numbers. Before leaving Lake Clowey all the Northern Indians who had assembled there prepared their arms for the encounter, and did not forget to make shields before they left the woods of Clowey. These shields were composed of thin boards about three-quarters of an inch thick, two feet broad, and three feet long, and were intended to ward off the arrows of the Eskimo.

When the now large expedition reached a river with the fearful name of Congecathawhachaga, they found a portion of the tribe known as Copper Indians,[1] and these had never before seen a white man. They gave a very friendly reception to Hearne on account of Matonabi.

"They expressed as much desire to examine me from top to toe as a European naturalist would a nondescript animal. They, however, found and pronounced me to be a perfect human being, except in the colour of my hair and eyes; the former, they said, was like the stained hair of a buffalo's tail, and the latter, being light, were like those of a gull. The whiteness of my skin also was, in their opinion, no ornament, as they said it resembled meat which had been sodden in water till all the blood was extracted. On the whole I was viewed as so great a curiosity in this part of the world that during my stay there, whenever I combed my head, some or other of them never failed to ask for the hairs that came off, which they carefully wrapped up, saying: 'When I see you again, you shall again see your hair'."

[1] Or "Tantsawhûts". Like the "Dog-rib" Indians, mentioned farther on, they belonged to the "Northern", Tinné, Athabaskan type.

The Copper Indians sent a detachment of their men in the double capacity of guides and warriors, and the whole party now turned towards the north-west, and after some days' walking reached the Stony Mountains. "Surely no part of the world better deserves that name", wrote Hearne. They appeared to be a confused heap of stones quite inaccessible to the foot of man. Nevertheless, with the Copper Indians as guides, they got over this range, though not without being obliged frequently to crawl on hands and knees. This range, however, had been so often crossed by Indians coming to and fro that there was a very visible path the whole way, the rocks, even in the most difficult places, being worn quite smooth. By the side of the path there were several large, flat stones covered with thousands of small pebbles. These marks had been gradually built up by passengers going to and fro from the copper mines in the far north. The weather all this time, although the month was July, was very bad—constant snow, sleet, and rain. Hearne seldom had a dry garment of any kind, and in the caves where they lodged at night the water was constantly dropping from the roof. Their food all this time was raw venison. One snowstorm which fell on them was heavier than was customary even in the winter, but at last the weather cleared up and sunshine made the journey far more tolerable.

As they descended the northern side of the Stony Mountains they crossed a large lake, passing over its unmelted ice, and called it Musk-ox Lake, from the number of these creatures which they found grazing on the margin of it.

This was not the first time that Hearne had seen the musk ox. These animals were wont to come down as far south as the shores of Hudson Bay.

On the northern side of the Stony Mountains Hearne was taken by the Indians to see a place which he called Grizzly-bear Hill, which took its name from the numbers of those animals (presumably what we call grizzly bears) which resorted here for the purpose of bringing forth their young in a cave in this hill. On the east side of the adjoining marsh Hearne was amazed at the sight of the many hills and dry ridges, which were turned over like ploughed land by the long claws of these bears in searching for the ground squirrels and mice which constitute a favourite part of their food. It was surprising to see the enormous stones rolled out of their beds by the bears on these occasions.

As they neared the Coppermine River the weather became very warm, and the country had a good supply of firewood. Reindeer were abundant, and, the Indians having killed some of these, Hearne sat down to the most comfortable meal he had had for some months.

It was a kind of haggis, called by the Amerindians "biati", made with the blood of the reindeer, a good quantity of fat shredded small, some of the tenderest of the flesh, together with the heart and lungs, cut, or more commonly torn, into small slivers—all which would be put into the stomach, and roasted by being suspended before the fire by a string. Care had to be taken that it did not get too much heat at first, as the bag would thereby be liable to be burnt and the contents be let out. When it was sufficiently done it emitted steam, "which", writes Hearne, "is as much as to say: 'Come, eat me now'; and if it be taken in time, before the blood and other contents are too much done, it is certainly a most delicious morsel, even without pepper, salt, or any other seasoning."

It was now almost impossible to sleep at night for the mosquitoes, which swarmed in myriads as soon as the warmth of the sun melted the ice and snow. When Hearne actually reached the banks of the Coppermine River he was a little disappointed at its appearance, as it seemed to be only one hundred and eighty yards wide, shallow, and full of shoals. The Chipewayan Amerindians with him now sent out their spies to try and locate the Eskimo. Presently they found that there were five tents of them on the west side of the river.

"When the Indians received this intelligence no further attendance or attention was paid to my survey, but their whole thoughts were immediately engaged in planning the best method of attack, and how they might steal on the poor Eskimo the ensuing night and kill them all when asleep. To accomplish this bloody design more effectually the Indians thought it necessary to cross the river as soon as possible; and, by the account of the spies, it appeared that no part was more convenient for the purpose than that where we had met them, it being there very smooth, and at a considerable distance from any fall. Accordingly, after the Indians had put all their guns, spears, shields, &c., in good order, we crossed the river. . . .

"When we arrived on the west side of the river, each painted the front of his shield; some with the figure of the sun, others with that of the moon, several with different kinds of birds and beasts of prey, and many with the images of imaginary beings, which, according to their silly notions, are the inhabitants of the different elements, Earth, Sea, Air, &c. On enquiring the reason of their doing so, I learned that each man painted his shield with the image of that being on which he relied most for success in the intended engagement. Some were content with a single representation; while others, doubtful, as I suppose, of the quality and power of any single being, had their shields covered to the very margin with a group of hieroglyphics quite unintelligible to everyone except the painter. Indeed, from the hurry in which this business was necessarily done, the want of every colour but red and black, and the deficiency of skill in the artist, most of those paintings had more the appearance of a number of accidental blotches, than 'of anything that is on the earth, or in the water under the earth'. . . .

"After this piece of superstition was completed, we began to advance towards the Eskimo tents; but were very careful to avoid crossing any hills, or talking loud, for fear of being seen or overheard by the inhabitants."

When the attacking party was within two hundred yards of the Eskimo tents, they lay in ambush for some time, watching the motions of their intended victims; and here the Indians wanted Hearne (for whom they had a sincere affection) to stay till the fight was over; but to this he would not consent, lest, when the Eskimo came to be surprised, they should try every way to escape, and, finding him alone, kill him in their desperation.

While they lay in ambush the Northern Indians performed the last ceremonies which were thought necessary before the engagement. These chiefly consisted in painting their faces: some all black, some all red, and others with a mixture of the two; and to prevent their hair from blowing into their eyes, it was either tied before or behind, and on both sides, or else cut short all round. The next thing they considered was to make themselves as light as possible for running, which they did by pulling off their stockings, and either cutting off the sleeves of their jackets, or rolling them up close to their armpits; and though the mosquitoes at that time "were so numerous as to surpass all credibility", yet some of the Indians actually pulled off their jackets and entered the lists nearly or quite naked. Hearne, fearing he might have occasion to run with the rest, thought it also advisable to pull off his stockings and cap, and to tie his hair as close up as possible.

By the time the Indians had made themselves thus "completely frightful", it was nearly one in the morning. Then, finding all the Eskimo quiet in their tents, they rushed forth from their ambuscade, and fell on the poor, unsuspecting creatures, unperceived till they were close to the very eaves of the tents. A horrible massacre forthwith took place, while Hearne stood neutral in the rear.

"The scene was shocking beyond description. The poor unhappy victims were surprised in the midst of their sleep, and had neither time nor power to make any resistance; men, women, and children, in all upward of twenty, ran out of their tents stark naked, and endeavoured to make their escape; but the Indians having possession of all the landside, to no place could they fly for shelter. One alternative only remained, that of jumping into the river; but, as none of them attempted it, they all fell a sacrifice to Indian barbarity!

"The shrieks and groans of the poor expiring wretches were truly dreadful; and my horror was much increased at seeing a young girl, seemingly about eighteen years of age, killed so near me, that when the first spear was stuck into her side she fell down at my feet, and twisted round my legs, so that it was with difficulty that I could disengage myself from her dying grasp. As two Indian men pursued this unfortunate victim, I solicited very hard for her life; but the murderers made no reply till they had stuck both their spears through her body, and transfixed her to the ground. They then looked me sternly in the face, and began to ridicule me by asking if I wanted an Eskimo wife; and paid not the smallest regard to the shrieks and agony of the poor wretch, who was twining round their spears like an eel!"

On his requesting that they would at least put the woman out of her misery, one of the Indians hastily drew his spear from the place where it was first lodged, and pierced it through her breast near the heart. The love of life, however, even in this most miserable state, was so predominant, that "though this might justly be called the most merciful act that could be done for the poor creature, it seemed to be unwelcome, for, though much exhausted by pain and loss of blood, she made several efforts to ward off the friendly blow." . . . "My own situation and the terror of my mind at beholding this butchery, cannot easily be conceived, much less described; though I summed up all the fortitude I was master of on the occasion, it was with difficulty that I could refrain from tears; and I am confident that my features must have feelingly expressed how sincerely I was affected at the barbarous scene I then witnessed; even at this hour I cannot reflect on the transactions of that horrid day without shedding tears."

There were other Eskimo on the opposite shore of the river. Though they took up their arms to defend themselves, they did not attempt to abandon their tents, for they were utterly unacquainted with the nature of firearms; so much so that when the bullets struck the ground, they ran in crowds to see what was sent them, and seemed anxious to examine all the pieces of lead which they found flattened against the rocks. At length one of the Eskimo men was shot in the calf of his leg, which put them in great confusion. They all immediately embarked in their little canoes, and paddled to a shoal in the middle of the river, which being somewhat more than a gunshot from any part of the shore, put them out of the reach of our barbarians.

"When the savages discovered that the surviving Eskimo had gained the shore above-mentioned, the Northern Indians began to plunder the tents of the deceased of all the copper utensils they could find; such as hatchets, bayonets, knives, &c., after which they assembled on the top of an adjacent hill, and, standing all in a cluster, so as to form a solid circle, with their spears erect in the air, gave many shouts of victory, constantly clashing their spears against each other, and frequently calling out *tima! tima!*[1] by way of derision to the poor surviving Eskimo, who were standing on the shoal almost knee deep in water."

"It ought to have been mentioned in its proper place,"

[1] "*Tima* in the Eskimo language is a friendly word similar to *what cheer?*"—Hearne.

writes Hearne, after describing further atrocities, "that in making our retreat up the river, after killing the Eskimo on the west side, we saw an old woman sitting by the side of the water killing salmon, which lay at the foot of the fall as thick as a shoal of herrings. Whether from the noise of the fall, or a natural defect in the old woman's hearing, it is hard to determine, but certain it is, she had no knowledge of the tragical scene which had been so lately transacted at the tents, though she was not more than two hundred yards from the place. When we first perceived her she seemed perfectly at ease, and was entirely surrounded with the produce of her labour. From her manner of behaviour, and the appearance of her eyes, which were as red as blood, it is more than probable that her sight was not very good; for she scarcely discerned that the Indians were enemies, till they were within twice the length of their spears of her. It was in vain that she attempted to fly, for the wretches of my crew transfixed her to the ground in a few seconds, and butchered her in the most savage manner. There was scarcely a man among them who had not a thrust at her with his spear; and many in doing this aimed at torture rather than immediate death, as they not only poked out her eyes, but stabbed her in many parts very remote from those which are vital.

"It may appear strange that a person supposed to be almost blind should be employed in the business of fishing, and particularly with any degree of success; but when the multitude of the fish is taken into the account, the wonder will cease. Indeed they were so numerous at the foot of the fall, that when a light pole, armed with a few spikes, which was the instrument the old woman used, was put under water, and hauled up with a jerk, it was scarcely possible to miss them. Some of my Indians tried the method, for curiosity, with the old woman's staff, and seldom got less than two at a jerk, sometimes three or four. Those fish, though very fine, and beautifully red, are but small, seldom weighing more (as near as I could judge) than six or seven pounds, and in general much less. Their numbers at this place were almost incredible, perhaps equal to anything that is related of the salmon in Kamschatka, or any other part of the world."

Hearne seems to have been so intent on geographical discovery that he did not allow his feelings to influence him very long against the society of his Amerindian companions, who apparently sat down and ate a dish of salmon with him an hour or so after they had killed this last old woman! The Indians now told him that they were ready again to assist him in making an end of his survey, and apparently on foot, for the Coppermine River was not navigable here, even for a boat.

Thus, first of all white men coming overland, he reached the sea coast of the Arctic Ocean. The tide was then out, and a good deal of the sea surface was covered with ice, on which he observed many seals lying about. Along the sea coast and river banks were many birds; gulls, divers or loons, golden plovers, green plovers, curlews, geese, and swans. The country a little way inland was obviously inhabited by numbers of musk oxen, reindeer, bears, wolves, gluttons, foxes, polar hares, snowy owls, ravens, ptarmigans, gopher ground-squirrels, stoats (ermines), and mice. In this region also he saw a bird which the Copper Indians called the Alarm Bird. He tells us that in size and colour it resembles a "Cobadekoock"; but as none of us know what that is, we can only go on to imagine that the Alarm Bird was a kind of owl, as Hearne says it was "of the owl genus". When it perceived people or beasts it directed its way towards them immediately, and, after hovering over them for some time, flew over them in circles or went away with them in the same direction as they walked. All this time the bird made a loud screaming noise like the cry of a child. These owls were sometimes accustomed to follow the Indians for a whole day, and the Copper Indians believed that they would in some way conduct them to herds of deer and musk oxen, which without the birds' assistance might never be found. They also warned Indians of the arrival of strangers. The Eskimo, according to Hearne, paid no heed to these birds, and it was thus that they allowed themselves to be surprised and massacred, for if they had looked out from the direction in which the Chipewayans were lying in ambush, they would have seen a large flock of these owls continually flying about and making sufficient noise to awaken any man out of the soundest sleep.

The country on either side of the estuary of the Coppermine River was not without vegetation. There were stunted pines and tufts of dwarf willows, and the ground was covered with a lichen or herb, which the English of the Hudson's Bay Company knew by the name of Wishakapaka,[1] and which they dried and used instead of tea. There were also cranberry and heathberry bushes, but without fruit. The scrub grew gradually thinner and smaller as one approached the sea, and at the mouth of the river there was nothing but barren hills and marsh.

The unfortunate Eskimo of this region, judging by the examples seen by Hearne, were of low stature, with broad thickset bodies. Their complexion was a dirty copper colour, but some of the women were almost fair and ruddy. Their dress, their arms and fishing tackle were precisely similar to those of the Greenland Eskimo. Their tents were made of deerskins, and were pitched in a circular form. But these were only their summer habitations, those for the winter being partly underground, with a roof framework of poles, over which skins were stretched; and of course Nature did the rest, covering the roof with

[1] *Ledum palustre.*

several feet of snow. Owing to being almost entirely surrounded by snow, these winter houses were very warm. Their household furniture consisted of stone kettles and wooden troughs of various sizes, also dishes, scoops, and spoons made of musk-ox horns. The stone kettles (which some people think they borrowed from the Norse discoverers of America in the eleventh century) were as large as to be capable of containing five or six gallons. They were, of course, carved out of solid blocks of stone, every one of them being ornamented with neat moulding round the rims, and some of the large ones with fluted work at each corner. In shape they were oblong, wider at the top than the bottom, and strong handles of solid stone were left at each end to lift them up.

The Eskimo hatchets were made of a thick lump of copper about five or six inches long, and one and a half to two inches broad. They were bevelled away at one end like a chisel. This piece of copper was lashed into the end of a piece of wood about twelve or fourteen inches long. The men's daggers and the women's knives were also made of copper. The former were in shape like the ace of spades, and the handle was made of reindeer antler.

With the Eskimo was a fine breed of dogs, with erect ears, sharp noses, bushy tails. They were all tethered to stones to prevent them from eating the flesh that was spread all over the rocks to dry. Apparently, these beautiful dogs were left behind still tethered by the wicked Amerindians, after the massacre of their owners. Hearne, however, noticed with these Coppermine River Eskimo that the men were entirely bald, having all their head hair pulled out by the roots. The women wore their hair at the usual length.

Before leaving this region to return southwards, Hearne was led by the Indians to one of the copper mines about thirty miles south-east of the river mouth. It was no more than a jumble of rocks and gravel, which had been rent in many ways, apparently by an earthquake shock. This mine was at the time of Hearne's visit very poor in copper, much of the metal having already been removed.

The Copper Indians set a great value on this native metal even at the present day, and prefer it to iron for almost every use except that of a hatchet, a knife, and an awl. "For these three necessary implements", writes Hearne, "copper makes but a very poor substitute."

On the return journey, in the course of which the Great Slave Lake—which Hearne calls "Lake Athapuscow"—was discovered and crossed on the ice, the party travelled so hard and stayed so seldom to rest that Hearne suffered terribly with his legs and feet. "I had so little power to direct my feet when walking, that I frequently knocked them against the stones with such force, as not only to jar and disorder them, but my legs also; and the nails of my toes were bruised to such a degree, that several of them festered and dropped off. To add to this mishap, the skin was entirely chafed off from the tops of both my feet, and between every toe; so that the sand and gravel, which I could by no means exclude, irritated the raw parts so much, that for a whole day before we arrived at the women's tents, I left the print of my feet in blood almost at every step I took. Several of the Indians began to complain that their feet also were sore; but, on examination, not one of them was the twentieth part in so bad a state as mine. This being the first time I had been in such a situation, or seen anybody foot-foundered, I was much alarmed, and under great apprehensions for the consequences. Though I was but little fatigued in body, yet the excruciating pain I suffered when walking had such an effect on my spirits, that if the Indians had continued to travel two or three days longer at that unmerciful rate, I must unavoidably have been left behind; for my feet were in many places quite honeycombed by the dirt and gravel eating into the raw flesh."

"Among the various superstitious customs of those people, it is worth remarking, and ought to have been mentioned in its proper place, that immediately after my companions had killed the Eskimo at the Copper River, they considered themselves in a state of uncleanness, which induced them to practise some very curious unusual ceremonies. In the first place, all who were absolutely concerned in the murder were prohibited from cooking any kind of victuals, either for themselves or others. As luckily there were two in company who had not shed blood, they were employed always as cooks till we joined the women. This circumstance was exceedingly favourable on my side; for had there been no persons of the above description in company, that task, I was told, would have fallen on me; which would have been no less fatiguing and troublesome, than humiliating and vexatious.

"When the victuals were cooked, all the murderers took a kind of red earth, or ochre, and painted all the space between the nose and chin, as well as the greater part of their cheeks, almost to the ears, before they would taste a bit, and would not drink out of any other dish, or smoke out of any other pipe, but their own; and none of the others seemed willing to drink or smoke out of theirs."

He goes on to relate that they practised the custom of painting the mouth and part of the cheeks before each meal, and drinking and smoking out of their own utensils, till the winter began to set in, and during the whole of that time they would never kiss any of their wives or children. They refrained also from eating many parts of the deer and other animals, particularly the head, entrails, and blood; and during their "uncleanness" their food was never cooked in water, but dried in the sun, eaten quite raw, or broiled. When the time arrived that was to put an end to these ceremonies, the men, without a female being present, made a fire at some distance from the tents, into which they threw all their ornaments, pipe stems, and dishes, which were soon consumed to ashes; after which a feast was prepared, consisting of such articles as they had long been prohibited from eating, and when all was over each man was at liberty to eat, drink, and smoke as he pleased, "and also to kiss his wives and children at discretion, which they seemed to do with more raptures than I had ever known them to do it either before or since".

On the 11th of January, as some of Hearne's companions were hunting, they saw the track of a strange snowshoe, which they followed, and at a considerable distance came to a little hut, where they discovered a young woman sitting alone. As they found that she understood their language, they brought her with them to the tents. On examination she proved to be one of the Western Dog-rib Indians, who had been taken prisoner by the Athapaska Indians in the summer of 1770. From these, in the following summer, she had escaped, with the intention of returning to her own country, but the distance being so great, and the way being unknown to her, she forgot the track, so she built the hut in which they found her, to protect her from the weather during the winter, and here she had resided from the first setting in of the cold weather. For seven months she had seen no human face. During all this time she had supported herself in comparative comfort by snaring grouse, rabbits, and squirrels; she had also killed two or three beaver, and some porcupines. That she did not seem to have been in want was evident, as she had a small stock of provisions by her when she was discovered, and was in good health and condition; and Hearne thought her "one of the finest women", of the real Indian type, that he had seen in any part of North America.

"The methods practised by this poor creature to procure a livelihood were truly admirable, and are great proofs that necessity is the real mother of invention. When the few deer sinews that she had an opportunity of taking with her were all expended in making snares and sewing her clothing, she had nothing to supply their place but the sinews of the rabbits' [he means hares'] legs and feet; these she twisted together for that purpose with great dexterity and success. The rabbits, &c., which she caught in those snares, not only furnished her with a comfortable subsistence, but of the skins she made a suit of neat and warm clothing for the winter. It is scarcely possible to conceive that a person in her forlorn situation could be so composed as to be capable of contriving or executing anything that was not absolutely necessary to her existence; but there were sufficient proofs that she had extended her care much farther, as all her clothing, beside being calculated for real service, showed great taste and exhibited no little variety of ornament. The materials, though rude, were very curiously wrought and so judiciously placed as to make the whole of her garb have a very pleasing, though rather romantic, appearance.

"Her leisure hours from hunting had been employed in twisting the inner rind or bark of willows into small lines, like net twine, of which she had some hundred fathoms by her; with this she intended to make a fishing net as soon as the spring advanced. It is of the inner bark of willows, twisted in this manner, that the Dog-rib Indians make their fishing nets, and they are much preferable to those made by the Northern Indians.

"Five or six inches of an iron hoop, made into a knife, and the shank of an arrowhead of iron, which served her as an awl, were all the metals this poor woman had with her when she eloped, and with these implements she had made herself complete snowshoes, and several other useful articles.

"Her method of making a fire was equally singular

and curious, having no other materials for that purpose than two hard sulphurous stones. These, by long friction and hard knocking, produced a few sparks, which at length communicated to some touchwood (a species of fungus which grew on decayed poplars); but as this method was attended with great trouble, and not always with success, she did not suffer her fire to go out all the winter. . . ."

Hearne regained Prince of Wales's Fort on Hudson Bay in June, 1772. Subsequently he was dispatched, in the year 1774, to found the first great inland trading station and fort of the Hudson's Bay Company which was established at any considerable distance westward of Hudson Bay—the first step, in fact, which led to this chartered company becoming in time the ruler and colonizing agent of Alberta and British Columbia. Hearne chose for his station of "Cumberland House" a site at the entrance to Pine Island Lake on the lower Saskatchewan River.

In 1775 he became Governor of his old starting-point on Hudson Bay—Fort Prince of Wales. During the American war with France, the French admiral, La Pérouse, made a daring excursion into Hudson Bay (1782), and summoned Hearne to surrender his fort. This he felt obliged to do, not deeming his small garrison strong enough to resist the French force.

Samuel Hearne returned to England in 1787, and died (probably in London) in 1792.

# CHAPTER XI

## Alexander Mackenzie's Journeys

It has been already mentioned that the conquest of Canada by the British led to a great increase in travel for the development of the fur trade. Previously, under the French, permission was only granted to a few persons to penetrate into the interior to trade with the natives, commerce being regarded as a special privilege or monopoly to be sold or granted by the Crown. But after the British had completely assumed control, nothing was done to bar access to the interior. So long as the Catholic missionaries had been practically placed in charge of the Amerindians, and had served as buffers between them and unscrupulous traders, they—the Amerindians—had been saved from two scourges, smallpox and strong drink.[1] But now, unhappily, all restrictions about trade in alcohol were removed. In their eagerness to obtain ardent spirits and "high" wine, the Indians eagerly welcomed British traders and French Canadians in their midst. The fur trade developed fast. The Hudson's Bay Company had established its trading stations only in the vicinity or on the coasts of that inland sea, far away from the two Canadas, from the Middle West and the vast North West. After a little reluctance and suspicion, most of the northern Amerindian tribes were persuaded to deflect their caravans from the routes leading to Hudson Bay, and to meet the British, the New Englander ("Bostonian"), and the French Canadian traders at various rendezvous on

[1] See Sir Alexander Mackenzie's *Travels*, p. 5.

Lake Winnipeg and its tributary lakes and rivers. The principal depot and starting-point for the north-west traders was *Grand Portage*, on the north-west coast of Lake Superior, whence canoes and goods were transferred by a nine-mile portage to the waters flowing to Rainy Lake, and so onwards to the Winnipeg River and the vast system of the Saskatchewan, the Red River, and the Assiniboine.

Amongst the pioneers in this new development of the fur trade, who became also the great explorers of northernmost America, was Alexander Henry (already described), THOMAS CURRIE, JAMES FINLAY, PETER POND,[1] JOSEPH and BENJAMIN FROBISHER, and SIMON M'TAVISH. These and some of their supporting merchants in Montreal resolved to form a great fur-trading association, the celebrated North-west Trading Company, and did so in 1784.

Two of the Montreal merchant firms participating in this confederation (Gregory and M'Leod) were inclined to play a somewhat independent part, and called themselves the New North-west Trading Company. They had the foresight to engage as their principal agents in the north-west (Sir) ALEXANDER MACKENZIE and his cousin RODERICK MACKENZIE. Both these young men were Highlanders, probably of Norse origin. Alexander Mackenzie was born at Stornoway, in the Island of Lewis (Hebrides), in 1763. He was only sixteen when he started for Canada to take up a position as clerk in the partnership concern of Gregory & M'Leod at Montreal.

It may be said here briefly that this "New North-west Company" went at first by the nickname of "The Little Company" or "The Potties", this last being an Amerindian corruption of the French *Les Petits*. Later it developed into the "X. Y. Company", or "Sir Alexander

[1] Peter Pond was a native of Connecticut, and in the opinion of his trading associates rather a ruffian. He was strongly suspected of having murdered an amiable Swiss fur trader named Wadin, and at a later date he actually did kill his trading partner, Ross.

Mackenzie & Co.". Although much in rivalry with the original "Nor'-westers", the rivalry never degenerated into the actual warfare, the indefensible deeds of violence and treachery, which later on were perpetrated by the Hudson's Bay Company on the agents of the North-west, and returned with interest by the latter. Often the New North-west agents and the original Nor'-westers would camp or build side by side, and share equably in the fur trade with the natives; their canoemen and French-Canadian *voyageurs* would sing their boating songs in chorus as they paddled side by side across the lakes and down the rivers, or marched with their heavy loads over the portages and along the trails. Eventually, in 1804, the X. Y. Company and the North-west fused into the North-west Trading Company, which until 1821 fought a hard fight against the encroachments and jealousy of the Hudson's Bay Company.

During the period, however, from 1785 to 1812 the men of the north-west, of Montreal, and Grand Portage (as contrasted with those of Hudson Bay) effected a revolution in Canadian geography. They played the rôle of imperial pioneers with a stubborn heroism, with little thought of personal gain, and in most cases with full foreknowledge and appreciation of what would accrue to the British Empire through their success. It is impossible to relate the adventures of all of them within the space of any one book, or even of several volumes. Moreover, this has been done already, not only in their own published journals and books, but in the admirable works of Elliot Coues, Dr. George Bryce, Dr. S. J. Dawson, Alexander Ross, and others. I must confine myself here to a description of the adventures of Sir Alexander Mackenzie, with a glance at incidents recorded by Simon Fraser and by Alexander Henry the Younger.

Mackenzie, having been appointed at the age of twenty-two a partner in the New North-west Company, proceeded to Grand Portage in 1785, and by the year 1788 (after founding Fort Chipewayan on Lake Athabaska) conceived the idea of following the mysterious Slave River to its ultimate outlet into the Arctic or the Pacific Ocean. He left Fort Chipewayan on June 3, 1789, accompanied by four French-Canadian *voyageurs*, two French-Canadian women (wives of two *voyageurs*), a young German named John Steinbruck, and an Amerindian guide known as "English Chief". This last was a follower and pupil of the Matonabi who had guided Hearne to the Coppermine River and the eastern end of the Great Slave Lake. The party of eight whites packed themselves and their goods into one birch-bark canoe. English Chief and his two wives, together with an additional Amerindian guide and a hunter, travelled in a second and smaller canoe. The expedition, moreover, was accompanied as far as Slave River by LE ROUX, a celebrated French-Canadian exploring trader who worked for the X. Y. Company. The journey down the Slave River was rendered difficult and dangerous by the rapids. Several times the canoes and their loads had to be lugged past these falls by an overland portage. Mosquitoes tortured the whole party almost past bearance. The leaders of the expedition and their Indian hunter had to be busily engaged (the Indian women also) in hunting and fishing in order to get food for the support of the party, who seemed to have had little reserve provisions with them. Pemmican was made of fish dried in the sun and rubbed to powder. Swans, geese, cranes, and ducks fell to the guns; an occasional beaver was also added to the pot. When they reached the Great Slave Lake they found its islands—notwithstanding their barren appearance—covered with bushes producing a great variety of palatable fruits—cranberries, juniper berries, raspberries, partridge berries, gooseberries, and the "pathogomenan", a fruit like a raspberry.

Slave Lake, however, was still, in mid-June, under the spell of winter, its surface obstructed with drifting ice. In attempting to cross the lake the frail birch-bark canoes ran a great risk of being crushed between the ice floes. However, at length, after halting at several islands and leaving Le Roux to go to the trading station he had founded on the shores of Slave Lake, Mackenzie and his two canoes found their way to the river outlet of Slave Lake, that river which was henceforth to be called by his name. Great mountains approached near to the west of their course. They appeared to be sprinkled with white stones, called by the natives "spirit stones"—indeed over a great part of North America the Rocky Mountains were called "the Mountains of Bright Stones"—yet these brilliant patches were nothing more wonderful than unmelted snow.

A few days later the party encountered Amerindians of the Slave and Dog-rib tribes, who were so aloof from even "Indian" civilization that they did not know the use of tobacco, and were still in the Stone Age as regards their weapons and implements. These people, though they furnished a guide, foretold disaster and famine to the expedition, and greatly exaggerated the obstacles which would be met with—rapids near the entrance of the tributary from Great Bear Lake—before the salt water was reached.

The canoes of these Slave and Dog-rib tribes of the Athapaskan (Tinné) group were covered, not with birch bark, but with the bark of the spruce fir.

The lodges of the Slave Indians were of very simple structure: a few poles supported by a fork and forming a semicircle at the bottom, with some branches or a piece of bark as a covering. They built two of these huts facing each other, and made a fire between them. The furniture consisted of a few dishes of wood, bark, or horn. The vessels in which they cooked their victuals were in the shape of a gourd, narrow at the top and wide at the bottom, and made of *wátápé*.

This was the name given to the divided roots of the spruce fir, which the natives wove into a degree of compactness that rendered it capable of containing a fluid. Wátápé fibre was also used to sew together different parts of the bark canoes. They also made fibre or thread from willow bark. Their cooking vessels made of this wátápé not only contained water, but water which was made to boil by putting a succession of hot stones into it. It would, of course, be impossible to place these vessels of fibre on a fire, and apparently none of the Amerindians of temperate North America knew anything about pottery. Those that were in some degree in touch with the Eskimo used kettles or cauldrons of stone. Elsewhere the vessels for boiling water and cooking were made of bark or fibre, and the water therein was made to boil by the dropping in of red-hot stones. The arrows of these Slave Indians were two and a half feet long, and the barb was made of bone, horn, flint, or copper. Iron had been quite lately introduced, indirectly obtained from the Russians in Alaska. Their spears were pointed with barbed bone, and their daggers were made of horn or bone. Their great club, the *pógamagán*, was made of a reindeer's antler. Axes were manufactured out of a piece of brown or grey stone, six to eight inches long and two inches thick. They kindled fire by striking together a piece of iron pyrites and touchwood, and never travelled without a small bag containing such materials.

The Amerindians along the lower Mackenzie had heard vague and terrible legends about the Russians, far, far away on the coast of Alaska; they were represented as beings of gigantic stature, and adorned with wings; which, however, they never employed in flying (possibly the sails of their ships). They fed on large birds, and killed them with the greatest ease. They also

c 312

BIG-HORNED SHEEP OF ROCKY MOUNTAINS

possessed the extraordinary power of killing with their eyes (no doubt putting up a gun to aim), and they travelled in canoes of very large dimensions.

"I engaged one of these Indians," writes Mackenzie, "by a bribe of some beads, to describe the surrounding country upon the sand. This singular map he immediately undertook to delineate, and accordingly traced out a very long point of land between the rivers . . . which he represented as running into the great lake, at the extremity of which he had been told by Indians of other nations there was a white man's fort." The same people described plainly the Yukon River westward of the mountains, and told Mackenzie it was a far greater stream than the one he was exploring. This was the first "hint" of the existence of the great Alaskan river which was ever recorded. They also spoke to Mackenzie of "small white buffaloes" (? the mountain goat), which they found in the mountains west of the Mackenzie.

Whenever and wherever Mackenzie's party met these northernmost tribes of Athapascan Indians they were always ready to dance in between short spells of talking. This dancing and jumping was their only amusement, and in it old and young, male and female, went to such exertions that their strength was exhausted. As they jumped up and down they imitated the various noises produced by the reindeer, the bear, and the wolf.

In descending the Mackenzie River, and again on the return journey upstream, Mackenzie notices the abundance of berries on the banks of the river, especially the kind which was called "pears" by the French Canadians. These were of a purple hue, rather bigger than a pea, and of a luscious taste. There were also gooseberries and a few strawberries. Quantities of berries were collected and dried, but while on the lower Mackenzie the expedition fed mainly on fat geese. On the beach of the great river they found an abundance of a sweet fragrant root which Mackenzie calls "liquorice".

Mackenzie seemed to think that along the lower Mackenzie River, near the sea, there were not only reindeer, bears, wolverines, martens, foxes, and hares, but a species of white buffalo or white musk ox, which may have been the mountain goat above referred to. He noted, in the cliffs or banks of the lower Mackenzie, pieces of "petroleum" which bore a resemblance to yellow wax but was more friable. His Indian guide informed him that rocks of a similar kind were scattered about the country at the back of the Slave Lake, near where the Chipewayans collected copper. If so, there may be a great oilfield yet to be discovered in Arctic Canada.

On the river coming out of the Bear Lake Mackenzie discovered coal; the whole beach was strewn with it. He was attracted towards it by seeing smoke and noticing a strong sulphurous smell. The whole bank of the river was on fire for a considerable distance, and he thought this was due to the natives having camped there and set fire to the coal in the bank from their hearths. But subsequent travellers have also found this lignite coal burning to waste, and imagine that, being full of gas, it catches fire spontaneously if any landslip or other accident exposes it to moist air. In 1906 it was still burning!

According to Mackenzie, the ground in the regions about the lower reaches of the Mackenzie River is always frozen at least five inches down from the surface, yet he found small spruce trees growing in patches near the delta of this river, besides pale-yellow raspberries of an agreeable flavour, and a great variety of other plants and herbs.

As the expedition drew near to the estuary of the great Mackenzie River a range of lofty snowy mountains rose into sight on the west. These mountains were said by the natives to swarm with large bears—probably of the huge chocolate-coloured Alaska type; and again a mention was made of "small white buffaloes", which were in all probability the large white mountain goat (*Oreamnus*). The Amerindians along the river greatly magnified the dangers, predicting impassable rapids between the confluence of the Great Bear River and the sea. But these stories were greatly exaggerated. Every now and then the river would narrow and flow between white precipitous limestone walls of rock, but there was no obstacle to navigation, though it was very deep and the current fast.

The travellers now began to get within touch of the Eskimo and to hear of their occasional raids up the river from the sea. They were said to use slings, from which they flung stones with such dexterity as to prove formidable in their fights with the Amerindians, who regarded them with great respect, the more so because of their intercourse with the mysterious white people (Russians) from whom they obtained iron.

Mackenzie just managed to reach within sight of the sea, beyond the delta of the river, his most northern point being about 69° 14″ north latitude. Hence he gazed out northwards over a vast expanse of piled-up ice in which several small islands were embedded. In the spaces of open water whales were visible (the small white whale, *Beluga*). The water in between the islands was affected by the tide. The travellers had, in fact, reached the Arctic ocean. But, owing to the fickleness of their guides, and the danger of being detained by some obstacle in these northern latitudes without proper supplies for the winter, Mackenzie was afraid to stay for further investigations, and on July 16, 1789, turned his back on the sea and commenced his return journey up the stream of the great river which was henceforth to bear his name.

The strength of the current made the homeward travel

much more lengthy and tedious. The Indians of the party were troublesome, and the principal guide, English Chief, was sulky and disobedient. This man had insisted on being accompanied by two of his wives, of whom he was so morbidly jealous that he could scarcely bring himself to leave them for an hour in order to go hunting or to prospect the country; consequently he did little or nothing in the killing of game, and this kept the expedition on very small rations. Mackenzie got wroth with him, and so gave him a sound rating. This irritated English Chief to a high degree, and after a long and vehement harangue he burst into tears and loud and bitter lamentations. Thereat his friends and wives commenced crying and wailing vociferously, though they declared that their tears were shed, not for any trouble between the white man and English Chief, but because they suddenly recollected all the friends and relations they had lost within the last few years! "I did not interrupt their grief for two hours, but as I could not well do without them, I was at length obliged to sooth it and induce the chief to change his resolution (to leave me), which he did with great apparent reluctance."

Later on English Chief told Mackenzie that he feared he might have to go to war, because it was a custom amongst the Athapaskan chiefs to make war after they had given way to the disgrace attached to such a feminine weakness as shedding tears. Therefore he would undertake a warlike expedition in the following spring, but in the meantime he would continue with Mackenzie as long as he wanted him.

Mackenzie, rejoining Le Roux at the Slave Lake, safely reached his station at Fort Chipewayan on September 12, 1789, just as the approach of winter was making travel in these northern regions dangerous to those who relied on unfrozen water as a means of transit.

Mackenzie seems to have been a little disappointed with the results of his northward journey; perhaps he had thought that the outlet of Slave Lake and the Mackenzie River would be into the Pacific, the *Mer de l'Ouest* of his Canadian *voyageurs*. Yet he must have realized that he had discovered something very wonderful after all: the beginning of Alaska, the approach to a region which, though lying within the Arctic circle, has climatic conditions permitting the existence of trees, abundant vegetation, and large, strange beasts, and which, moreover, is highly mineralized. His work in this direction, however (and that of Hearne), was to be completed in the next century by SIR JOHN FRANKLIN, SIR GEORGE BACK, SIR JOHN RICHARDSON, and SIR JOHN ROSS—all knighthoods earned by magnificent services in geographical exploration—and by THOMAS SIMPSON, Dr. John Rae,[1] WARREN DEASE, JOHN M'LEOD, ROBERT CAMPBELL, and other servants of the Hudson's Bay Company.

In October, 1792, Mackenzie had determined to make a great attempt to reach the Pacific Ocean. By this time he and his colleagues had explored the Peace River (the main tributary of Slave Lake), and had realized that they could travel up it into the heart of the Rocky Mountains. He wintered and traded at a place which he called "New Establishment", on the banks of the Peace River, near the foothills of the Rocky Mountains. He left this station on May 9, 1793, accompanied by ALEXANDER MACKAY,[2] six French Canadians, and two Indian guides. They travelled up the Peace River in a twenty-five-foot canoe, and at first passed through scenery the most beautiful Mackenzie had ever beheld. He describes it as follows:—

"The ground rises at intervals to a considerable

[1] See p. 125.

[2] Alexander Mackay long afterwards left the service of the North-west Company, and was killed by savages on the Alaska coast, near Nutka Sound.

height, and stretching inwards to a considerable distance: at every interval or pause in the rise, there is a very gently ascending space or lawn, which is alternate with abrupt precipices to the summit of the whole, or at least as far as the eye could distinguish. This magnificent theatre of nature has all the decorations which the trees and animals of the country can afford it: groves of poplars in every shape vary the scene; and their intervals are enlivened with vast herds of elks and buffaloes: the former choosing the steeps and uplands and the latter preferring the plains. At this time the buffaloes were attended with their young ones, who were striking about them; and it appeared that the elks would soon exhibit the same enlivening circumstance. The whole country displayed an exuberant verdure; the trees that bear a blossom were advancing fast to that delightful appearance, and the velvet rind of their branches reflecting the oblique rays of a rising or setting sun, added a splendid gaiety to the scene which no expressions of mine are qualified to describe."

Of course, as they neared the Rocky Mountains the navigation of the Peace River became more and more difficult. At last they left the river to find their way across the mountains till they should reach the headwaters of a stream flowing towards the Pacific Ocean. Sometimes they only accomplished three miles a day, having to carry all their goods and their canoe. The mountainous country was covered with splendid forests of spruce, pine, cypress, poplar, birch, willow, and many other kinds of trees, with an undergrowth of gooseberries, currants, and briar roses. The travellers generally followed paths made by the elks,[1] just as in the dense forests of Africa the way sometimes is cleared for human travellers by the elephant. Every now and again they resumed their journey on the

[1] For the word "elk" Mackenzie uses "moose deer". "Elk" in the Canadian Dominion is misapplied to the great Wapiti red deer.

river between the falls and cascades. The mountains seemed to be a solid mass of limestone, in some places without any covering of foliage.

"In no part of the north-west", writes Mackenzie, "did I see so much beaver work" (along the eastern branch of the Peace River). In some places the beavers had cut down acres of large poplars, and were busily at work on their labours of dam-making during the night, between the setting and the rising sun.

Gnats and mosquitoes came with the intense heat of June to make life almost unbearable. As they got close to the Rocky Mountains they encountered Amerindians who had never seen a white man before, and who at first received them with demonstrations of great hostility and fright. But owing to the diplomatic skill of Mackenzie they gradually yielded to a more friendly attitude, and here he decided to camp until the natives had become familiarized with him and his party, and could give them information as to his route. But they could only tell that, away to the west beyond the mountains, a month's travel, there was a vast "lake of stinking water", to which came, for purposes of trade, other white men with vessels as big as islands.

These Rocky Mountain Indians made their canoes from spruce bark[1] in the following manner: The bark is taken off the spruce fir to the whole length of the intended canoe, only about eighteen feet, and is sewed with *wàtàpé* at both ends. Two laths are then laid across the end of the gunwale. In these are fixed the bars, and against them the ribs or timbers, that are cut to the length to which the bark can be stretched; and to give additional strength, strips of wood are laid between them. To make the whole water-tight, gum is abundantly employed.

Obtaining a guide from these people, Mackenzie continued his journey along the Parsnip, or southern branch

[1] See p. 281.

of the upper Peace River, partly by water, partly by land, till he reached its source,[1] a lake, on the banks of which he saw innumerable swans, geese, and ducks. Wild parsnips grew here in abundance, and were a grateful addition to the diet of the travellers. As to birds, they not only saw blue jays and yellow birds, but the first humming bird which Mackenzie had ever beheld in the north-west.[2]

From this tiny lake he made his way over lofty mountains to another lake at no great distance, and from this a small stream called the Bad River flowed southwards to join a still bigger stream, which Mackenzie thought might prove to be one of the branches of the mighty Columbia River that flows out into the Pacific through the State of Oregon. It really was the Fraser River, and of the upper waters of the Fraser Mackenzie was the discoverer.[3]

Their experiences down the little mountain stream which was to take them into the Fraser nearly ended in complete disaster. "The violence of the current being so great as to drive the canoe sideways down the river, and break her by the first bar, I instantly jumped into the water and the men followed my example; but before we could set her straight, or stop her, we came to deeper water, so that we were obliged to re-embark with the utmost precipitation. . . . We had hardly regained our situations when we drove against a rock which shattered the stern of the canoe in such a manner, that it held only by

[1] Mr. Burpee points out that this was really the southernmost source of the mighty congeries of streams which flowed northwards to form the Mackenzie River system. Having traced the Mackenzie to the sea, its discoverer now stood four years afterwards at its most remote source, 2420 miles from its mouth at which he had seen the ice floes and the whales.

[2] Humming birds arrive annually in British Columbia between April and May, and stay there till the autumn. They winter in the warmer parts of California.

[3] The great surveyor and map maker, David Thompson, was the first white man to reach the upper waters of the *Columbia* River. The Fraser River was afterwards followed to its outlet in the Straits of Georgia (opposite Vancouver Island) by Simon Fraser.

C 312 Photo. Thompson

THE UPPER WATERS OF THE FRASER RIVER

the gunwales, so that the steersman could no longer keep his place. The violence of this stroke drove us to the opposite side of the river, which is but narrow, when the bow met with the same fate as the stern. . . . In a few moments, we came across a cascade which broke several large holes in the bottom of the canoe, and started all the bars. . . . The wreck becoming flat on the water, we all jumped out . . . and held fast to the wreck; to which fortunate resolution we owed our safety, as we should otherwise have been dashed against the rocks by the force of the water, or driven over the cascades. . . . At length we most fortunately arrived in shallow water, and at a small eddy, where we were enabled to make a stand, from the weight of the canoe resting on the stones, rather than from any exertions of our exhausted strength. . . . The Indians, when they saw our deplorable situation, instead of making the least effort to help us, sat down and gave vent to their tears."

Nobody, however, had been killed, though much of the luggage was lost, and what remained had to be spread out to dry. Many of Mackenzie's people, however, when they took stock of their misfortunes, were rather pleased than otherwise, as they thought the disaster would stop him from any further attempt to reach the Western Sea. He wisely listened to their observations without replying, till their panic was dispelled, and they had got themselves warm and comfortable with a hearty meal and a glass of rum; though a little later only by their indifferent carelessness they nearly exploded the whole of the expedition's stock of gunpowder.

Fortunately the weather was fine. Mackenzie and his fellow countryman, Mackay, allowed nothing to dismay them or damp their spirits. Bark was obtained from the forest, the canoe was repaired, and they heard from their guide that this violent little stream would before long join a great and much smoother river. But they were tormented with sandflies and mosquitoes, and a day or two afterwards the guide bolted, while the expedition had to cross morasses in which they were nearly engulfed, and the water journey was constantly obstructed by driftwood. Nevertheless, at last they had "the inexpressible satisfaction of finding themselves on the bank of a navigable river on the western side of the first great range of mountains". Here they re-embarked, and were cheerful in spite of heavy rain.

As they paddled down this great stream, more than two hundred yards wide, snow-capped mountains rose immediately above the river. The current was strong, but perfectly safe. Flocks of ducks, entirely white, except the bill and a part of the wing, rose before them. Smoke ascending in columns from many parts of the woods showed that the country was well inhabited, and the air was fragrant with the strong odour of the gum of cypress and spruce fir.

Then came a series of cascades and falls and a most arduous portage of the heavy canoe. These labours were somewhat lightened by the discovery of quantities of wild onions growing on the banks; but these, when mixed with the pemmican, on which the party was subsisting, stimulated their appetites to an inconvenient degree, seeing that they were on short commons. Meeting with strange Indians they found no one to interpret, and had to use signs. But on the banks of the Fraser they were lucky enough to find the "real red deer", the great wapiti stag, which is absent from the far north-west, beyond the region of the Saskatchewan. The canoe was loaded with venison. The banks of the Fraser River sank to a moderate height and were covered with poplars and cypresses, birch trees, junipers, alders, and willows. The deserted house or lodge of some Amerindian tribe was visited on the banks. It was a finer structure than anything that Mackenzie had seen since he left Fort Michili-Makinak in upper

Canada. It had been constructed for three families. There were three fireplaces and three beds and a kind of larder for the purpose of keeping fish. The whole "lodge" was twenty feet long by three wide, and had three doors. The walls were formed of straight spruce timbers with some skill of carpentry. The roof was covered with bark, and large rods were fixed across the upper part of the building, where fish might hang and dry.

As they continued to descend the Fraser River, with here and there a rapid which nearly swamped the canoe, and lofty cliffs of red and white clay like the ruins of ancient castles (stopping on their way to bury supplies of pemmican against their return, and to light a fire on the top of the burial place so as to mislead bears or other animals that might dig it up), they were more or less compelled to seek intercourse with the new tribes of Amerindians, whose presence on the river banks was obvious. As usual, Mackenzie had to exercise great bravery, tact, and guile to get into peaceful conversation with these half-frightened, half-angry people. The peacemaking generally concluded with the distribution of trinkets amongst the men and women, and presents of sugar to the children. Talking with these folk, however, through such interpreters as there were amongst the Indians of his crew, he learnt that lower down on the Fraser River there was a peculiarly fierce, malignant race, living in vast caves or subterranean dwellings, who would certainly massacre the Europeans if they attempted to pass through their country on their way to the sea. He therefore stopped and set some of his men to work to make a new canoe. He noticed, by the by, that these Amerindians of the Fraser had small pointed canoes, "made after the fashion of the Eskimo".

Renewing their voyage, they reached a house the roof of which just appeared above the ground. It was deserted by its inhabitants, who had been alarmed at the approach of the white men, but in the neighbourhood appeared gesticulating warriors with bows and arrows. Yet these people of underground houses turned out to be friendly and very ready to give information, partly because they were in communication with the Amerindian tribes to the east of the Rocky Mountains. From the elderly men of this tribe Mackenzie ascertained that the Fraser River flowed south by east, was often obstructed by rapids, and, though it would finally bring them to a salt lake or inlet, and then to the sea, it would cause them to travel for a great distance to the south. He noticed the complete difference in the language of these Atna or Carrier Indians[1] and that of the Nagailer or Chin Indians of the Athapaskan group on the eastern side of the Rocky Mountains.

He, however, learnt from these Atna Indians that although the Fraser was out of the question as a quick route to the sea, if he retraced his journey a little up this river he would find another stream entering it from the west, and along this they could travel upstream. And then the route to the water "which was unfit to drink", and the region to which came people with large ships, would be of no great length. Accordingly, after having had a tree engraved with Mackenzie's name and the date, by the bank of the Fraser River, the expedition returned to the subterranean house which they had seen the day before.

"We were in our canoe by four this morning, and passed by the Indian hut, which appeared in a state of perfect tranquillity. We soon came in sight of the point where we first saw the natives, and at eight were much surprised and disappointed at seeing Mr. Mackay and our two Indians coming alone from the ruins of a house that had been partly carried away by the ice and water, at a short distance below the place where we had appointed

1 Apparently these were of the Sikanni tribe, and only another branch of the great Tinné (Athapaskan) stock.

to meet. Nor was our surprise and apprehension diminished by the alarm which was painted in their countenances. . . . They informed me they had taken refuge in that place, with the determination to sell their lives . . . as dear as possible. In a very short time after we had separated, they met a party of the Indians, whom we had known at this place, and were probably those whom we had seen landing from their canoe. These Indians appeared to be in a state of extreme rage, and had their bows bent, with their arrows across them. The guide stopped to ask them some questions, which our people did not understand, and then set off with his utmost speed. Mr. Mackay, however, followed, and did not leave him till they were both exhausted with running. . . . The guide then said that some treacherous design was meditated against them, . . . and conducted them through very bad ways as fast as they could run. When he was desired to slacken his pace, he answered that they might follow him in any manner they pleased, but that he was impatient to get to his family, in order to prepare shoes and other necessaries for his journey. They did not, however, think it prudent to quit him, and he would not stop till ten at night. On passing a track that was but lately made, they began to be seriously alarmed, and on enquiring of the guide where they were, he pretended not to understand. Then they all laid down, exhausted with fatigue, and without any kind of covering; they were cold, wet, and hungry, but dared not light a fire, from the apprehension of an enemy. This comfortless spot they left at the dawn of day, and, on their arrival at the lodges, found them deserted; the property of the Indians being scattered about, as if abandoned for ever. The guide then made two or three trips into the woods, calling aloud, and bellowing like a madman. At length he set off in the same direction as they had come, and had not since appeared. To heighten their misery, as they did not find us at the place appointed, they concluded that we were all destroyed, and had already formed their plan to take to the woods, and cross in as direct a line as they could proceed, to the waters of the Peace River, a scheme which could only be suggested by despair. They intended to have waited for us till noon, and if we did not appear by that time, to have entered without further delay on their desperate expedition."

Making preparations for warfare, if necessary, yet neglecting no chance of re-entering into friendly relations with the natives, Mackenzie set to work to repair the wretched canoe, which was constantly having holes knocked through her. He dealt tactfully with the almost open mutiny of his French Canadians and Indians. At last everyone settled down to the making of a new canoe, on an island in the river where there were plenty of spruce firs to provide the necessary bark. Even here they were plagued with thunderstorms. Nevertheless, the men set to work, and as they worked Mackenzie addressed them with simple fervour, saying he knew of their plans to desert him, but, come what might, *he* was resolved to travel on to the westwards until he reached the waters of the Pacific.

This calmed down the mutineers, and, to the great relief of all concerned, that very afternoon the runaway guide of the Atna people returned and apologized for having deserted them. He then offered once again to conduct them to the seacoast. Nevertheless, again he fled, and Mackenzie was obliged to guide the expedition, according to the information he had gathered from the natives, up the small western affluent of the upper Fraser, which he called the West Road River (now known as the Blackwater).

His perseverance was rewarded, for after proceeding up this river for some distance he saw two canoes coming towards them containing the runaway guide and six of his relations. The guide was dressed in a painted beaver robe, and looked so splendid that they scarcely knew him again. Once more he declared it really was his intention not to disappoint them. Soon afterwards they landed, buried their property and provisions, and placed their canoe on a stage, shaded by a covering of small trees and branches from the sun. Each man carried on his back four bags and a half of pemmican, of an average weight of eighty-five pounds, or other loads (instruments, goods for presents, ammunition, &c.) of ninety pounds in weight. Moreover, each of the Canadians carried a gun. The Amerindian servants of the expedition were only asked to carry loads of forty-five pounds in weight. Mackenzie's pack, and that of his companion, Mackay, amounted to about seventy pounds. Loaded like this they had to scramble up the wooded mountains, first soaked in perspiration from the heat and then drenched with heavy rain. Nevertheless they walked for about thirteen miles the first day. Now they began to meet natives who were closely in touch with the seacoast, which lay to the west at a distance of about six days' journey.

"We had no sooner laid ourselves down to rest last night than the natives began to sing, in a manner very different from what I had been accustomed to hear among savages. It was not accompanied either with dancing, drum, or rattle; but consisted of soft, plaintive tones, and a modulation that was rather agreeable: it had somewhat the air of church music." The country through which they travelled abounded in beavers. It was the month of July, however, and they were harassed with thunderstorms, some of which were followed by hailstones as big as musket balls. After one such storm the ground was whitened for two miles with these balls of ice.

In order not to be deserted by all of their new guides, Mackenzie was obliged to insist on one of them sharing his hut. This young Amerindian was dressed in beaver garments which were a nest of vermin. His hair was greased with fish oil, and his body smeared with red earth, so that at first Mackenzie thought he would never be able to sleep; but such was his fatigue that he passed a night of profound repose, and found the guide still there in the morning. In this region he notes that the balsam fir of Canada was abundant, the tree which provided the gum that cured Cartier's expedition of scurvy. Some of the natives with whom they now came into contact were remarkable for their grey eyes, a feature often observed amongst the Amerindians of the North Pacific coast

"On observing some people before us, our guides hastened to meet them, and, on their approach, one of them stepped forward with an axe in his hand. This party consisted only of a man, two women, and the same number of children. The eldest of the women, who probably was the man's mother, was engaged, when we joined them, in clearing a circular spot, of about five feet in diameter, of the weeds that infested it; nor did our arrival interrupt her employment, which was sacred to the memory of the dead. The spot to which her pious care was devoted contained the grave of a husband and a son, and whenever she passed this way she always stopped to pay this tribute of affection."

By this time, exposure to wind and sun, the attacks of mosquitoes and flies, the difficulty of washing or of changing their clothes, had made all the Europeans of the party as dark in skin colour as the Amerindians, so that such natives as they met who had the courage to examine them, did so with the intention of discovering whether they had any white skin left. The natives whom they now encountered (belonging to the maritime tribes) were comely in appearance, and far more cleanly than the tribes of the north-west. As already mentioned, they had grey eyes, sometimes tinged with hazel. Their stature was noble, one man measuring at least six feet four inches.

They were clothed in leather, and their hair was nicely combed and dressed with beads. One of a travelling band of these Indians, finding that Mackenzie's party was on short rations and very hungry, offered to boil them a kettle of fish roes.

"He took the roes out of a bag, and having bruised them between two stones, put them in water to soak. His wife then took an handful of dry grass in her hand, with which she squeezed them through her fingers. In the meantime her husband was employed in gathering wood to make a fire, for the purpose of heating stones. When she had finished her operation, she filled a *wâtâpé* kettle nearly full of water, and poured the roes into it. When the stones were sufficiently heated, some of them were put into the kettle, and others were thrown in from time to time, till the water was in a state of boiling. The woman also continued stirring the contents of the kettle, till they were brought to a thick consistency; the stones were then taken out, and the whole was seasoned with about a pint of strong rancid oil. The smell of this curious dish was sufficient to sicken me without tasting it, but the hunger of my people surmounted the nauseous meal. When unadulterated by the stinking oil these boiled roes are not unpalatable food."

Farther on their journey their hunger was alleviated by wild parsnips, also roots which appeared, when pulled up, like a bunch of white peas, with the colour and taste of a potato. On their way they were obliged to cross snow mountains, where the snow was so compact that their feet hardly made any perceptible impression. "Before us appeared a stupendous mountain, whose snow-clad summit was lost in the clouds." These mountains, according to the Indians, abounded in white goats.[1] Emerging from the mountains on to the lower ground, sloping towards the sea, at nightfall they came upon a native village

[1] *Oreamnus.*

in the thickness of the woods. Desperate with his fatigue, and risking any danger to obtain rest, Mackenzie walked straight into one of the houses, where people were busily employed in cooking fish, threw down his burden, shook hands with the people, and sat down.

"They received me without the least appearance of surprise, but soon made signs for me to go up to the large house, which was erected, on upright posts, at some distance from the ground. A broad piece of timber with steps cut in it led to the scaffolding even with the floor, and by this curious kind of ladder I entered the house at one end; and having passed three fires, at equal distances in the middle of the building, I was received by several people, sitting upon a very wide board, at the upper end of it. I shook hands with them, and seated myself beside a man, the dignity of whose countenance induced me to give him that preference. . . ."

Later on, this man, seeing Mackenzie's people arriving tired and hungry, rose and fetched from behind a plank, four feet wide, a quantity of roasted salmon. A whole salmon was offered to Mackenzie, and another to Mackay; half a salmon was given to each of the French Canadian *voyageurs*. Their host further invited them to sleep in the house, but, Mackenzie thinking it preferable to camp outside, a fire was lit to warm the weary travellers, and each was lent a thick board on which to sleep, so that he might not lie on the bare ground.

"We had not long been seated round the fire when we received a dish of salmon roes, pounded fine and beat up with water so as to have the appearance of a cream. Nor was it without some kind of seasoning that gave it a bitter taste. Another dish soon followed, the principal article of which was also salmon roes, with a large proportion of gooseberries, and an herb that appeared to be sorrel. Its acidity rendered it more agreeable to my taste than the former preparation. Having been regaled with these delicacies, for such they were considered by that hospitable spirit which provided them, we laid ourselves down to rest with no other canopy than the sky. But I never enjoyed a more sound and refreshing rest, though I had a board for my bed and a billet for my pillow."

The gooseberries, wortleberries, and raspberries which Mackenzie ate at this hospitable village were the finest he ever saw or tasted of their respective kinds. They were generally eaten together with the dry roes of salmon. Salmon was the staple food of the country, and very abundant in the river which Mackenzie was following down to the Pacific shore. The fish were usually caught in weirs, and also by dipping nets. The natives were so superstitious about the salmon, that they believed they would give offence to the spirits if they ate any other animal food, especially meat. They would scarcely allow Mackenzie to carry venison in his canoe, in case the salmon should smell it and abandon the river.

After this welcome rest they embarked in two canoes on the stream which Mackenzie calls the Salmon River. The stream was rapid, and they proceeded at a great rate, stopping every now and then to get out and walk round salmon weirs. Nevertheless, although other Indians ran before them announcing their approach towards a village, the noise of which was apparent in the distance, they were received at this place in a very hostile way, the men rapidly arming themselves with bows and arrows, spears, and axes. But Mackenzie walked on alone to greet them, and shook hands with the nearest man. Thereupon an elderly man broke from the crowd and took Mackenzie in his arms. Another then came and paid him the same compliment. One man to whom he presented his hand broke the string of a handsome robe of sea-otter skin and threw it over Mackenzie.

The chief made signs to the white men to follow him to his house, which Mackenzie found to be of larger dimensions and better materials than any he had yet seen. "Very clean mats" were spread in this house for the chief, his counsellors, and the two white men. A small roasted salmon was then placed before each person.

"When we had satisfied ourselves with the fish, one of the people who came with us from the last village approached, with a kind of ladle in one hand, containing oil, and in the other something that resembled the inner rind of the cocoanut, but of a lighter colour. This he dipped in the oil, and, having eaten it, indicated by his gestures how palatable he thought it. He then presented me with a small piece of it, which I chose to taste in its dry state, though the oil was free from any unpleasant smell. A square cake of this was next produced, when a man took it to the water near the house, and having thoroughly soaked it, he returned, and, after he had pulled it to pieces like oakum, put it into a well-made trough, about three feet long, nine inches wide, and five deep. He then plentifully sprinkled it with salmon oil, and manifested by his own example that we were to eat of it. I just tasted it, and found the oil perfectly sweet, without which the other ingredient would have been very insipid. The chief partook of it with great avidity after it had received an additional quantity of oil. This dish is considered by these people as a great delicacy; and on examination, I discovered it to consist of the inner rind of the hemlock pine tree, taken off early in summer, and put into a frame, which shapes it into cakes of fifteen inches long, ten broad, and half an inch thick; and in this form I should suppose it may be preserved for a great length of time. This discovery satisfied me respecting the many hemlock trees which I had observed stripped of their bark."

Mackenzie found some of the older men here with long beards, and to one of them he presented a pair of scissors for clipping his beard.

After describing some remarkable oblong "tables" (as they might be called) of cedar wood — twenty feet long by eight feet broad — made of thick cedar boards joined together with the utmost neatness, and painted with hieroglyphics and the figures of animals; and his visit to a kind of temple in the village, into the architecture of which strangely carved and painted figures were interwoven; Mackenzie goes on to relate an episode giving one a very vivid idea of the helplessness of "native" medicine in many diseases.

He was taken to see a son of the chief, who was suffering from a terrible ulcer in the small of his back, round which the flesh was gangrened, one of his knees being afflicted in the same way. The poor fellow was reduced to a skeleton, and apparently drawing very near to death.

"I found the native physicians busy in practising their skill and art on the patient. They blew on him, and then whistled; at times they pressed their extended fingers with all their strength on his stomach; they also put their forefingers doubled into his mouth, and spouted water from their own with great violence into his face. To support these operations the wretched sufferer was held up in a sitting posture, and when they were concluded he was laid down and covered with a new robe made of the skin of a lynx. I had observed that his belly and breast were covered with scars, and I understood that they were caused by a custom prevalent among them of applying pieces of lighted touchwood to their flesh, in order to relieve pain or demonstrate their courage. He was now placed on a broad plank, and carried by six men into the woods, where I was invited to accompany them. I could not conjecture what would be the end of this ceremony, particularly as I saw one man carry fire, another an axe, and a third dry wood. I was, indeed, disposed to suspect that, as it was their custom to burn the dead, they intended to relieve the poor man from his pain, and perform the last sad duty of surviving affection. When they had advanced a short distance into the wood, they laid him upon a clear spot, and kindled a fire against his back, when the physician began to scarify the ulcer with a very blunt instrument, the cruel pain of which operation the patient bore with incredible resolution. The scene afflicted me, and I left it."

The chief of this village had probably met Captain Cook about ten years before. He had been down in a large canoe[1] with forty of his people to the seacoast, where he saw two large vessels.

Farther down the river the natives, instead of regaling them with fish, placed before them a long, clean, and well-made trough full of berries, most of them resembling blackberries, though white in colour, and others similar to huckleberries. In this region the women were employed in beating and preparing the inner rind of the juniper bark, to which they gave the appearance of flax, and others were spinning with a distaff; again, others were weaving robes of this fibrous thread, intermixed with strips of sea-otter skin. The men were fishing on the river with drag nets between two canoes, thus intercepting the salmon coming up the river.

At last, on Saturday, the 20th of July, 1793, they emerged from the Salmon River into an arm of the sea (probably near King Island). The tide was out and had

[1] Mackenzie thus describes one of the large sea-going canoes of the coast natives: "This canoe was built of cedar, forty-five feet long, four feet broad, and three and a half in depth. It was painted black and decorated with white figures of different kinds. The gunwale fore and aft was inlaid with the teeth of the sea otter." He adds that "these coast tribes (north of Vancouver Island and of Queen Charlotte Sound) had been in indirect contact with the Spaniards since the middle of the sixteenth century, and with the Russians from the middle of the eighteenth century. Therefore, from these two directions they had learnt the use of metal, and had obtained copper, brass, and iron. They may possibly have had copper earlier still from the Northern Indians on the other side of the Rocky Mountains; but brass and iron they could, of course, only have obtained from Europeans. They had already become very deft at dealing with these metals, and twisted the iron into collars which weighed upwards of twelve pounds, also beating it into plates for their daggers and knives."

left a large space covered with seaweed. The surrounding hills were involved in fog. . . . The bay appeared to be some three miles in breadth, and on the coast the travellers saw a great number of sea otters.[1] At two in the afternoon the swell was so high, and the wind, which was against them, so boisterous, that they could not proceed along the seacoast in their leaky canoe. A young chief who had come with them as one of their guides, and who had been allowed to leave when the seacoast was reached, returned bearing a large porcupine on his back. He first cut the animal open and threw its entrails into the sea, then singed the skin and boiled it in separate pieces; nor did he go to rest till, with the assistance of two others who happened to be awake, every morsel of it had been devoured. This was fortunate, because their stock of provisions was reduced to twenty pounds' weight of pemmican, sixteen pounds of rice, and six pounds of flour amongst ten men, "in a leaky vessel, and on a barbarous coast".

The rise and fall of the tide here was noted at fifteen feet in height. Mr. Mackay collected a quantity of small mussels, which were boiled and eaten by the two Scotchmen, but not by the Canadians, who were quite unacquainted with sea shellfish.

Near Point Menzies, which had already been reached and named by Captain VANCOUVER in the spring of 1793 on his great voyage of discovery up the North American coast,[2] Alexander Mackenzie met a party of Amerindians,

[1] These *may* have been small seals, but the sea otter (*Enhydris lutris*), now nearly extinct, was at one time found in numbers along the north-west American coast, from the Aleutian Islands and Alaska to Oregon. Owing to persecution it now leads an almost entirely aquatic life, resting at times on the masses of floating seaweed.

[2] GEORGE VANCOUVER (born about 1758, and probably descended from Dutch or Flemish ancestors) was one of the great pioneers of the British Empire. His name is commemorated in Vancouver's Island, an important portion of British Columbia. Vancouver entered the navy when only thirteen, sailed with Captain Cook, and eventually was appointed to command a naval expedition sent out in 1791 to survey and take over from the Spaniards the north-west American coast north of Oregon. It is remark-

amongst whom was a man of insolent aspect, who, by means of signs and exclamations, made him understand that he and his friends had been fired at by a white man named Makuba (Vancouver), and that another white man, called "Bensins", had struck him on the back with the flat of his sword. This man more or less compelled Mackenzie to accompany him in the direction of his village, and on the way explained that "Makuba" had come there with his "big boat". Indeed, Mackenzie's party perceived the remains of sheds or buildings on the shore where Europeans had probably made a camp, and here they established themselves, taking up a position of defence, because the attitude of the natives was rather threatening.

At this camp there was a rock, and on this Alexander Mackenzie, mixing up some vermilion or red clay in melted grease, inscribed in large characters the following words: "Alexander Mackenzie, from Canada, by land, the twenty-second of July, one thousand seven hundred and ninety-three". He then shifted his camp to a place three miles to the north-east, below a precipice from which issued streams of fine water as cold as ice. And here he took careful observations with his astronomical and surveying instruments, in order to fix his position. Fortunately the day was one of bright sunshine. Otherwise, had there been a long persistence of cloud, he might have been obliged to leave the Pacific coast without being able to fix precisely the place where he had reached the sea.

Then he yielded to the passionate desire of his people to withdraw inland from the possibly dangerous inhabitants of the coast, and returned with them to the encamp-

able that he should only have missed Mackenzie's arrival at Point Menzies by about two months. With what amazed rejoicing would these two heroic explorers have greeted one another had they met on this remote point of the Pacific coast, the one coming overland (so to speak) from Quebec and the Atlantic, and the other all the way by sea from Falmouth via the Cape of Good Hope, Australia, New Zealand, Tahiti, and Hawaii.

ment where the porcupine had been eaten. Here the guide made off into the woods. Mackenzie followed him, and thus reached a village from which two men issued armed with daggers and intending to attack him. While stopping to defend himself, many other people assembled, and amongst them he recognized the irritating person who incessantly repeated the names "Makuba" and "Benzins". However, this threatened danger was narrowly averted, and eventually they left the village with a supply of food; but also in a state of considerable irritation with—fleas! For some of the houses of these Pacific coast villages swarmed with fleas to such an extent that Mackenzie and his men were obliged to take to the water to rid themselves of these vermin, which swarmed also on the ground that was bare of grass.

The return journey up the Salmon River was a series of bewildering vicissitudes. Sometimes Mackenzie and his party were received in the most threatening way by persons who had been warm friends on their downward journey, then seemingly inevitable war was transformed into peace, but guides deserted, or the Amerindians from across the Rocky Mountains attempted to mutiny. However, they struggled through all their difficulties, till at last they reached the place known as the Friendly Village, and were here fortunately received with great kindness, being once more entertained "with the most respectful hospitality". "In short, the chief behaved to us with so much attention and kindness that I did not withhold anything in my power to give which might afford him satisfaction. . . . I presented him with two yards of blue cloth, an axe, knives, and various other articles. He gave me in return a large shell which resembled the under shell of a Guernsey oyster, but was somewhat larger. Where they procure them I could not discover, but they cut and polish them for bracelets, ear-rings, and other personal ornaments. . . ."

The women of this place were employed in boiling sorrel and different kinds of berries in large square kettles made of cedar wood. This pottage, when it had attained a certain consistency, they took out with ladles, and poured it into frames about twelve inches square. These were then exposed to the sun, until their contents became so many dried cakes. This was their principal article of food, and probably of traffic. These people had also made portable chests of cedar, in which they packed these cakes, as well as their salmon, both dried and roasted. The only flesh they ate in addition to the salmon was that of the sea otter and the seal; except that one instance already mentioned of the young Indian who feasted on the flesh of the porcupine.

"Their faces are round, with high cheekbones, and their complexion between olive and copper. They have small grey eyes with a tinge of red, . . . their hair is of a dark-brown colour." The men wore their hair long, and either kept it well combed and hanging loose over the shoulders, or plaited it and bedaubed it with brown earth so as to make it quite impervious to the comb. Those who adopted this fashion had to carry a bone bodkin about with them to ease the frequent irritation which arose from the excessive abundance of vermin in their hair.

The women, on the other hand, usually wore their hair short. Mackenzie noticed that the infants had their heads enclosed with boards covered with leather, to press the skull into the shape of a wedge. The women wore a fringed apron, and over that a long robe made of skins or leather, either loose or tied round the middle with a girdle. Over these in wet weather was worn a cap in the shape of an inverted bowl or dish. The men also wore this cap, and in cold weather used the robe, but in warm weather went about in no clothing at all, except that their feet were protected with shoes made of dressed elks' skins. In wet weather, over their robe they wore a circular mat with an opening in the middle sufficiently large to admit the head. This, spreading over the shoulders, threw off the wet. As compared with the Indians of the Rocky Mountains and the great plains, the men and boys were very cleanly, being constantly in the water. The women, however, were dirty.

At the end of July, 1793, Mackenzie left what he calls the Friendly Village, and prepared to return to the east across the Rocky Mountains, having distributed to each man about twenty pounds weight of smoked salmon, flour, and pemmican. The fatigue of ascending the precipices of the mountains was past description. When they arrived at a spot where water could be obtained, and a camp made, they were in such an extremity of weariness they could hardly crawl about to gather wood for the purpose of making a fire; but two hours afterwards the Amerindians of their party arrived and came to their assistance. Then when they were sitting round a blazing fire, and some of their fatigue had lessened, they could sit and talk of past dangers, and indulge in the delightful reflection that they were thus far advanced on their homeward journey. "Nor was it possible to be in this situation without contemplating the wonders of it. Such was the depth of the precipices below, and the height of the mountains above, with the rude and wild magnificence of the scenery around, that I shall not attempt to describe such an astonishing and awful combination of objects. . . . Even at this place, which is only, as it were, the first step towards gaining the summit of the mountains, the climate was very sensibly changed. The air that fanned the village which we left at noon, was mild and cheering; the grass was verdant, and the wild fruits ripe around it. But here the snow was not yet dissolved, the ground was still bound by the frost, the herbage had scarce begun to spring, and the crowberry bushes were just beginning to blossom."

Eventually they found their canoe, and the property which they had left behind, in perfect safety. At this camp, where the canoe had been left behind, many natives arrived both from the upper and lower parts of the river, all of them dressed in beaver robes, which they were ready enough to sell for large knives. It struck Alexander Mackenzie as being very extraordinary that these people, who had left absolutely untouched the property stored at this place—when anyone passing by could have stolen it and never have been detected—should now be so ready to pilfer articles and utensils from the camp. So many small things had been picked up and taken away by them, when coming to sell their beaver robes, that he was obliged to take some action. So, before all these beaver-clad Amerindians had departed on their westward journey, he told the rearguard that he had noticed the thefts, and scarcely thought their relations who were guilty of stealing realized the awful mischief that would result from this dishonesty; that they were on their way now to the sea to procure large quantities of salmon from the rivers, but the salmon, which was absolutely necessary to their existence, came from the sea which belonged to the white men, and it only needed a message from the white men to the powers of nature to prevent the fish coming up from the sea into the rivers; and if this word were spoken they and their children might starve. He consequently advised them to hurry after their friends, and see that all the stolen articles were sent back. This plan succeeded. The stolen articles were restored, and then Mackenzie purchased from these people several large salmon, and his party enjoyed a delicious meal.

Mackenzie declared that there were no bison to be found on the west side of the Rocky Mountains[1] (British Columbia), and no wolves.

[1] He was not quite accurate: there were a few "wood" bison in the north and east of British Columbia.

Resuming their journey up the Fraser River, they passed through the narrow gut between mountainous rocks, which on the outward journey had been a passage of some risk. But now the state of the water was such that, they got up without difficulty, and had more time to examine these extraordinary rocks, which were as perpendicular as a wall, and gave the traveller the idea of a succession of enormous Gothic cathedrals. With little difficulty they transported their canoe across the water parting to the Peace River.

As they began to glide down this stream, homeward bound, they noticed at the entrance of a small tributary an object which proved to be four beaver skins hung up to attract their attention. These were the skins which had been given to Mackenzie as a present by a native as he travelled westwards. Not wishing to add to his loads, he had left the skins behind, saying he would call for them on his return. Mackenzie imagined, therefore, that, being under the necessity of leaving the river, this Indian had hung up the skins in the hope that they would attract the attention of the travellers on their return. "To reward his honesty, I left three times the value of the skins in trade goods in their place." As the Peace River carried them away from the great mountains, and the plains extended before their sight, they stopped to repair the canoe and to get in supplies of food from the herds of game that were visible. They began with a hearty meal of bison beef. "Every fear of future want was removed." Soon afterwards they killed an elk, the carcass of which weighed over two hundred and fifty pounds. "As we had taken a very hearty meal at one o'clock, it might naturally be supposed that we should not be very voracious at supper; nevertheless, a kettleful of elk flesh was boiled and eaten, and that vessel replenished with more meat and put on the fire. All that remained of the bones, &c., were placed after the Indian fashion round the fire to roast, and at ten the next morning the whole was consumed by ten persons and a large dog, who was allowed his share of the banquet. Nor did any inconvenience result from what may be considered as an inordinate indulgence."

On the 24th of August, 1793, Mackenzie was back again at Fort Chipewayan, after an absence of eleven months, having been the first white man to cross the broad continent of North America from the Atlantic to the Pacific, north of Mexico.

# CHAPTER XII

## Mackenzie's Successors

The Spaniards of California had been aware in the middle of the eighteenth century that there was a big river entering the sea to the north of the savage country known as Oregon. The estuary of this river was reached in May, 1792, by an American sea captain of a whaling ship—ROBERT GRAY, of Boston. He crossed the bar, and named the great stream after his own ship, the *Columbia*. Five months afterwards (October, 1792) Lieutenant BROUGHTON, of the Vancouver expedition, entered the Columbia from the sea, explored it upstream for a hundred miles, and formally took possession of it for the King of Great Britain. The news of this discovery reached Alexander Mackenzie (no doubt after his return from his overland journey to the Pacific coast), and he at once jumped to the conclusion that the powerful stream he had discovered in the heart of the Rocky Mountains, and had partially followed on its way to the Pacific, must be the Columbia. As a matter of fact it was the river afterwards called Fraser.

If you look at the map of British North America, and then at the map of Russian Asia—Siberia—you will notice a marked difference in the arrangement of the waterways. Those of the Canadian Dominion, on the whole, flow more eastwards and westwards, or at any rate radiate in all directions, so as to constitute the most wonderful system of natural canals possessed by any country or continent. On the contrary, the rivers of Siberia flow usually in somewhat parallel lines from south to north. Siberia also is far less well provided than British North America with an abundance of navigable rivers, streams, and great lakes. Therefore the traveller in pre-railway days wishing to cross Siberia from west to east or east to west was obliged to have recourse to wheeled traffic, to ride, or to walk. Consequently, until the beginning of the twentieth century, the "exploitation" (or turning to useful account) of Siberia was a far more difficult process than the development of North America, once the question of British *versus* French or Spanish was settled. Siberia at one time was almost as rich in fur-bearing animals as British North America; yet so difficult was transport (and so severe were the rigours of the climate) that the Russians, once they reached the shores of the Pacific at the beginning of the eighteenth century, began to stretch out their influence to the opposite peninsula of Alaska mainly on account of the fur trade. For it was easier and less expensive to bring furs from Alaska round Cape Horn, or the Cape of Good Hope, to Europe than to convey them overland from eastern Siberia. Then, also, the Chinese market was becoming of importance to the fur trade. Already Mackenzie, at the end of the eighteenth century, is found considering whether a sea trade between China and a British port on the North Pacific coast could not be arranged so as to develop a profitable market among the mandarins and grandees of the Celestial Empire for a good proportion of the North-west Company's skins.

Peter Pond, already referred to on p. 278, is said to have expressed his intention (in 1788) of going to treat with the Empress Catherine II for a Russian occupation of the Alaskan and Columbian coasts. For this reason, or the mere desire to have a proportion of this fur-producing country, the Emperor Paul, in 1799, created a Russian Chartered Company to occupy the Alaska and north Columbian coasts. Great Britain offered no objection—

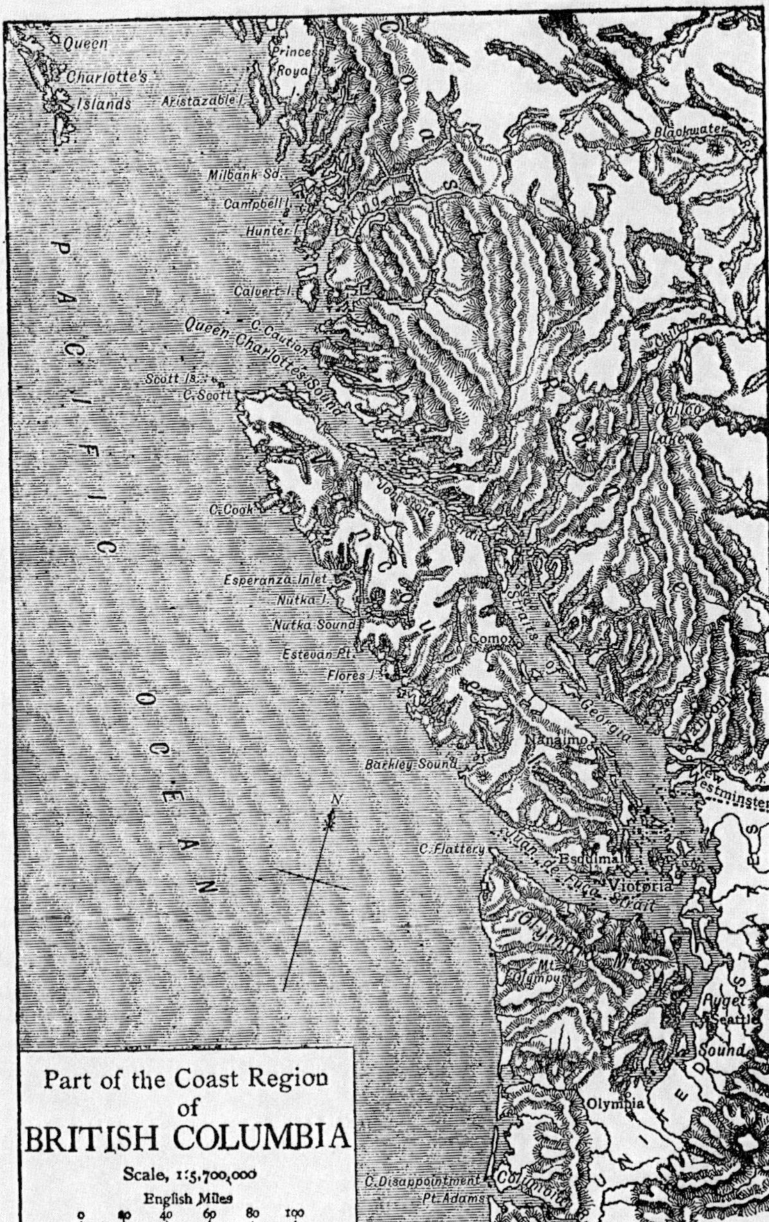


Part of the Coast Region of BRITISH COLUMBIA

Scale, 1:5,700,000

English Miles

0 20 40 60 80 100

in spite of having acquired some rights here by an agreement with Spain—and that is why, when you look at the map of the vast Canadian Dominion, you find with surprise that it has been robbed (one might almost say) of at least half of its legitimate Pacific seaboard. The Russian Company was allowed to claim the north Columbian coast between Alaska proper and Queen Charlotte Islands.

In 1867 the Russian Government sold all Alaska and the north Columbian coast to the United States, partly to annoy Great Britain, whom it had not forgiven for the Crimean War.

You will have noticed that quite a number of United States citizens (mostly born British subjects in New England) had taken part in the north-west fur trade immediately after the British conquest of Canada disposed of French monopolies. There were Jonathan Carver and Peter Pond, for example; and a much more worthy person than the last named—Daniel W. Harmon, a New Englander, who entered the service of the North-west Company in 1800, and followed in Mackenzie's footsteps to the upper Fraser River and the vicinity of the Skeena. Simon Fraser also, whose tracing of the Fraser River from its upper waters to the Pacific coast we shall presently deal with, was a native of Vermont, though his father came from Scotland. The furs which began to penetrate into the United States by way of Detroit and Niagara, the rising scale of luxury in dress in the towns of the eastern seaboard of the United States, the voyages of American whalers up the west coast of North America (including the discovery of the Columbia River in 1792 by Captain Robert Gray), the purchase of Louisiana from the Emperor Napoleon in 1804—with the vague claim it gave to the coast line of Oregon on the Pacific: all these circumstances inspired far-sighted persons in the United States at the beginning of the nineteenth century with a wish to secure for their Government and commerce a share in the fur trade and in these wonderful new lands of the Pacific watershed. American ships (whaling ships) had already become accustomed to sail round Cape Horn and to visit the Oregon and Alaskan coasts. The American Government therefore, immediately after the Louisiana purchase, dispatched an American expedition under Captains Meriwether Lewis and Jonathan Clarke to travel up the Missouri River and so across the mountains to the coast of Oregon, a wonderful expedition, which they carried out with great success in two years (1804-6), reaching the lower Columbia River and following it down to the sea.

Consequently, with all this in the air, it is not very surprising that the far-sighted John Jacob Astor, a wealthy German merchant of New York, should have conceived the idea of founding a great American fur-trading company and of establishing it at the mouth of the Columbia River.

At the beginning of the nineteenth century he had entered into arrangements with an Anglo-Canadian Company (the Mackinaw), which worked the southernmost part of Canada, to fuse its enterprise with his, and thus founded the *South-west Company*, the name of which (at any rate in current speech) was afterwards changed into the Pacific Fur-trading Company. After attempting in vain to come to a working arrangement with the great North-west Company, he decided to act quite independently and to establish the headquarters of his new concern at the mouth of the Columbia River. Accordingly, the expedition was sent out in duplicate to the mouth of the Columbia River, one-half going a six-months' voyage round Cape Horn in a sailing ship, the *Tonquin*, and the other marching overland or canoeing on lakes and rivers in eighteen months from Montreal via the Mississippi and Missouri. These two parties together founded "Astoria", at the mouth of the Columbia. But most of Astor's employees were British subjects derived from men of the

c 312 Photo. Thompson

THE KOOTENAY OR HEAD STREAM OF THE COLUMBIA RIVER

North-west and Mackinaw Companies; and when, in 1812, war broke out between the United States and Great Britain, a British war vessel came up the Pacific coast to Astoria and promptly turned it into "Fort George". Forthwith the North-west Company bought up the derelict property of Mr. Astor's Company from his not very honest British employees, and the few Americans in the concern retreated inland, and, after almost incredible sufferings from the attacks of unfriendly Indians, succeeded in reaching the Mississippi.

This Columbia River had in reality been discovered at its sources, and traced down to the sea, between 1807 and 1811 by DAVID THOMPSON (once a Blue-coat boy in London; from 1784 to 1792 in the service of the Hudson's Bay Company, and after that one of the most famous of the Nor'-westers). The upper course of this river and its northern affluents were annexed as British by David Thompson; the lower course did not at once become the political property of the United States, but was considered vaguely to be the joint property of both nations, till the Oregon settlement of 1846. By the treaty of 1792, the southern boundary of central Canada was agreed upon as being the 49th degree of north latitude, but only between the Lake of the Woods and the Rocky Mountains. The agreement of 1846 continued the 49th degree boundary to the shore of the Pacific opposite Vancouver Island.

Prominent among the agents of the North-western Company who followed Sir Alexander Mackenzie as a pioneer towards the Pacific shores was ALEXANDER HENRY THE YOUNGER,[1] regarding whose journeys some extracts may be given.

The first entry in his diary of 1799 is not particularly romantic, but shows some of the unexpected dangers attending the life of an adventurer in the far north-west.

[1] The nephew of the Alexander Henry already mentioned as an explorer between 1761 and 1775.

He had been riding through the Assiniboin country in the autumn of 1799, probably after one of the very indigestible meals which he describes here and there in his pages. Alone, and crossing an open plain swarming with wolves, he was seized suddenly with a violent colic, the pain of which was so terrible that he could not remain in the saddle. He dismounted, hobbled his horse, and threw himself on the grass, where he lay in agony for two hours, expecting every moment would be his last, till, quite exhausted, he fell asleep. He was awakened, however, by the howling of the wolves advancing to tear him to pieces; yet he was so weak that he was scarcely able to mount his horse, and then could only proceed at a slow walk, with the wolves snapping at his horse's heels.

Near the site of the present city of Winnipeg, in the late summer of 1800, he and his expedition were much troubled by swarms of water snakes. They were harmless but not pleasant in their familiarity, for they entered the tents and took refuge in the explorers' beds; and as they apparently came from their breeding places in Amerindian graves which covered the remains of people who had died of smallpox in a recent epidemic, they were additionally loathsome.

Smallpox indeed played a very important part in the historical development of western North America. Prior to 1780 the Amerindian tribes between the upper Mississippi and the Rocky Mountains, and between the Saskatchewans and the Missouri, were numerous and warlike. At first, about 1765, they received in very friendly fashion the pioneer British traders and French Canadians who attempted to resume the fur trade where it had been dropped by the French monopolists in 1760. But fifteen years afterwards, enraged at the violence and wrongdoing of the British and Canadian traders, and maddened by strong drink, they were planning a universal massacre of the whites, when suddenly smallpox (introduced by the Spaniards into New Mexico) came on them as a scourge, which destroyed whole tribes, and depopulated much of western North America.

Alexander Henry had many adventures with the bison of the plains. Here is one of them.

"Just as I came up to him at full speed and prepared to fire, my horse suddenly stopped. The bull had turned about to face my horse, which was naturally afraid of buffaloes, and startled at such a frightful object; he leaped to one side to avoid the bull. As I was not prepared for this I was pitched over his head, and fell within a few yards of the bull's nose; but fortunately for me he paid no more attention to my horse than to me. The grass was long, and I lay quiet until a favourable opportunity offered as he presented his placotte. I discharged both barrels of my double gun at him; he turned and made one plunge toward me, but had not time to repeat it before he fell, with his nose not more than three paces off. . . . I had to return on foot as my horse had bolted."

At this place—near the Red River (the season September)—the country swarmed with big game such as North America will never see any more: enormous numbers of bison, of wapiti or Canadian red deer, moose or elk, prong-buck, and of grizzly bears and black bears who followed the herds to attack them. The rivers swarmed with otters and beavers. The ground along the banks of the river was worn into a smooth, hard pavement by the hoofs of the thousands of buffaloes. Racoons, red foxes, wolves, and pumas frequented the bush country and the chumps of forest. A large white wolf, prowling rather imprudently, came within a few yards of Henry, and was shot dead. "We observed on the opposite beach no fewer than seven bears drinking all at the same time. Red deer were whistling in every direction, but our minds were not sufficiently at ease to enjoy our situation." Large flocks of swans (*Cygnus columbianus*) rose out of the Red River apparently in a state of alarm and confusion, possibly caused by the many herds of buffaloes rushing down to the river to drink. At night everything was quiet except the bellowing of buffaloes and the whistling of red deer. "I climbed up a tall oak at the entrance of the plain, from the top of which I had an extensive view of the country. Buffalo and red deer were everywhere in sight passing to and fro."

But the prairie had its nuisances as well as its wonders of animal life. From the end of April to the end of July the woods and grass swarmed with ticks (*Ixodes*), which covered the clothes of the Europeans and entered their ears and there caused serious inflammations. They would in time get such a firm hold by the insertion of their heads into the skin that they could not be removed without pulling the body from the head, which caused a terrible itching lasting for months. If left alone they adhered to the flesh until they swelled to the size of a musket ball, when they fell off of themselves. In the summertime gadflies were exasperating in their attacks on men and cattle. Mosquitoes were a veritable plague, and midges also, between June and the end of September.

Not the least of the terrors of life in the far north-west in those days was the vermin that collected in the houses or huts built for a winter sojourn. It is frequently mentioned, in the records of the pioneers, how the lodges or tents of the Amerindians swarmed with fleas and lice. Henry notes on the 19th of April, 1803: "The men began to demolish our dwelling houses, which were built of bad wood, and to build new ones of oak. The nests of mice we found, and the swarms of fleas hopping in every direction, were astonishing."

Henry reached the Pacific coast in 1814, by way of the Kootenay, Spokane, and Columbia River route, which had been discovered by David Thompson. He describes well the forests of remarkable trees on this portion of the Pacific coast, opposite the south end of Vancouver Island: the crooked oaks loaded with mistletoe, the tall wild cherry trees, the hazels with trunks thicker than a man's thigh, the evergreen arbutus, the bracken fern, blackberries, and black raspberries; and the game in these glades of trees and fern: small Columbian *Mazama* deer, large lynxes, bears, gluttons, wolves, foxes, racoons, and squirrels. Overhead soared huge Californian condors (*Pseudogryphus*).

Henry was drowned in 1812 in the estuary of the Columbia River, through the capsizing of a boat.

The question of the identity of the great river flowing to the Pacific from near the headwaters of the Peace—the river which Mackenzie had discovered and been forced to leave—was finally decided by SIMON FRASER, one of the most celebrated among the North-west Company's pioneers. Like Mackenzie, he believed this stream to be the upper Columbia.

Accompanied by John Stuart and Jules Quesnel, he left the Fraser River at its junction with the Nechaco on May 22, 1807, and, keeping as near as he could to the course of the river, found himself in the country of the Atna tribe, Amerindians of a diminutive size but active appearance, from whom he obtained an invaluable guide and faithful interpreter, Little Fellow, but for whose bravery, wise advice, and clever diplomacy the journey must have ended in disaster or disappointment—a remark which might be made about nearly all the Amerindian guides of the pioneers.

The Atna Indians were dressed in skins with the hair outside, and were armed with bows and arrows. They besmeared their bodies with fish oil and red earth, and painted their faces in different colours. Bison were quite unknown to them, being very seldom found in those latitudes on the western side of the Rocky Mountains. The country of the Atna Indians on the upper Fraser abounded in elk, wapiti, reindeer, bighorn sheep, mountain goats,[1] and beaver.

Here is a description by Fraser of some of the rapids in the upper part of the river named after him.

"The channel contracts to about forty yards, and is enclosed by two precipices of immense height, which bending towards each other make it narrower above than below. The water which rolls down this extraordinary passage in tumultuous waves and with great velocity has a frightful appearance. However, it being impossible to carry canoes by land, all hands without hesitation embarked, as it were, *à corps perdu* upon the mercy of this awful tide. Once engaged, the die was cast. Our great difficulty consisted in keeping the canoes in the middle of the stream, that is, clear of the precipice on the one side, and of the gulfs formed by the waves on the other. Thus, skimming along as fast as lightning, the crews, cool and determined, followed each other in awful silence, and when we arrived at the end we stood gazing at each other in silent gratification at our narrow escape from total destruction. . . . I scarcely ever saw anything so dreary and dangerous in any country (such precipices, mountains, and rapids), and I still seem to see, whichever way I turn my eyes, mountains upon mountains whose summits are covered with eternal snow."

They had to take to these same mountains, the river being unnavigable. The Asketti Indians brought them different kinds of roots, especially wild onions boiled into a syrup, excellent dried salmon, and some berries. These Indians had visited the seacoast, and had seen ships of war come there with white men, "very well dressed, and very proud, for," continued the chief, getting up and clapping his two hands upon his hips, and then striding

[1] This remarkable beast (*Oreamnus*) they called "Aspai", and wove from its white wool an excellent cloth for their clothing.

c 312

A HUNTER'S "SHACK" IN BRITISH COLUMBIA: AFTER A SUCCESSFUL SHOOT OF BLUE GROUSE

about the place with an air of importance, "this is the way they go". In this country of the Hakamaw and Asketti Indians, dogs were much in use for carrying purposes, and could draw from one hundred to one hundred and fifty pounds. They were considered by the French Canadians very good eating, though only the smaller kinds were eaten, the large dogs being of another race and having a rank taste. They also shaved these dogs in the summer time, and wove rugs from their hair. These rugs were striped in different colours, crossing at right angles, and resembling at a distance a Highland plaid.

The tombs of the Indian villages on this western side of the Rocky Mountains were superior to anything that Fraser had ever seen amongst savages. They were about fifteen feet long, and of the form of a chest of drawers. Upon the boards and posts, beasts and birds were carved in a curious but crude manner, and pretty well proportioned. Returning to the river, when the worst of the rapids were passed, they descended it rapidly, helped by a strong current, and at length entered a lake where they saw seals, which showed that they had got near to the Pacific Ocean. They also beheld a round mountain, the now celebrated Mount Baker, which is visible from so much of the surrounding country of British Columbia and Vancouver Island. The trees were splendid, junipers thirty feet in circumference in their trunks and two or three hundred feet high. Mosquitoes, however, were in clouds. Nearer to the coast the Indians often appeared in the distance like white men, for the very literal reason that they had covered their skins with white paint. Their houses were built of cedar planks, and were six hundred and forty feet long by sixty feet broad, all under one roof, but of course separated into a great number of partitions for different families. On the outside the boards (as Mackenzie had noticed) were carved with figures of men, beasts, and birds as large as life. Simon Fraser, however, when he reached sea water, near the site of New Westminster, was greatly disappointed that any view of the main ocean should be obstructed by distant lands. He had believed all along that he was tracing the far-famed Columbia River to its entrance into the Pacific Ocean; and now that, instead of this, he had discovered an entirely new river, henceforth to be called after him but without so long a course as the Columbia, his vanity was hurt.

The Amerindians of the sea coast, opposite Vancouver Island, showed hostility to Fraser's party, as they had done farther north to Mackenzie. The Canadian *voyageurs* got alarmed, and told Fraser's assistant, John Stuart, that they had made up their minds to return by land across the Rocky Mountains. Fraser and the other officers of the expedition joined in arguing with them and recalling them to their senses. Finally each member of the party swore a solemn oath before Almighty God that they would sooner perish than forsake in distress any of the crew in the present voyage. After this ceremony was over all hands dressed in their best apparel, and each took charge of his own bundle. They therefore returned as much as possible by the Fraser River, and only took to the mountains when obliged by the rapids. They had to pass many difficult rocks, defiles, precipices, in which there was a beaten path made by the natives, and made possible by means of scaffolds, bridges, and ladders, so peculiarly constructed that it required no small degree of necessity, dexterity, and courage in strangers to undertake them. For instance, they had to ascend precipices by means of ladders composed of two long poles placed upright, with sticks tied crosswise with twigs; upon the end of these others were placed, and so on to any height; add to this that the ladders were often so slack that the smallest breeze put them in motion, swinging them against the rocks, while the steps leading from scaffold to scaffold were so narrow and irregular that they could scarcely be traced by the feet without the greatest care and circumspection; but the most perilous part was when another rock projected over the one they were clearing.

The Hakamaw Indians certainly deserved Fraser's grateful remembrance for their able assistance throughout these alarming situations. The descents were, if possible, still more difficult; in these places the white men were under the necessity of trusting their property to the Indians, even the precious guns were handed from one Indian to another; yet they thought nothing of it, they went up and down these wild places with the same agility as sailors do on a ship. After escaping innumerable perils in the course of the day, the party encamped about sunset, being supplied by the natives with plenty of dried fish.

Thus the main lines of the exploration of the great Canadian Dominion were completed. Alexander Mackenzie went to England in 1799 and received a knighthood for his remarkable achievements. On his return he first definitely created the New North-west or "X. Y." Company, and then brought about its fusion (after several years of bitter rivalry) with the old North-west Company; and it was this united and strengthened organization which, between 1804 and 1819, sent out so many bold pioneers to fill in the details of the map between the Columbia and Missouri on the south, and the Great Slave Lake and Liard River on the north. But during these years the energies of the Hudson's Bay Company were reviving under a strange personality—THOMAS DOUGLAS, EARL OF SELKIRK. Lord Selkirk conceived the idea of putting new life into the Hudson's Bay Company, reviving the monopolies of trading granted in its old charter, and turning its vague rights to land into the absolute ownership of the enormous area of North America north and west of the Canadian provinces. No regard of course was paid to any rights of the natives, who as a matter of fact were dying out rapidly from the effects of bad alcohol and epidemic diseases.

His motive was to establish large colonies of stalwart Highlanders as the tenants of a Chartered Company. Alexander Mackenzie had already called the north-west country "New Caledonia". Lord Selkirk wished to make it so in its population.

Already he had been instrumental in establishing a Scottish colony on Prince Edward's Island,[1] which, after some difficulties at the beginning, had soon begun to prosper. Two or three years later he came to Montreal, and there collected all the information he could obtain from the partners in the North-west Company regarding the prospects of trade and colonization in the far west. In the year 1811 he had managed to acquire the greater part of the shares in the Hudson's Bay Company, and, placing himself at its head, he sent out his first hundred Highlanders and Irish to form a feudatory colony in the Red River district (the modern Manitoba). He also dispatched an official to govern what might be called the Middle West on behalf of the Hudson's Bay Company. This person, acting under instructions, claimed the whole region beyond the provinces of Upper and Lower Canada as the private property of the Hudson's Bay Company, on the strength of their antiquated charter issued by Charles II. The agents of the North-west Company were warned (as also the two or three thousand French Canadians and half-breeds in their pay) that henceforth they must not cut wood, fish or hunt, build or cultivate, save by the permission and as the tenants of the Hudson's Bay Company.

1 Prince Edward's Island is off the north coast of New Brunswick. It was named after Queen Victoria's father, the Duke of Kent.

It is not surprising that such an outrageous demand, when it was followed up by the use of armed force, soon provoked bloodshed and a state of civil war throughout the North-west Territories. Lord Selkirk himself took command on the Red River, with a small army of disciplined soldiers. At length, in 1817, the British Government intervened through the Governor-General of Canada, and in 1818 Lord Selkirk left North America disgusted, and two years afterwards died at Pau, in France, from an illness brought on by grief at the failure of his projects.

Sir Alexander Mackenzie also died suddenly in 1820, in Scotland. For twelve years he had been member of parliament for Huntingdon, and since 1812 had been the determined opponent in England of Lord Selkirk's plans of forcible colonization. After his death, however, in 1821, a sudden movement for reconciliation took place between the two Companies. Thenceforth the Hudson's Bay Company ruled over the vast regions of British North America, beyond Newfoundland, New Brunswick, Nova Scotia, and the two Canadian provinces. Under their government the work of geographical exploration went on apace. In 1834 one of their officers, J. M'Leod, discovered the Stikine River in northern British Columbia, and by 1848 J. Bell and Robert Campbell had revealed the Porcupine and Yukon Rivers. By the time Thomas Simpson, Warren Dease, and Dr. John Rae, on behalf of the Hudson's Bay Company; and Franklin, Back, Parry, Richardson, and M'Clintock, for the Imperial Government, had completed the explorations mentioned in Chapter VI, all the main features of Canadian geography were made known. The next series of pioneers were to be those of the mining industry—it was the discovery of gold in 1856 which created British Columbia; of agriculture—the wheat-growers of the Red River region made the province of Manitoba; of the steamboat; and above all the railway.

Developments of science scarcely yet dreamt of will demand in further time their pioneers, and these will not come from abroad, but will assuredly be found in this splendid Canadian people, the descendants of the men or of the types of men I have attempted to describe.